PENGUIN  C

HORACE
PERSIUS

Advisory Editor: Betty Radice

QUINTUS HORATIUS FLACCUS was born in 65 BC at Venusia in Apulia. His father, though once a slave, had made enough money as an auctioneer to send his son to a well-known school in Rome and subsequently to university in Athens. There Horace joined Brutus' army and served on his staff until the defeat at Philippi in 42 BC. On returning to Rome, he found that his father was dead and his property had been confiscated, but he succeeded in obtaining a secretarial post in the treasury, which gave him enough to live on. The poetry he wrote in the next few years impressed Virgil, who introduced him to the great patron Maecenas in 38 BC. This event marked the beginning of a life-long friendship. From now on Horace had no financial worries; he moved freely among the leading poets and statesmen of Rome; his work was admired by Augustus, and indeed after Virgil's death in 19 BC he was virtually Poet Laureate. Horace died in 8 BC, only a few months after Maecenas.

AULES PERSIUS FLACCUS was born in AD 34 in Etruria. Rich and well connected, he knew Lucan, Thrasea Paetus, and other members of the Stoic opposition to Nero's rule. His friendship with the philosopher Cornutus began when he was sixteen and remained a strong influence until his death at the age of twenty-seven. Although the satires are concerned with moral questions – a fact which endeared Persius to the Church Fathers and won him admiration in the Middle Ages and Renaissance – their main interest for us lies in their condensed, allusive, and highly metaphorical style.

NIALL RUDD is a graduate of Trinity College, Dublin. After lecturing in England during the fifties, he moved to Toronto where he wrote a book on Horace's *Satires*. Back in England, as Professor of Latin at Bristol, he published translations (including Juvenal's

Satires), commentaries (Horace's *Epistles II* and *Ars Poetica*) and literary studies (*Lines of Enquiry* and *The Classical Tradition in Operation*). Recently he has collaborated with R. G. M. Nisbet on a commentary on Horace, *Odes* III, and has prepared a text, translation and brief notes on Dr Johnson's Latin poems. He is now attached to the Department of English at Liverpool University.

HORACE
Satires and Epistles

PERSIUS
Satires

*A verse translation with an Introduction
and Notes by* NIALL RUDD

PENGUIN BOOKS

PENGUIN CLASSICS

Published by the Penguin Group
Penguin Books Ltd, 80 Strand, London WC2R 0RL, England
Penguin Group (USA) Inc., 375 Hudson Street, New York, New York 10014, USA
Penguin Group (Canada), 10 Alcorn Avenue, Toronto, Ontario, Canada M4V 3B2
(a division of Pearson Penguin Canada Inc.)
Penguin Ireland, 25 St Stephen's Green, Dublin 2, Ireland
(a division of Penguin Books Ltd)
Penguin Group (Australia), 250 Camberwell Road, Camberwell, Victoria 3124, Australia
(a division of Pearson Australia Group Pty Ltd)
Penguin Books India Pvt Ltd, 11 Community Centre,
Panchsheel Park, New Delhi – 110 017, India
Penguin Group (NZ), cnr Airborne and Rosedale Roads, Albany, Auckland 1310, New Zealand
(a division of Pearson New Zealand Ltd)
Penguin Books (South Africa) (Pty) Ltd, 24 Sturdee Avenue, Rosebank 2196, South Africa

Penguin Books Ltd, Registered Offices: 80 Strand, London WC2R 0RL, England

www.penguin.com

This translation of *The Satires of Horace and Persius* first published 1973
Revised edition, with Horace's *Epistles*, published 1979
Reprinted with revisions 1987
Reprinted with revisions 1997
Reprinted with revisions 2005

7

Set in 9.25/11 pt PostScript Adobe Sabon
Typeset by Rowland Phototypesetting Ltd, Bury St Edmunds, Suffolk
Printed in Great Britain by Clays Ltd, St Ives plc

ISBN-13: 978–0–140–45508–3
ISBN-10: 0–140–45508–6

www.greenpenguin.co.uk

Contents

Foreword to the Second Edition

This volume contains a revised version of the *Satires* of Horace and Persius. Although the basic sense has been changed at only half a dozen points, the rhythm has been made more regular by a reduction in the number of unstressed syllables.

For the sake of completeness a new translation of Horace's *Epistles* has now been included, and there have been consequential additions to the introduction, notes, bibliography, and index.

NR,
Bristol, 1979

Foreword to the 1997 Edition

The chronology of Horace, *Epistles II* and *Ars Poetica* has been brought into line with the view adopted in my commentary (1989). The text employed is still eclectic. Some fifty changes have been made in the translation for reasons of sense or rhythm. The bibliography has been brought up to date.

NR,
Bristol, 1996

Foreword to the 2005 Edition

Extensive changes have been made to produce a smoother and lighter versification. A few mistakes have been corrected; other areas remain largely the same.

NR,
Liverpool, May 2004

In memory of Betty Radice

Introduction

SATURA BEFORE HORACE

First a point of semantics. When the critic Quintilian, writing at the end of the first century AD, said that *satura* was entirely Roman (*satura quidem tota nostra est*),[1] he was referring to a specific genre of poetry, not to what we might call 'the satiric spirit'. The latter, as one would expect, is found in many areas of Greek literature, for example, the Homeric parodies, the lampoons of Archilochus, Aesop's fables, the comedies of Aristophanes, and Lucian's dialogues. It also occurs in a number of Roman writers who are not 'satirists', notably Lucretius, Ovid, and Tacitus. Conversely, *satura*, though usually in some sense satirical, is not invariably so. With Horace's description of his education (I. 6. 65–88), Persius' acknowledgement of his debt to Cornutus (5. 26–51), and Juvenal's passage on human sympathy (15. 131–58) we are given a respite from the ridicule of folly and vice.

The derivation of *satura* is uncertain. Some scholars would connect it with the Etruscan *satir*, which is supposed to mean 'speak', but the common view, which was certainly held by the Romans themselves, sees it as the feminine singular of *satur*, meaning 'full'. *Satura*, therefore, meant 'a full', and *saturae* 'fulls'. There is nothing odd in talking about 'fulls'. In the days before bottles became part of our national refuse everyone knew what was meant by taking back 'the empties'. But the noun understood with *satura* was not a bottle. Originally it was a dish (*lanx*), the *lanx satura* being a dish full of first fruits offered to the gods.

This, at any rate, is the most likely of the explanations offered by Diomedes, a grammarian of the fourth century AD.[2] He also records three others: (1) that *satura* was the name given to a kind of stuffing consisting of various ingredients. This usage is attested by the scholar Varro (first century BC), who seems to have found it in Plautus (late third, early second century BC); yet this is hardly as old as the usage connected with religious ritual; (2) that *satura* was a kind of law containing a number of different provisions. But the combination *lex satura* is not found. What we do get, in connection with legal and political acts, is the phrase *per saturam* (literally 'through a medley'), which presupposes that *satura* itself already meant 'a medley'; (3) that *satura* is derived from *satyri*, the wild and lustful attendants of Bacchus who are still to be seen in museums, chasing nymphs around the rims of Greek vases. This is etymologically impossible, though later the two roots became intertwined.

In the case of both the dish and the stuffing it is easy to see how the idea of variety was present from the very beginning. As time went on, this idea became predominant and *saturae* turned into mixtures or medleys.

The next piece of evidence comes from Livy.[3] In a brief account of the development of Roman drama, which is based on the work of Varro, he distinguishes five phases: (1) dignified dancing by Etruscans to the music of a pipe; (2) a burlesque of this by young Roman amateurs who exchanged raillery in improvised verses; (3) professional performances of *saturae* in which songs were now written out to go with the pipe; (4) plays with plots introduced by Livius Andronicus (i.e. comedies, which included music and dancing); (5) a return by young amateurs to improvised banter, which later became combined with Oscan farces.

As history this account does not bear examination. It is a tendentious construction designed to show how a complex art form emerged from simple beginnings. As such it proposes a set of relationships which never existed. Hence many scholars reject the whole passage and maintain that Livy's *saturae* were invented simply to explain the lyrical element in Roman comedy. Others, including myself, think that this is over-sceptical. The four other types of performance are all well authenticated; the *saturae* could be genuine too. Moreover Varro, whom Livy is copying, adds an etymological explanation of the term. He says that the *saturae* were 'full of tunes' (*impletae modis*). This could indicate that the old scholar knew of *saturae* being performed in the third century and felt called on to explain the term to his contemporaries, for whom *satura* was now a type of literature.

Satura first occurs in literature as the title of a play by Naevius, who was writing from about 240 BC to the end of the century. Naevius was a major poet with original ideas and a strongly Roman personality. In addition to tragedies and comedies he wrote an epic on the struggle against Carthage which had a considerable influence on the *Aeneid*. But unfortunately only fragments of his poetry survive, and from his

Satura we have no more than a single quotation: 'Why, pray, have you beaten the people of Saturn?' Therefore, although *Satura* was the title of a work by Naevius, we are not justified in assuming that the work itself was a mixture or medley.

With Ennius (239–169 BC) we are on firmer ground. His *Saturae* were undoubtedly medleys. Written in various metres, including iambics, trochaics, and hexameters, they contained very diverse material, e.g. a dispute between Life and Death, a proverb aimed at the over-meticulous ('to look for a knot in a bulrush'), ironical remarks about the writer himself ('I never poetize unless I've got gout'), and a fable about a lark in a cornfield, ending with the motto 'if you want something done do it yourself'. It is clear that these poems contained an element of criticism. There are attacks on a glutton, a slanderer, interfering nuisances, and (possibly) a parasite. But the victims are all types, without names or features. We do not even know who delivers the attack; in some cases it could be a character in a sketch. So it looks as if *saturae* had not yet become fully 'satirical'. Certainly, Ennius is never mentioned as a satirist by Horace, Persius, or Juvenal. Nevertheless, his type of medley was continued by his nephew Pacuvius, and it influenced the work of Varro, who in the first century BC composed mixtures of prose and verse – a form subsequently developed by Petronius and Seneca.

One more question before we leave Ennius: where did he get his title? No one really knows. If the stage *saturae* existed, it may have come from them. If we wish to stress the poet's Hellenistic side we can point to roughly similar titles in third-century Greek literature, e.g. *Atakta* ('Miscellanies'), used by Philetas and Euphorion, and *Soros* ('A Heap of Winnowed Grain') employed by Posidippus. Or perhaps Ennius himself thought of applying *satura* to poetry, just as a modern writer might publish a collection of essays under the title of 'Mixed Grill'.

The man acknowledged by Horace (I. 10. 48, II. 1. 63), Persius (I. 114–15), and Juvenal (I. 20 and 165–7) as the founder of their tradition, and therefore in a strict sense the first European satirist, was Gaius Lucilius, a wealthy knight from Suessa Aurunca on the borders of Campania and Latium. Lucilius began his satires in about 133 BC after returning from the Spanish wars, and continued to write until his death in Naples in 102. Unlike Ennius, whose great reputation rested on his epic and tragedy and whose *saturae* were in the nature of a light-hearted diversion, Lucilius never wrote anything else. He was a satirist first and last. After experimenting with various metres in his early work he eventually settled on the hexameter as the most suitable vehicle for his purpose. This decision stabilized the form of the genre.

In other respects, however, Lucilius maintained and indeed extended the range of Ennius' miscellany. The 1,300 fragments include dramatic scenes, fables, sermons, dialogues, letters, anecdotes, epigrams, and learned disquisitions. The subject-matter is correspondingly diverse, covering sailing and horsemanship, phonetics and orthography, medicine, cookery, politics, literature, ethics, and sex. Here are a few fragments by way of illustration, based on the text of Warmington (see Bibliography):

(1) The rat race:

But as it is, from dawn to dusk on holidays and workdays the whole populace, and their rulers too, mill about in the city square and never leave it. They all devote themselves to one and the same occupation and craft – to cheat with the maximum cunning, to fight cleverly, struggle charmingly, pretending they're good fellows and laying traps as if they were all mutual enemies. (W. 1145–51)

(2) Insincerity:

The chef doesn't care whether the bird has a spectacular tail provided it's plump. So friends are concerned with a man's nature, parasites with his money and possessions. (W. 761–2)

(3) Catering:

If you've enough cash you should also get a hefty bakeress – a massive woman who knows all about crisp Syrian loaves. (W. 1055–6)

(4) Deep-sea yarn:

But I saved the gear – mast, sails, everything – by promptly cutting the rope and freeing the halyard. (W. 617–18)

(5) An interrupted seduction:

She had just decided to give it to me, and I had put my clothes down on the bed. (W. 898–9)

(6) A trip south:

There all this was child's play and everything was free and easy; all free and easy, I say, and mere child's play and fun. But when we reached the outskirts of Setia, *that* was a tough haul – goat-forsaken mountains, each one an Etna and a rugged Athos. (W. 102–5)

(7) On the forthcoming fight:
'I'll just kill him and win, if that's what you want,' he said. 'But I guess this is what'll happen: first I'll take it on the face; then I'll leave my sword sticking in the stupid nut's belly and lungs. I hate the guy; for me it's a grudge fight. We won't hang around – just long enough for one of us to grab his sword. That's how mad I am; I hate the fellow's guts and can't wait to get at him.' (W. 176–81)

(8) *Les dames du temps jadis:*
Surely you don't think it impossible that any woman with 'lovely tresses' and 'lovely ankles' could have had breasts touching her womb and even her crotch; that Alcmena 'the wife of Amphitryon's bosom' could have been knock-kneed or bandy; and that others too, even Helen herself, that – (I won't say; think of it yourself and pick any two-syllable word you like) – that 'daughter of a noble sire', could have had some obvious blemish, a wart, a mole, a pock-mark, or one buck tooth? (W. 567–73)

(9) Manliness:
Manliness, Albinus, is the ability to pay what is actually due in our business dealings and social life. Manliness is the knowledge of what each issue involves for a man. Manliness is the knowledge of what is right, advantageous, and honourable for a man, what is good and likewise what is bad, what is disadvantageous, wrong, and dishonourable. Manliness is knowing the boundary and limit for acquiring riches. Manliness is the ability to pay wealth its due. Manliness is giving what is in fact owed to honour, being an enemy and an opponent of bad men and habits – a champion on the other hand of good men and habits, prizing the latter highly, wishing them well, and living on friendly terms with them; it means, furthermore, putting the interests of one's country first, then one's parents', then thirdly and lastly one's own. (W. 1196–1208)

(10) The last battle:
The Roman people has often been beaten by force and defeated in many battles – but never in a *war*; that's what matters. (W. 708–9)

(11) Government officials:
Publius Pavus Tuditanus was my chief finance officer in the land of Spain – a shifty shady character, one of those types, without a doubt. (W. 499–500)

    It wouldn't be so bad if I hadn't the Governor on my back needling me. As I say, he's the one who's tearing my guts out. (W. 501–2)

(12) A charmer:
> Of that crowd Lucius Trebellius ranks easily first; he causes fever, gloom, retching, and pus. (W. 531–2)

(13) As others see us:
> We've heard that some friends have been invited today including that horror Lucilius. (W. 929–30)

(14) Contentment:
> But to become an Asian tax-farmer, a revenue-official, instead of Lucilius – I don't want that; and I'm not changing this one thing for all the world. (W. 650–51)

The last two quotations illustrate the frank, informal way in which Lucilius wrote of himself. As Horace said:

In the past he would confide his secrets to his books, which he trusted,
like friends; and whether things went well or badly he'd always
turn to them: in consequence, the whole of the old man's life
is laid before us, as if it were painted on a votive tablet.

(II. 1. 30–33)

Lucilian satire was also personal in another sense: it attacked prominent contemporaries by name. See, for example, nos. 11–12 above. We are not in a position to assess how responsibly Lucilius used this weapon. Naturally he argued that his victims deserved such treatment and that he himself was the watchdog of society. But in any case he got away with it, partly because he was living in a free republic, partly because he belonged to the upper classes, but mainly because he enjoyed the friendship and protection of the powerful Scipio family. As a result, Lucilian satire, which contained several dramatic sketches, was the nearest equivalent the Romans knew to the comedy of Aristophanes.

The pugnacious element in Lucilius was always apparent. But whereas in the first century BC he is mentioned for other qualities too – Varro speaks of his 'slim' style, Cicero of his learning and charm, Horace of his wit and his easy informal manner – later writers refer only to his castigation of vice. No doubt such forthrightness seemed remarkable to Persius who was living under Nero, and to Juvenal who had experienced the tyranny of Domitian. These later satirists could not emulate the pioneer's frankness. Even Horace, who was writing in the last decade of the republic, had to tread very warily. Nevertheless, they all recognized that Lucilius had made criticism, in some form or other, an essential feature of the genre.

Finally it is worth pointing out that although Lucilius was at home in Greek literature and personally acquainted with the foremost Greek thinkers of his day, he was unmistakably a Roman poet. His writings had a Roman setting, portrayed Roman conditions and personalities, and (as we see in nos. 9–10 above) presented a hard-headed Roman outlook on life. They brought something fresh and vigorous into the European tradition, and their disappearance is one of the tragedies of literary history.

At this point, before proceeding to the section on Horace, the reader may well prefer to read the translation.

HORACE

If originality is thought of as the invention of new genres, then Lucilius had no rival in Latin literature – Petronius is no exception. But most ancient writers, Greek and Roman, showed their originality by producing innovations within some traditional form with a fixed metre and a certain range of mood and subject. These limits were no disadvantage. To imagine that a poet felt cramped and confined by his chosen metre is like suggesting that a squash-player feels restricted by the walls of his court. Mood and subject were more vaguely defined. There were certain general expectations, but poets were allowed a good deal of flexibility in their treatment. Virgil transformed pastoral by expansion. That is, he incorporated in his *Eclogues* some elements which were Theocritean but non-bucolic (e.g., the spells of Simaetha in *Idyll* 2) and other elements which weren't Theocritean at all (e.g., the plight of an evicted peasant). Horace worked in the opposite direction, transforming Lucilian satire by reduction and refinement.

He concentrated on a few central themes – mainly the perennial enslavement of men to money, power, superstition, and sex. At the same time he drew on a much smaller fund of vocabulary and idiom, eliminating Greek, which Lucilius had employed for technical precision, stylishness or parody, and greatly restricting the use of vulgarisms, archaisms, dialect words, and comic coinages. If we possessed the whole of Lucilius, no doubt we could see that from time to time this greater refinement was purchased at the cost of some vigour and spontaneity. But this was not always the case. The history of

architecture frequently shows how a superior technique of construc-
tion allows a greater economy of material and a greater degree of
lightness and elegance without any loss of strength.

Lucilius was often clumsy and repetitious, Horace almost never. As
a brief illustration, compare these two passages, which refer to the
fable of the fox and the sick lion. (The fox is addressing the lion who
is crouching in a cave.)

> What does it mean and how does it come about that the tracks face
> inwards and towards you and all point forwards?
>
> (W. 1119–20)

> Because those footprints scare me; all of them lead in your direction, none
> of them back.
>
> (Horace, *Epistles* I. 1.74–5)

Horace's neatness is also partly a result of his metrical dexterity.
Lucilius permitted himself a large number of elisions in any given
passage – so large that, according to Horace, it looked as if his only
concern was to force something into six feet (I. 10. 59–60). Horace's
own rate of elision is less than half as high. On the other hand Horace
is more free in his use of enjambment. That is, he lets the sense flow
on from one line to the next, often making his pauses *within* the verse.
This contributes to the easy conversational effect implied in the Latin
sermo (causerie), a name which Horace used for both his *Satires* and
Epistles. Neatness, rapidity, elegance, and ease – these are among the
classical qualities of style affirmed by Horace in *Satires* I. 10, and
particularly in vv. 7–15:

> So it's not enough to make your listener bare his teeth
> in a grin – though I grant there's some virtue even in that.
> You need terseness, to let the thought run freely on
> without becoming entangled in a mass of words that will hang
> heavy on the ear. You need a style which is sometimes severe,
> sometimes gay, now suiting the role of an orator or poet
> now that of a clever talker who keeps his strength in reserve
> and carefully rations it out. Humour is often stronger
> and more effective than sharpness in cutting knotty issues.

That quotation raises the question of wit and humour. Here too
Horace operated within narrower limits, partly because of his tempera-
ment and partly because he had a stricter conception of the decorum

demanded by the genre. In his view both the artistic and moral effects of satire were weakened if there was too large a proportion of buffoonery, coarseness, and abuse.

The names in Horatian satire fall into several categories. Some belong to living people, some to the dead, some to people who, though dead, have survived as types (like our Crippen or Hitler), and some to people who were formerly attacked by Lucilius. Others are 'significant' names (like Porcius the glutton), others are drawn from mythology, and one or two seem to be metrical substitutions (viz. Pitholeon for Pitholaus, Heliodorus for Apollodorus). So it is plain that Horace was not primarily concerned to attack contemporary individuals. Those whom he did attack were seldom people of any importance in society.

This marks a notable departure from Lucilius, and the explanation must lie to a large extent in Horace's background and career. He had no advantages of birth, being the son of an emancipated slave from Venusia, a remote country town in southern Italy (see map on p. 21). Nothing is known of his mother, but his father was clearly an astute and enterprising man. He had made a fair amount of money as an auctioneer's agent, and so when he recognized his son's talent he was able to have him educated in Rome. A brief but memorable account of this period is given in *Satires* I. 6. 71–88. After that, Horace continued his studies at Athens, where he must have known a number of well-to-do young Romans like Valerius Messalla and Cicero's son Marcus.

In September 44 BC, six months after the assassination of Caesar, Brutus arrived at Athens to recruit officers for his army. Horace, who was now twenty-one years old, signed up and two years later at Philippi he was in command of a legion. After that defeat, which was a disaster for the republican cause, Horace was pardoned by the Triumvirs (Antony, Octavian, and Lepidus) and allowed to return to Italy. His father was now dead, and the farm which he would have inherited had been confiscated. Through his contacts he succeeded in finding a job in the treasury which gave him enough money to live on and enough leisure to do some writing. But when, on the recommendation of Virgil and Varius, Maecenas offered him patronage he was quick to accept it. That was in 37 BC. Two years later he published his first collection of satires.

Horace's admission to the circle of Maecenas was a sign of his growing reputation. Yet his position was rather delicate. As a dependant, without private means or family connections, who had fought on the wrong side in a civil war, he could not afford to antagonize Octavian (the future Augustus) or any of his supporters. And no doubt this in part explains the comparatively innocuous nature of his satire. Yet one must also add (for it is usually forgotten) that in the years preceding Actium – say from 35 to 31 BC – Horace had ample opportunity to attack Octavian's enemies, especially Mark Antony. The air was thick with propaganda and personal abuse. Yet he never joined in. In fact the more security he acquired the milder his work became, until in the end he abandoned satire altogether.

Since, in a famous essay on satire, Horace has been called 'a temporizing poet, a well-mannered court slave . . . who is ever decent because he is naturally servile',[4] it is also worth pointing out that in the ten years after Philippi Horace never wrote a word in praise of Octavian, even though he had fought on his side against Pompey's son, Sextus, in 36 BC. It is only in the latest satires and epodes, which were written in the year after Actium, that he mentions the future emperor specifically. And even then the tone is hardly deferential (see *Satires* II. 1. 18–20, 5. 62–3, 6. 52–6).

This political disenchantment was not offset by any religious faith. In Horace's view the gods did not direct human affairs or offer hope of personal survival. Had he been a mystic he might still have contemplated them as patterns of perfection, but in fact his interests were focused entirely on man. Politics, then, were nonsense and religion didn't count. There remained only the world of personal relations. Even here Horace was a realist. He didn't expect too much of himself or anyone else. Yet he did believe that men could spare themselves a great deal of misery by acceptance, restraint, good humour, and tolerance, and that these virtues might be promoted by taking thought. Hence, whereas Juvenal works on the emotions by presenting a series of vivid pictures, Horace operates on the intellect by various rational procedures.

First, although there are minor differences, each poem has usually one main section devoted to a single vice, e.g. greed (I. 1), adultery (I. 2), unfairness (I. 3), ambition (I. 6), gluttony (II. 2). Even when several vices are presented, as in II. 3 and II. 7, they are treated in an orderly way and are grouped under some general heading such as madness or servitude.

Second, if we leave aside the entertainment pieces (nos, 5, 7, 8, and 9 of Book I), we find that the satirical attack is conducted in the form of an argument or debate. Take, for example, the following passage:

> You like to be well thought of; no songs are sweeter to the ear
> than songs of praise. But the bigger the turbot and dish the bigger
> the scandal, not to mention the waste of money. Also your uncle

and the neighbours will be furious; you'll lose your self-respect and resolve
on suicide – except you'll be so broke that you won't have a penny
for a rope.

   'You can talk like that to Trausius,' he says, 'for he
deserves it. But I have a large income and a bigger fortune
than three kings put together.'

     'Well then, can't you think of a better way
to get rid of your surplus? Why should any decent man
be in need when you are rich? Why are the ancient temples
of the gods falling down? Why, if you've any conscience,
don't you give something from that pile you've made to the land of your
                [birth?
           (II. 2. 94–105)

Notice the structural function of 'but', 'not to mention', 'also'; and
the objection from the accused, answered by 'well then' (*ergo*), 'why',
'why'. The poem, in fact, has a dialectical framework, even though
the progress from one phase of the argument to the next is often
concealed by some clever transitional device which gives the appear-
ance of casual improvisation.

 Third, the satirist rarely adopts a truculent, insulting manner. He
doesn't try to establish too much; he hears objections; makes con-
cessions. And so at the end of the poem the reader feels not only that
he has been listening to a reasonable man, but also that the ethical
point at issue has been made progressively clearer and more precise.
The same is true of the literary satires. A good example is the tenth
satire of Book I which opens like this:

 True, I did say that Lucilius' verses lurched
 awkwardly along. Which of his admirers is so perverse
 as not to admit it? But he is also praised on the same page
 for scouring the city with caustic wit. While granting him this,
 however, I cannot allow the rest as well, for then
 I should have to admire the mimes of Laberius for their poetic
               [beauty.

The poem then goes on to explore Horace's attitude to Lucilius,
elucidating his mixed feelings of respect and dissatisfaction.

 The moral ideas propounded are straightforward and intelligible,
drawn in the main from that large central area where the different
schools overlapped. Thus whether the reader was Stoic, Academic, or
Epicurean he would readily accept the contention that happiness was

not ensured by wealth, and that it was always endangered by avarice, gluttony, adulterous intrigues, and the struggle for power. Only features that fell outside this central area came in for ridicule – for example the dirtiness and boorish manners of the Cynics, the Stoic contention that all sins were equally serious, and the obsession with gastronomy which was popularly ascribed to the Epicureans. Horatian satire may therefore be called conservative in that it mocked deviations from commonly accepted norms. The ethical content was in no way original, and Horace never imagined it was. His purpose was rather to use these traditional ideas as standards for judging the faults of his own time. As a result, although the presentation of the argument is often subtle and sophisticated, in the end we can be pretty sure where Horace stands.

In that last assertion some critics would want to substitute 'the satirist' for 'Horace', maintaining that the opinions of the historical Horace are undiscoverable and in any case irrelevant. This theory, which abandons the poet's mind or personality as an object of critical discussion and concentrates instead on his masks or *personae*, is part of a reaction which has taken place in the last twenty-five years against the excesses of biographical scholarship. The reaction has been largely beneficial in that readers born before 1940 are now unlikely to forget that the poem itself should occupy the centre of the critic's attention. But like all reactions it has been too sweeping. Some poets are indeed anonymous or inscrutable; but not all. Others, like Horace, not only invite our acquaintance but provide historically verifiable information about themselves. Therefore, although it is too large a question to discuss here, I would contend that while Horace undoubtedly employs different *personae*, such as Ofellus, Damasippus, Fundanius, and others, these do not prevent us from making some valid inferences about his own views and attitudes.

Horace, then, offered a critique of vice and folly, and he certainly did not share the view, which is widely held today, that a man's behaviour is totally unaffected by what he reads. Nevertheless it would be wrong to regard him as a reforming satirist, if by this one means a writer who sets out to influence society at large. For although he aimed to stimulate people's moral awareness, he had no missionary zeal, and he never sought a wide audience. Moreover, the purpose of his work was not solely – perhaps not even primarily – didactic. He wrote to give pleasure, to entertain people with his deft presentation of ideas, his amusing anecdotes, and his skilful adjustment of the hexameter to the rhythms of educated conversation. In the *Ars Poetica* (343) he was to say omne tulit punctum qui miscuit utile dulci.

Over the centuries the *Satires* have won many votes for that same combination of utility and delight.

Yet the *Satires*, along with the *Epodes*, form only the initial phase of Horace's poetic development. After 30 BC he turned to themes of love, death, and patriotism which had already figured in the *Epodes* but were quite beyond the limits of satire. This period culminated in the publication of three books of *Odes* (23 BC), a work which established Horace as Rome's first lyric poet. He then reverted to the hexameter, not for satire but for verse epistles. Here again Lucilius had paved the way. We have a fragment of an epistle complaining to a friend who had failed to visit him when sick (W. 186–93); and it also looks as if Lucilius had given some thought to the general question of an epistle's literary status (W. 401–10). But the idea of composing a whole book of verse epistles was something quite novel. The flavour of the pieces was also distinctively Horatian. They were addressed to Horace's circle of acquaintances; they provided a good deal of information about the poet's opinions and way of life; and their reflections on friendship, contentment, and civilized behaviour were conveyed in a characteristically Horatian manner.

Since, however, that manner is one of sophisticated variety, it does not lend itself easily to generalization. For example, are the epistles of Book I (published in 19 BC) 'real letters'? Some critics believe they are; others hold that they are rather thoughts or recommendations cast in an epistolary form; others again maintain that they are both private letters *and* general reflections. Each of these positions tends to assume that all the pieces satisfy the same criteria. Yet this is not the case. In *Epistles* I. 3, for instance, Horace asks Julius Florus various questions about himself and his friends, and looks forward to receiving an answer; *Epistles* I. 8 contains a specific message for Celsus Albinovanus ('Don't let success go to your head'); in *Epistles* I. 9 the situation is less straightforward. (Presumably Horace had in some way recommended Septimius to Tiberius, but the epistle itself, which is mainly about Horace's scruples, can hardly constitute the original recommendation.) And in *Epistles* I. 6 we have a causerie on peace of mind, which begins 'Dear Numicius' and ends with a brief farewell.

But we cannot stop here, for we have not decided what the criteria of a 'real letter' actually are. To illustrate the difficulty let us put four questions: (1) Were the epistles addressed to real people? (2) Were they spontaneous? (3) Was their primary purpose to communicate with the recipient (conveying statement, question or command)?

(4) Were they actually sent? The answers, crudely, are as follows: (1) Yes, if we allow that I. 20 is ultimately meant for the Sosii (as I. 13 is ultimately meant for Augustus). (2) No. They are highly finished poems, and such objects take time to construct. (But are 'real letters' always spontaneous?) (3) In some cases probably yes, in others certainly no. (But don't we sometimes write 'real letters' in the hope of clearing our own minds of some intellectual or personal problem?) (4) We cannot be sure, but it is reasonable to believe that most of them were. At least we should not assume that because an epistle is largely general (like I. 6) it could not have been sent. Educated Romans enjoyed discussing ethical questions more than we do.

So as usual the question of reality is obscure and difficult. But luckily our enjoyment of the poems does not depend on the answer. Nor need we trouble overmuch about the book's structure and arrangement. It is true that if we regard no. 20 as an epilogue (as it is), then the collection is framed by nos. 1 and 19, addressed to Maecenas, and by nos. 2 and 18, addressed to Lollius; we can also see that the regularly spaced 7 and 13 are intended for Maecenas and Augustus respectively, and that the central piece (no. 10) is addressed to Aristius Fuscus – friend, critic, schoolmaster, and a man of no political importance. But on the whole very little emerges when the epistles are laid side by side like bricks. It is much more illuminating to see them as forming a web of interrelated ideas. The reader will identify several of the strands for himself; but to get some conception of the book's full richness and complexity he should consult the chapter entitled 'The Texture of Argument' in M. J. McGann, *Studies in Horace's First Book of Epistles*, Bruxelles, 1969.

McGann has also written the best guide to *Epistles* II. 2.[5] This long poem, composed in 19 or 18 BC, takes the form of an elaborate excuse for not supplying the lyrics which Julius Florus had expected: I was always lazy and never pretended to be anything else; nowadays I'm comfortably off and don't need the money; Rome is impossible – the noise is appalling, and I dislike the mutual congratulation of the literary set; writing poetry is hard work – not just a pleasant pastime for amateurs; and anyhow at my age one becomes interested in more serious matters, like philosophy. Within this framework there are passages of great vividness and diversity, including autobiography, complaints about city life, and amusing stories like those about Lucullus' soldier and the lunatic from Argos. Pope's *Imitation* is well worth reading. It is not an antiquarian exercise, but an eighteenth-century poem in its own right, and English commentators have noted

a number of brilliant gains vis-à-vis the original. But there were losses
too, as Pope would have been the first to admit.

Odes IV, published in 13 BC has an autumnal quality. Virgil and
Cinara are dead; Phyllis will be the last of Horace's loves; though not
forgotten (11. 17–20), Maecenas is not addressed; he has now little
political influence. New stars are rising – Tiberius and Drusus, Iullus
Antonius, Paulus Fabius Maximus; Horace wishes them well, but they
are not of his generation. Yet there is no bitterness; on the contrary
Horace enjoys recognition, and his loyalty to Augustus – the ruler who
had made it possible for his talent to ripen in peace – is undiminished.

In writing that book Horace had broken his resolution to give up
lyric poetry (*Epistles* I. 1. 10, reaffirmed in *Epistles* II. 2), a change of
mind referred to in *Epistles* II. 1. 111–12. The same poem speaks of
the religious honours being paid to Augustus (15–16) – honours which
probably began in 12 BC when he became Pontifex Maximus. So the
epistle seems to have appeared in that year. According to Suetonius it
was prompted by Augustus, who after reading certain hexameter
poems (doubtless epistles, but we do not know exactly which) com-
plained that Horace had not addressed him. Here then we have a long
epistle on a topic of general interest, viz. the position of the poet in
contemporary society, but which has at the same time cleverly twisted
into its fabric three substantial sections devoted to Augustus himself
(1–19, 214–28, 245–70). In addition, the subject-matter is, as always,
selected, shaped, and presented so as to express the poet's own point
of view:

> It makes me annoyed that a thing should be faulted, not for being
> crudely or clumsily made, but simply for being recent,
> and that praise and prizes should be asked for the old, instead of
> [forbearance.

Because Horace is now a classic, it is easy to forget that in his own
day he was not just a modern poet but also a daring innovator who
had to win acceptance in the face of conservative taste.

The work referred to by Quintilian (VIII. 3. 60) as the *Ars Poetica*
was probably addressed to Lucius Calpurnius Piso (the Pontifex) and
his sons in 10 BC (See pp. 20–21 of my commentary.) The greater
detachment from contemporary controversies also suggests that it
came after rather than before *Epistles* II. 1. Apart from the date, there
are two other long-standing problems about the *Ars Poetica*, namely
its structure and its relevance. Is there, as many have thought, a

division between *ars* (1–294) and *artifex* (295–476)? Should we go
further and subdivide *ars* into *poema* (style) and *poesis* (content)?
Advocates of this idea point out that the same three terms were used
by Neoptolemus of Parium (a scholar-poet of the third century BC)
and that, according to Porphyrion (a commentator of the third century
AD), Horace 'gathered together the precepts of Neoptolemus of Parium
on the art of poetry, admittedly not all, but the most significant'.
But can we be sure that *poema* and *poesis* had these functions in
Neoptolemus? And what degree of precision can be attributed to
Porphyrion? This controversy can best be studied in the books of
Brink and Williams (see Bibliography). Here one need only remark
that if Horace took over this tripartite scheme (as he may well have
done), he so blurred the lines of demarcation that the separate parts
were no longer plainly apparent to his readers. And so the scheme as
such can hardly have been of central importance.

The question of relevance arises in connection with the passages on
tragedy, comedy, and satyr-drama. Was Horace hoping to encourage
and assist some budding playwrights? If so, one wonders how vital
new dramatic writing was under Augustus, and whether someone was
really thinking of attempting a satyr play. Unfortunately the evidence
is frustratingly slender.[6] But perhaps it is wrong to imagine that Horace
was addressing himself to any actual situation. In that case he would
have written about drama because, since the time of Aristotle, that
had been a central area of critical concern, and because the subject
provided topics for satire, moral affirmation, and general reflections
on life. This may be the right approach, but if so we must acknowledge
that the *Ars Poetica* has no unity of intent; for several other sections
of the poem are clearly related to Roman literary life. Again, however,
our enjoyment of the work does not depend on possessing the right
answer to this problem. Whatever view we adopt, we can appreciate
that the *Ars Poetica* covers an immense historical scope, and has
exercised a powerful influence on European literary theory. It handles
a variety of topics with lightness, humour, and good sense; and as no
one had ever written a poem on poetics it remains a work of impressive
originality.

When he died in November, 8 BC, only two months after Maecenas,
Horace had completed what he himself had earlier referred to as 'a
monument more lasting than bronze'. Yet when we hear his name we
don't really think of a monument. We think rather of a voice which
varies in tone and resonance but is always recognizable, and which by
its unsentimental humanity evokes a very special blend of liking and
respect.

PERSIUS

On 4 December AD 34, almost a century after Horace's birth, another, very different, Flaccus was born. This was Aules Persius Flaccus, and his birthplace was the Etruscan town of Volaterrae. He himself was a knight and he had a number of senators among his relatives and friends. So it is not wholly surprising to learn from his ancient biography that he left a sum of two million sesterces on his death.[7] Persius went to school at Volaterrae until the age of eleven. Then he moved to Rome where he was taught language and literature by the brilliant but dissolute Remmius Palaemon, and then public speaking by Verginius Flavus. Finally, when he was sixteen, he came under the influence of the Stoic Cornutus, a freedman from the household of Seneca. Dramatist, scholar, and thinker, Cornutus was a man of real intellectual distinction. He did a great deal to assist the development of the young Persius, who had lost his father at the age of six; and in the fifth satire he is warmly thanked for his kindness. When Persius died, aged only twenty-seven, Cornutus advised his mother to suppress his juvenilia, which included a tragedy and (apparently) a collection of travel poems. But he arranged for the *Satires* to be edited for publication by the poet Caesius Bassus, a friend addressed in no. 6.

We are told that when they appeared the *Satires* caused a lot of interest – largely, no doubt, among the intelligentsia. They were praised by Lucan, Quintilian, and Martial,[8] and their combination of high-mindedness and stylistic peculiarity ensured their survival among theologians and scholars of the middle ages. The date of the first edition (Rome, 1470) put the *Satires* among the earliest printed works. In the last five hundred years they have been read in sixty translations, and their influence has been out of all proportion to their size.

There are only six poems and a prologue, containing in all less than seven hundred lines. The range of illustrative material is correspondingly limited. We hear of contemporary poetry and the audiences for whom it catered at dinner-parties, recitals, and theatre performances. There are several passages about schoolboys and students; and a number of references to special skills, e.g., pottery, agriculture, navigation, and especially medicine. Attacks are made on anti-Greek prejudice and on ignorant misconceptions of religion. Some use is made of Greek characters (e.g., Socrates and Alcibiades), and there is an excerpt from a scene of Menander. A few references are made to Roman public life – e.g., court scenes, ceremonies of manumission, triumphal processions and shows. So there is, if you like, a certain degree of variety; but the area of interest is much smaller than Horace's and minute in comparison with that of Lucilius.

All this would not prove that Persius lived a quiet life, but that is certainly the impression given in his biography. We hear of no military exploits, no perils by sea, no commercial or erotic adventures. On the contrary we are told that the poet had a very gentle disposition and a young girl's modesty. He was handsome, good, clean-living, and devoted to his female relatives. Much of his time seems to have been spent in talking and thinking about philosophy. On his death he left Cornutus seven hundred volumes on Stoicism.

Yet although Persius did not seek a wide range of experience it does not follow that the whole of his life was sheltered and secure. He may have run considerable risks by writing as he did. This is a rather debatable question, but as it has a bearing on our assessment of the *Satires* we must consider the more important pieces of evidence.

First, the poet's family connections. Persius was related to Arria, the wife of Thrasea Paetus, and to her even more famous mother. The elder Arria's husband, Caecina Paetus, had taken part in an abortive plot against the Emperor Claudius. When he was sentenced she showed him how to die by stabbing herself and then handing him the sword saying 'It doesn't hurt, Paetus' (Pliny, 3. 16). We know that as a boy Persius had written verses on her bravery.

More important, Persius was a friend of Thrasea Paetus for ten years and occasionally accompanied him on journeys abroad. Thrasea belonged to a senatorial family from Padua, an area with a strong sense of the past. Significantly he wrote a book on Cato, who in imperial times represented the essence of the old republican spirit. Thrasea was also a Stoic. This must have had some bearing on his political attitude; for although in theory Stoics favoured monarchy if the monarch was a good man, it soon became clear that Nero was the very antithesis of the Stoic ideal. At first Thrasea tried to cooperate. He held the consulship in AD 56. But after that he became more and more disenchanted. In AD 59 Nero had his mother murdered. The senate, with its usual servility, was giving thanks for the Emperor's lucky escape when Thrasea walked out in disgust. He deplored the growing frivolity and licentiousness of court life, and did not conceal his contempt for the musical and theatrical performances in which Nero took part. In AD 62 he opposed the death penalty in the case of a man who had written abusive verses about Nero, and he further annoyed the Emperor by securing the abolition of automatic votes of thanks to provincial governors. All this happened before Persius' death in November, AD 62. Shortly after, Thrasea withdrew from public life, but this did not save him from being executed in AD 66 on a charge of treason.

In the spring of AD 65, less than three years after the death of Persius, there was an unsuccessful plot against Nero. In the ensuing purge many famous men perished, including Seneca, who was acquainted with Persius, and Lucan, who had been a fellow student. Others were driven into exile, notably Persius' former teachers, Verginius Flavus and Cornutus. Had the poet himself been alive he could hardly have escaped. It would be naïve to plead that his poetry did not constitute a political act. In an autocracy anything that offends the dictator is a political act, and some passages of Persius could certainly have given offence.

Before considering what they were we should recall that among the various kinds of poetry being written at the time were Latin versions of the *Iliad*, tragedy (by Seneca), pastoral (by Calpurnius), elegy (by Cocceius Nerva), and miscellaneous compositions by Lucan. In many cases the authors were known personally to Nero. Tacitus (*Annals* 14. 16) says that some of the minor talents would have dinner with the Emperor and then spend the evening reading poetry to each other and improvising verses together. Nero's own compositions included an epic on Troy in more than one book, a piece on Attis and another on the Bacchanals which he recited accompanying himself on the lyre, and various minor poems, some erotic, some satiric. He was insatiable in his desire for applause and could be highly sensitive to adverse criticism (Suetonius, *Nero* 25).[9]

Now in the first satire we find adverse comment on a Latin version of the *Iliad*, on tragedy, elegy, epyllia, and romantic epic. Scorn is directed at the recitations and improvisations of wealthy Romans around the dinner-table. And particular reference is made to drivel written about Attis and the Bacchanals. In view of these facts it seems rather perverse to deny that the Emperor and his friends could have been included in Persius' condemnation. On the other hand, it is going too far to suggest that Nero was singled out for ridicule and that the whole satire focuses on him. It is not certain that the verses quoted in I. 93 ff. and 99 ff. were written by Nero himself, and even if they were that would not alter the fact that the satire was meant to have a general application. This is also the main objection to the story that at v. 121 Persius actually wrote *auriculas asini Mida rex habet* – 'King Midas has an ass's ears', and that Cornutus changed *Mida rex* to *quis non* to avoid offending Nero. The story is more likely to have arisen from the presence of the words *Mida rex* as a marginal gloss on v. 121.

We shall therefore confine ourselves to believing that in *Satires* I

Persius attacked various kinds of poetry which were being written by wealthy dilettanti, including Nero and his circle. If this is true, then the satire was quite a daring piece of work, even though it wasn't published in the poet's lifetime.

Persius was the most doctrinaire of the Roman satirists in that he kept more closely than the others to a single philosophical school. In the first satire (123–4) he speaks highly of the Greek fifth-century comedy because it castigated folly, but he despises the romantic sentimental verse written in Alexandria and imitated by Catullus, Ovid, and their successors. He also dislikes the bombastic rhetoric of Roman tragedy. These opinions are in line with the Stoic view that poetry should above all have a moral function. The Stoics also held that if a man had one vice it affected his whole nature. Hence a degenerate character would manifest itself in degenerate literary tastes. The belief that the style is the man receives its classic statement in Seneca's 114th letter.

The positive Stoic conviction underlying *Satires* 2 is that the true object of prayer is to align one's own will with that of God. This purpose is commonly frustrated by the frivolous desires of the flesh (62–7).

The first half of *Satires* 3 reminds us of the emphasis which the Stoics placed on the education of the will. In 66 ff. we are told how the fundamental questions about life are answered by philosophy – a theme which has many parallels in Seneca, Epictetus, and Marcus Aurelius. And the final section, from v. 88 on, employs the Stoic metaphor of the philosopher as doctor of the soul. Seneca and Epictetus also insist that constant self-examination is necessary if one is to make any progress towards virtue. That is the central message of *Satires* 4.

The fifth satire describes how the Stoic Cornutus taught Persius that the only true freedom was moral freedom. This central tenet of the school was summed up in the saying, 'all fools are slaves; only the wise are free'.

These are just a few examples of Stoic theory in Persius. It must be added, however, that by this time Stoicism had become very eclectic. For example, although the dualism of mind and body (*Satires* 2) is found in Stoics like Poseidonius and Seneca, it goes back to Plato and beyond him to the Pythagoreans. The call for self-knowledge (*Satires* 4) is one of the oldest elements in Greek thought – the maxim 'know thyself' was inscribed above the portals of Apollo's temple at Delphi. And certainly the Stoics were not the only people to stress the moral function of poetry (*Satires* 1). Finally, the theme of *Satires* 6 is that the sensible man will use what he has and will not struggle to amass a fortune for his heir. The same advice can be found in Plato, Aristotle, the Cynics, and the Epicureans. It is therefore perhaps a mistake to lay too great a stress on the purely Stoic side of Persius.

Furthermore, the modern reader is not primarily interested in Persius as an expositor of ethical ideas. The ideas themselves are traditional. It is the form in which they are presented that catches our attention. To amplify this would involve an essay on Persius' style, and that would be inappropriate here. I can only give a few examples from the Prologue.

Persius begins by disclaiming inspiration: he has not drunk from Hippocrene. But he doesn't put it so simply. He translates the Greek Hippocrene – 'horse spring' – into Latin, choosing the pedestrian word for horse. The result is *fons caballinus* – 'cart-horse spring', instead of *fons equinus* – 'steed spring'. That is not how Nathaniel Hawthorne and his predecessors spoke of Pegasus. One thinks rather guiltily of the massive dray depicted by Rubens in 'Perseus frees Andromeda'.

The satirist goes on to say that he had nothing to do with the *Heliconides* ('maids of Helicon') – a word found nowhere else; he is not a full member of the bards' fraternity, only a *semipaganus* ('half clansman') – another unique word. The established poets who line the walls of the public libraries have ivy licking their busts. The graphic and semi-derisive *lambunt* – 'lick', which suggests that every piece of ivy is like a fawning animal, is typical of Persius. He ends by saying (ironically, for he was well off) that the prospect of cash makes all kinds of uninspired people poetic:

> If cash sends out a tempting ray of hope,
> then raven poets and magpie poetesses
> you'd swear were singing Pegasus' nectar-flow.

The middle line has the unusual device of two nouns juxtaposed, the first functioning as an adjective. Not only that, the device occurs twice in the one line – *corvos poetas et poetridas picas*. Finally, linking up with the allusion to Pegasus in v. 1, we have the extraordinary line

> cantare credas Pegaseium nectar.

Theocritus had spoken of the Muse letting nectar drop on a poet's mouth. A critic of Horace's accuses him of believing that he alone distils the honey of poetry. But it took Persius to describe someone as 'singing nectar'. Also, he couples the noun with the adjective

Pegaseium (a form found nowhere else) which means 'pertaining to Pegasus', hence 'inspired by the Muses'.

This compressed, allusive, metaphorical style is at once the delight and the despair of the translator. If he irons out every peculiarity he is doing violence to the poet. If he always gives a literal rendering the result will in many cases be unintelligible. So he must simply use his judgement as best he can and hope that the over-all effect is reasonably accurate.

A NOTE ON SOME TRANSLATIONS OF
HORACE AND PERSIUS

For a long time the only translation of Horace's *Satires* readily obtainable in England was the Loeb version by H. R. Fairclough first printed in 1926. Fairclough was a sound scholar, and except in a very few cases he gave an accurate rendering of the Latin. But apart from the question of price and format, there ought surely to be more than one type of translation available. Fairclough's is in prose, which by definition involves a loss of rhythmical regularity. And the prose itself is often rather stilted. Here is the opening of the famous encounter with the pest on the Sacred Way (I. 9):

> I was strolling by chance along the Sacred Way, musing after my fashion on some trifle or other, and wholly intent thereon, when up there runs a man I knew only by name and seizes me by the hand: 'How d'ye do, my dearest fellow?' 'Pretty well, as times are now,' I answer, 'I hope you get all you want.'

I doubt if that represents the spoken English of any place or period. The earlier prose version by E. C. Wickham (1903), which Fairclough should have acknowledged, varies quite a lot in fluency, but it usually keeps close to the Latin. I have frequently consulted both these translations and am much in their debt.

The last verse translation to appear in England was that of John Conington (1874). Written in ten-syllable rhyming couplets, it is a work of great dexterity which can still be read with pleasure. Here is his rendering of the same passage of I. 9:

> Along the Sacred Road I strolled one day,
> Deep in some bagatelle (you know my way),

> When up comes one whose name I scarcely knew –
> 'The dearest of dear fellows! how d'ye do?'
> He grasped my hand – 'Well thanks: the same to you.'

As it happens, those five lines correspond to five in the original, but such compression could not be maintained. A little later the pest says of himself:

> 'There's not a man can turn a verse so soon,
> Or dance so nimbly when he hears a tune:
> While, as for singing – ah! my forte is there:
> Tigellius' self might envy me, I'll swear.'

'When he hears a tune', 'ah! my forte is there', and 'I'll swear' are all imported to eke out the rhyme. As a result of such expansion Conington's translation of I. 9 has 109 verses to Horace's 78. In defence it might be argued that, since Horace averages about fifteen syllables to a line as opposed to Conington's ten, Conington is justified in taking half as many lines again. But even if that were granted a more serious difficulty would remain, namely that the rhyming couplets make the sense-units too short and regular. The metre can still be used to translate Ovid's elegiacs – if one has the elegance and ingenuity of Mr L. P. Wilkinson. But it is really too tight a jacket for the Horatian *sermo*. This may sound an odd contention in view of the achievements of Pope, but then Pope was not translating; he was imitating. This allowed him to omit much of the original and to bring in characteristically brilliant effects of antithetical wit.

Consider vv. 7–14 of his dialogue with Fortescue in imitation of *Satires* II. 1:

> P. Timorous by nature, of the rich in awe,
>   I come to counsel learned in the law:
>   'You'll give me, like a friend both sage and free,
>   Advice; and (as you use) without a fee.'
> F. I'd write no more.
> P.   'Not write? but then I think,
>   And for my soul I cannot sleep a wink,
>   I nod in company, I wake at night,
>   Fools rush into my head, and so I write.'

Delightful, but only the tiniest nucleus comes from Horace, as a literal rendering will show: 'Trebatius, advise me what to do.' 'Take a rest.'

'You mean not write verses at all?' 'I do.' 'Dammit that *would* be the best thing, but I can't get to sleep.'

Even when full credit is given to these versions, the obvious fact remains that rhyming couplets would not do for a modern translation. They do not allow the thought to flow on in a conversational style, and they demand conventional licences of diction and word-order which are not granted today.[10] These were doubtless among the points in Professor Smith Palmer Bovie's mind when he produced his verse translation in 1959. Based on stress instead of rhyme, the rendering is fluent, contemporary, and often amusing. I did not consult it when preparing the present version, but I remember noting when I read it ten years ago that it did not attempt to keep very close to the Latin, and that from time to time it jazzed up the original by inserting intellectual jokes. For example, the phrase from I. 2. 113 *Inane abscindere soldo* (to mark off solid from void) is rendered 'to distinguish between romance and mere sexistentialism', and vv. 11–12 of I. 8 appear thus:

> A plebeian community sepulchre, 'Parasites Lost'
> (for guys like Pantolabus or that fool Nomentanus).

The situation with Persius was rather similar. There were two good prose translations – Conington (revised by Nettleship, 1893) and Ramsay (1918); one clever version in rhyming couplets (Tate, 1930); and a lively American rendering by Merwin (1961) in lines of five or six beats.[11]

As in the case of Horace, only the modern translator is capable of facing the obscene passages, scarce though they are. Tate justifies his evasions by a sophistical epigram: 'to turn physiological accuracy into literary indecency is not the function of a translator' (Introduction, p. 3). Conington in the Preface to his Horace is more candid: 'I have omitted two entire satires and several passages from others. Some of them no one would wish to see translated: some, though capable of being rendered without offence a hundred or even fifty years ago, could hardly be so rendered now' (i.e., in 1874). These two quotations show how the Victorian sense of propriety was already developing as the great lady ascended the throne, and how it still prevailed in the years preceding the Second World War. Its passing is not, perhaps, a matter for unmixed relief, but, however that may be, a translator can no longer claim that he is prevented from giving an honest rendering of his author by the delicacy of public taste.

The present translation is in verse because a prose rendering, apart from being superfluous, did not seem to offer much challenge. If this sounds rash, it must be remembered that satire was the least 'inspired' and the most relaxed and conversational of all the poetic genres. Like several recent translators I have chosen a line of six variable beats with a sufficient number of dactyls or anapaests to recall the movement of the original.[12] Since this is a rather rambling form, it seemed best, in the hope of achieving economy, to have the same number of verses as the original poems, and to reproduce their strong pauses when these occurred at the end of a line. For example, Horace I. 1 has full stops or question marks at the end of vv. 3, 5, 8, and 10. These are observed in the translation.

Stress, unlike quantity, is sometimes a rather subjective thing. Take the opening line of Horace I. 1:

How is it, Maecenas, that no one is content with his own lot?

The problem is confined to the first three words. In conversation we might say, 'how is it' or, more emphatically, 'how is it'. In this case, if we want to be accurate, we must say 'how is it'; otherwise the line will have one beat too many. Other lines can be read correctly in more than one way. One other point to bear in mind, though it may be rather obvious, is that pronouns carry a stress when emphasized. I have seldom thought it necessary to indicate this with italics. In the matter of stress, then, there is bound to be some variation between one reader and another. All I would claim is that every line can be read in a natural way with six beats.

In 1987 a new version of Persius, with the genuine taste of 'bitten nails' (I. 106), was published by Guy Lee. In the dilemma mentioned on p. 31 above he tends, perhaps rightly, to favour strangeness over accessibility. William Barr's commentary is an added bonus.

NOTES

1. Quintilian, *Institutiones Oratoriae* X. 1. 93.
2. A full account of the *satura*-question is given by C. A. Van Rooy and by M. Coffey (see Select Bibliography, p. 209).
3. Livy 7. 2.
4. Dryden, *Discourse Concerning the Original and Progress of Satire.* See W. P. Ker's edition of Dryden's essays, Oxford, 1926, vol. 2, pp. 86–7. There is a discussion of Dryden's essay in the appendix of

the present author's book *The Satires of Horace* (hereafter referred to as *SH*).

5.   *Rheinisches Museum* 97 (1954) 343–58.

6.   The question of satyrs in Rome is explored by T. P. Wiseman in *Journal of Roman Studies* 78 (1988) 1–13. See also the points made on pp. 30–31 of my commentary (Select Bibliography, p. 210).

7.   This short biography, based on material collected towards the end of the first century AD, will be found in the Loeb translation of Suetonius, vol. 2.

8.   Lucan, as quoted in the biography of Persius; see the Loeb translation of Suetonius, vol. 2, p. 496. Quintilian X. 1. 94; Martial IV. 29. 7.

9.   Cf. Tacitus, *Annals* 16.22 (Thrasea) and perhaps also 14.48 (Antistius); Dio 62.29 (Cornutus). This is somewhat modified by Suetonius, *Nero* 39, but that passage says nothing of attacks on the Emperor's poetry, and it does mention two cases of banishment.

10.   These points apply even more to the eight-syllable couplet. See Cowper's version of Horace I. 9.

11.   For earlier verse translations see W. Frost, 'English Persius: The Golden Age', *Eighteenth-Century Studies* 2 (1968) 77–101.

12.   The only exception is the Prologue of Persius, which is rendered in five-stress lines.

HORACE
Satires

BOOK I

SATIRE I

'Why are men discontented with their jobs? Presumably because they
would prefer to do something else. Yet if they were given the opportu-
nity to change they would most likely refuse it. A man will say that
he puts up with his job simply in order to save enough for his retire-
ment. But such men often continue to work even when they have
made sufficient money.' By now (v. 40) it appears that discontent is
in some way connected with greed. In the main section of the poem
(41–107) Horace talks to a miser who puts forward various arguments
in defence of greed. Finally at v. 108 the opening topic is reintroduced
in a modified form. 'As a result of envious greed few people can say
that they've had a happy life.'

How is it, Maecenas, that no one is content with his own lot –
whether he has got it by an act of choice or taken it up
by chance – but instead envies people in other occupations?
'It's well for the merchant!' says the soldier, feeling the weight of
[his years
and physically broken down by long weary service.
The merchant, however, when his ship is pitching in a southern gale,
cries 'Soldiering's better than this! Of course it is! You charge,
and all in a moment comes sudden death or the joy of victory.'
The expert in law and statute longs for the farmer's luck
when before daylight an anxious client knocks on his door.   10
The other, dragged up to town from the country to appear in court,
swears that only city folk know what happiness is.

To quote all the other examples would exhaust that windbag Fabius.
But I shan't keep you – here's what I'm getting at: suppose a god
were to say 'Behold, here am I, ready to grant

your wishes. You who just now were a soldier shall become a
                                                    [merchant,
and you who just now were a lawyer shall become a farmer. Right!
Exchange roles and away you go. What are you waiting for?'
they'd refuse, even though they could have their heart's desire.
20 Why should Jupiter keep his patience? He might well puff out
his cheeks in anger and vow with every justification
never again to be so obliging as to heed their prayers.

Again, not to skip over the subject with a laugh like someone
telling a string of jokes – and yet what harm can there be
in presenting the truth with a laugh, as teachers sometimes give
their children biscuits to coax them into learning their ABC?
However, joking aside, let's take the matter seriously.
That fellow turning the heavy soil with his rough plough,
the crooked barman, the soldier, and the sailors who dash so bravely
30 across the seven seas maintain that their only object
in enduring hardship is to make their pile, so when they are old
they can then retire with an easy mind. In the same way
the tiny ant with immense industry (for he is their model)
hauls whatever he can with his mouth and adds it to the heap
he is building, thus making conscious and careful provision for the
                                                    [future.
Then, as the year wheels round into dismal Aquarius, the ant
never sets foot out of doors but, very sensibly, lives
on what he has amassed. But you – neither scorching heat nor the
                                                    [cold
of winter can divert you from your money-grubbing; fire, tempest,
                                                    [sword –
40 nothing can stop you; no one else must be richer than you.
Why have a huge mass of silver and gold if it makes you
so nervous that you dig a hole in the ground and furtively bury it?
    'If you once broke in on it you'd soon be down to your last
                                                    [penny.'
If you don't break in on it what's so fine about having a heap?
Suppose your floor has threshed a hundred thousand bushels,
that doesn't mean your stomach will hold any more than mine.
If you belonged to a slave-gang and happened to be carrying the
                                                    [bread-bag
on your aching shoulders, you wouldn't get any more than the chap
who had carried nothing. Tell me, if a man lives within nature's

limits, what matter whether he has a hundred or a thousand acres   50
of ploughed land?
                    'But it's nice to draw from a big pile!'
But if you let us draw the same amount from our *little* pile,
why should your granaries be superior to our bins?
It's as if you needed only a jug or a glass of water
and said 'I'd sooner draw it from a big river than from this
piddling stream, although the amount would be just the same.'
That's how people who like more than their fair share
get swept away, bank and all, by the raging Aufidus,
while the man who wants only what he needs doesn't drink water
clouded with mud, nor does he lose his life in the torrent.   60

But many people are enticed by a desire which continually cheats
                                                    [them.
'Nothing is enough,' they say, 'for you're only worth what you
                                                    [have.'
What can you do with a man like that? You may as well tell him
to be miserable, since misery is what he enjoys. He's like the rich
Athenian miser who treated the people's remarks with contempt.
'The people hiss me,' he would say, 'but I applaud myself
when I reach home and set eyes on all the cash in my box!'

Tantalus thirstily strains at the waters eluding his lips –
what are you laughing at? Change the name and you are the subject
of the story. You scrape your money-bags together and fall asleep   70
on top of them with your mouth agape. They must remain unused
like sacred objects, giving no more pleasure than if painted on
                                                    [canvas.
Do you not realize what money is for, what enjoyment it gives?
You can buy bread and vegetables, half a litre of wine,
and the other things which human life can't do without.
Or maybe you prefer to lie awake half dead with fright,
to spend your days and nights in dread of burglars or fire
or your own slaves, who may fleece you and then disappear? For
                                                    [myself,
I think I can always do without blessing like those!

But if, you say, you happen to have caught a feverish chill,   80
or some other bit of bad luck has nailed you to your bed, you have
                                                    [someone

to sit beside you, prepare poultices, and get the doctor
to come and put you on your feet and restore you to your nearest
                                                [and dearest.
Don't you believe it. Your wife and son don't want you to recover.
Friends and neighbours, young and old, they all hate you.
Since you put money before all else small wonder that no one
offers you any affection. What do you do to earn it?
Or take your relatives, given you by nature with no effort
on your part – I suppose if you tried to hold and keep their love
you'd find it a futile waste of time, like training a donkey
to answer the rein and making him run in the Park races.

So let's put a limit to the scramble for money. As your wealth
                                                [increases
your fear of poverty should diminish, and having got what you
                                                [wanted
you ought to begin to bring that struggle to an end. Or else
you may finish up like Ummidius. The story won't take long:
this Ummidius was so rich that instead of counting
his money he weighed it, and so stingy that his clothes were never
better than a servant's, and yet to his dying day he was sure
he'd succumb to starvation. In fact he was split down the middle
                                                [with an axe
swung by a freedwoman, one of Clytemnestra's indomitable breed.

    'Well then, what do you want me to do? Live like Naevius
or Nomentanus?'
                    Ah, now you are setting together
things which are poles apart. When I urge you not to be a miser
I'm not saying you should be a rake and a wastrel. There is
a stage between the frigid midget and the massive vassal.
Things have a certain proportion. In short, there are definite limits;
if you step beyond them on this side or that you can't be right.

I return to my original point: must everyone, because of greed,
be at odds with himself and envy those in other occupations;
waste away because his neighbour's goat has more milk in her
                                                [udder;
and instead of comparing himself with the thousands who are
                                                [worse off,
struggle to outdo first him and then him? However fast
he runs there is always somebody richer just in front;

90

100

110

as when the teams spring from their pens and are swept along
in a flurry of hooves, the driver presses on the car ahead,
ignoring the one he has passed as it falls back among the stragglers.
So it is that we can rarely find a man who says
he has lived a happy life and who, when his time is up,
contentedly leaves the world like a guest who has had his fill.

Well, that's enough. I'd hate you to think I had pillaged the works   120
of old blood-shot Crispinus, so I shan't add another word.

SATIRE 2

*The opening section explores the idea that in avoiding one moral fault
fools lapse into its opposite (v. 24). From v. 28 on all the examples
given are of a sexual kind, and it becomes clear that the main theme
of the satire is folly as opposed to good sense in sexual relations. A
brief discussion of the structure will be found in the notes.*

*This is probably the earliest and certainly the bawdiest of all the
satires. None of the English commentators prints more than the first
twenty-eight lines. Pope wrote a very lively imitation entitled 'Sober
Advice from Horace'.*

The federated flute-girls' union, pedlars of quack medicines,
holy beggars, strippers, comics, and all that lot
are filled with sadness and dismay at the passing of Tigellius the
[singer;
he was such a *generous* person. This fellow here, however,
for fear of being called a wastrel would refuse a destitute friend
enough to keep out the cold and relieve the pinch of hunger.
If you ask another why, on receiving a splendid inheritance
from his father and grandfather, he is squandering it all on his
[greedy gullet,
ransacking the market for every kind of expensive food
with borrowed cash, he replies that he doesn't want to be thought   10
petty and mean. He is praised by some, condemned by others.

Fufidius, rich in land and equally rich in the money
he has lent, is afraid he may get the name of a spendthrift and
[waster.
So he charges five per cent per month – docked from the principal –

and the greater a man's distress the more relentlessly he hounds him.
He hunts for I.O.U.s from young men who have just
put on the adult toga and have stern fathers watching them.
Everyone who hears of him immediately says 'Good lord! But
[I take it
he lives on a scale in keeping with his income.' You'd scarcely
[believe
20 how harsh he is to himself. That father who appears in Terence's
play – I mean the one who has such a miserable time
after sending his son away – is less of a masochist than *he* is.

If anyone asks 'Now what's the point of all this?' I'll tell him:
In avoiding *one* sort of fault fools rush into its opposite.
Maltinus minces around with his tunic trailing low,
another has it hoisted obscenely up to his crotch, the refined
Rufillus smells of sweet cachous, Gargonius of goat.
There's no middle way. There are some who refuse to touch any
[women
unless their feet are concealed by a flounce sewn on their dress;
30 another must have the type that stands in a stinking brothel.
The sight of a certain aristocrat leaving a brothel drew
a famous remark from Cato: 'Keep up the good work!' he said.
'Whenever a young man's veins are swollen by accursed lust
he's right to go down to that sort of place instead of grinding
other men's wives.'
                    'I'd hate to be praised for a thing like that,'
Cupiennius says. (He fancies cunts which are dressed in white.)

It is worth your while to give ear, ye who wish ill success
to adulterous men, how on all sides they are beset by troubles,
how their pleasure is spoiled by many a pain, is won but rarely,
40 and then, as it often chances, amidst atrocious perils.
One has jumped from a roof, another has been flogged to death;
one while running away has blundered into a gang
of violent thugs; another has paid cash for his life;
another has been raped repeatedly by louts; there was even a case
where a man mowed the lover's balls and randy prick
with a sword. 'Perfectly legal,' said everyone. Galba dissented.

How much safer it is to do business with the second class –
freedwomen, I mean – though Sallust is as crazy over them
as the man who chases other men's wives. Now if Sallust wanted

to be kind and liberal in keeping with his means and the dictates of   50
                                                                    [reason,
showing at the same time a moderately generous spirit,
he would pay an adequate price which didn't involve ruin
and disgrace. Instead he smugly pats himself on the back
for this alone: 'I never touch a married woman.'
He is like Marsaeus, Miss Newcome's boyfriend, who once
                                                          [presented
his entire estate and family home to a striptease artist.
'I'd never have anything to do,' he said, 'with other men's wives.'
But you have with striptease artists and call-girls who damage your
                                                              [character
even worse than your finances. Or perhaps you think it's enough
to avoid the externals of adultery without avoiding the thing   60
that causes harm irrespective of class. To lose your good name
and to wreck your family inheritance is always wrong. What matter
whether your partner is a married lady or a wench with a cloak?

Villius who, thanks to Joy, was Sulla's son-in-law,
was sadly taken in by the name. He suffered enough –
and more; he was punched, attacked with a sword, and had the
                                                                [door
slammed in his face while Longarenus was inside.
Imagine him gazing on these disasters and hearing the voice
of his cock: 'What do you think you're doing? When my blood is up
I never insist, do I, on being provided with a cunt   70
descended from a mighty consul and veiled by a lady's robe?'
What would he say? 'But the girl has a most distinguished father!'
Nature's advice is directly opposed to *your* attitude
and much more sensible. She has ample wealth of her own
if only you would use it wisely and not confuse
wholesome with harmful. Do you think it's irrelevant whether your
                                                              [trouble
is your own fault or beyond your control? So stop chasing
married women or you may be sorry. You may well find
the pain and hardship far outweigh any real pleasure.
She may be decked in emeralds and snowy pearls, but that   80
doesn't give her a straighter leg or a softer thigh than Cerinthus
boasts. And often the girl with the cloak is better still.
Also she carries her wares without disguise, revealing
what she has for sale; if she possesses a good feature
she doesn't parade it and flaunt it while trying to hide her blemishes.

Sheiks have an interesting habit: when buying horses they cover
                                                          [them
before inspection, for fear a handsome shape with (as often)
a tender hoof underneath may fool the buyer as he gapes
at the lovely haunches, the small head, and the high neck.
90 And they're very wise. You mustn't examine the finest features
of a body with Lynx's eyes and then be as blind as Hypsaea
to defects. 'O legs! O arms!' But she has a small bottom,
a big nose, a short waist, and huge feet.

With a married lady you can't see a thing except her face.
The rest is covered by her long dress – unless she's a Catia.
If you want forbidden fruit protected by a wall (and that,
I may say, is what drives you crazy) you'll find a host of snags –
attendants, a litter, coiffeuses, female hangers-on,
a dress reaching to the ankles and on top of that a wrap –
100 a hundred things prevent you from getting a clear view.
With the other there's no problem. Her Coan silk allows you
to see her virtually naked, there's no chance of concealing
bad legs or ugly feet; you can check her profile.
Or perhaps you'd rather be taken in and fleeced of your money
before you inspect the goods?
                              The poet sings how the hunter
tracks the hare through the deep snow; when he sees it lying there
he won't touch it. Then he adds 'So with my love; it speeds
past what's ready to hand, pursuing what flies away.'
Do you think you'll succeed with the help of little ditties like that
110 in expelling the pain and turmoil and passion that vex your heart?
Would it not do more good to ask what limit nature
sets to desire, what privations she'll bear, and what
will cause her pain, and so distinguish solid from void?
When your throat is parched with thirst, do you insist on having
a golden tankard? When famished do you turn up your nose at all
but peacock and turbot? When your organ is stiff, and a servant girl
or a young boy from the household is near at hand and you know
you can make an immediate assault, would you sooner burst with
                                                        [tension?
Not me. I like sex to be there and easy to get.
120 'Not just yet', 'But I need more money', 'If my husband's away' –
that kind of girl's for the Gauls, Philodemus says; he goes
for the one who isn't too dear and who comes promptly when
                                                        [called.

She ought to be fair, well-poised, and smartly turned out, though
                                                            [she shouldn't
try to appear more tall or pale than she naturally is.
When a girl like that slips her left side under my right
she is Lady Ilia or Countess Egeria; I call her what I please.
No fear, while I'm fucking, that her husband will rush back to town,
the door crash open, the dog bark, and the house resound
with an awful din; that the woman, deathly white, will jump
out of bed, her accomplice shriek, and we'll all be in terror – the   130
                                                            [maid
for her legs, the guilty mistress for her dowry, and me for myself.
I have to run off barefoot with my clothes undone, or else
my cash or my arse or at least my respectability has had it.
It's tough to be caught; even Fabius would grant me that.

SATIRE 3

*The opening lines describe various kinds of unbalanced behaviour
exhibited by Tigellius the Sardinian. Then, after a brief transitional
passage (20–24), Horace goes on to deal with people's lack of toler-
ance in social relations. They criticize their friends' minor foibles
while remaining blind to their own. Such harshness is inconsistent and
unfair.*

   *In the second main section (76–118) Horace moves from friendship
to society as a whole. The argument now is 'Everyone is prone to do
wrong, so let us be fair in our punishments.' This plea for a sense of
proportion and a rational scale of penalties is directed against the
doctrinaire Stoics who maintained that all sins were equally culpable.*

   *The satire ends with a picture of the Stoic preacher, friendless and
ridiculous.*

Singers all have the same fault. When asked to perform
for their friends they never will; when no one asks them they never
stop. Tigellius, that typical Sard, had the same habit.
If Caesar, who could have made it an order, had merely requested
a song on the strength of his father's friendship and of his own,
he'd have wasted his time. Yet when in the mood the fellow would
                                                            [sing
at dinner through every course 'Come ye Bacchanals', ranging
from a high tenor to the lowest note the lyre can produce.

The man was a bundle of inconsistencies. Often he'd run
10 as if someone were after his blood; more often you'd think he was
                                                    [carrying
the sacred vessels of Juno. Sometimes he'd keep two hundred
servants, sometimes ten. After talking in lordly tones
about kings and princes, 'All I ask is a three-legged table,'
he'd say, 'clean salt in a shell, and a coat, however coarse,
to keep out the cold.' If you'd given a thousand pounds to that
                                                    [model
of thrift and simplicity, it would have burnt a hole in his pocket
in less than a week. He never went to bed until dawn,
and then snored all day. He was the most contradictory creature
that ever lived.
                        Now someone may say 'What about you?
20 Have *you* no faults?'
                              Oh yes! but they're different and perhaps less
                                                    [serious.
Once when Maenius was bitching about Newman, someone said
                                                    ['Hey there,
are you not conscious of what *you're* like? Or do you think *we* can
                                                    [fail
to be conscious of it?' 'I'm conscious but without a conscience,' said
                                                    [Maenius.
That sort of silly brazen egotism ought to be pilloried.

Before examining your own faults you smear ointment
on your bloodshot eyes, but when it comes to your friends' foibles
your sight is as sharp as an eagle's or the Epidaurian snake's.
Unfortunately they in their turn scrutinize *your* deficiencies.
So and so's a bit hot-tempered and not quite up to the curling
30 nostrils of modern society; he may cause amusement by his
                                                    [countrified
haircut, his sloppy toga, and the shoes a size too large
which barely stay on his feet. And yet he's a good man –
none better, *and* he's your friend, *and* a prodigious talent
lurks beneath that uncouth exterior. So give yourself a shaking
in case the seeds of wickedness have already been planted in you
by nature or by some bad habit. If you once neglect a field
bracken appears which eventually has to be burnt out.

Think instead of how a young man, blindly in love,
fails to notice his girl-friend's blemishes or even finds them

enchanting, as Balbinus did with the wen on Hagna's nose.   40
I wish we made the same mistake when judging our friends
and our moral language had a term of praise for this delusion.
If a friend has some defect, we shouldn't feel disgust
but behave like a father to his son. If the boy happens to squint,
his father calls him 'Castor'; if he's miserably undersized,
as was the case with Sisyphus the dwarf, he's called 'Smallie';
if his knees knock hard together he's 'Pigeon'; if his bandy legs
can hardly support him, the pet name used by his father is 'Bowie'.
So if one of your friends is a bit close-fisted, let's say he's thrifty;
if another is inclined to be tactless and loud-mouthed – well, he   50
                                                              [wants
his friends to think him sociable; or suppose he's rather ill-mannered
and outspoken to the point of rudeness, let's call him forthright and
                                                              [fearless.
Is he something of a hot-head? Then put him down as a keen type.
I really believe this habit both joins and cements friendships.

But in fact we turn the *good* qualities upside down
in our zeal to dirty a clean jar. If someone we know
is a decent and wholly unassuming fellow, we give him the nickname
'Slowcoach' or 'Fathead'; another avoids every trap
and never leaves himself open to hostile attack, because life
as we live it is a battlefield where envy is sharp and slanders   60
fly thick and fast; instead of saying he's jolly sensible
and no fool, we call him crafty and insincere.
If a man is rather uninhibited (the sort of fellow I would often
wish you to think *me*, Maecenas), breaking in
with some tiresome chatter when his friend is reading or quietly
                                                              [thinking,
we say 'He's got absolutely no *savoir faire*.' How casually
we endorse a law that is against ourselves! For no one is free
from faults; the best is the man who is hampered by the smallest.
                                                              [A kindly
friend will weigh, as is fair, my virtues against my failings,
and if he wants my affection he will come down on the side   70
of my virtues as being more numerous (if in fact they *are* more
                                                              [numerous!).
On that principle he will be weighed in the same scales.
If you expect your friend to put up with your boils
you'll forget about his warts. It's fair that anyone who asks
indulgence for his faults should grant the same in return.

Since, then, anger and the other failings so deeply rooted
in human folly can't be cut out once and for all,
why doesn't Reason employ weights and measures of her own
and curb offences with the type of punishment suited to each?
80 Suppose a servant, told to remove a dish, has a lick
at the half-eaten fish and the lukewarm sauce; if his master hanged
                                                                [him
sane people would swear he was more insane than Labeo.
How much madder and graver a fault is this: a friend
commits some trivial offence which you really ought to ignore
if you're not to appear churlish; yet you loathe him heartily and
                                                                [dodge him
like a fellow who owes Ruso money and is bound to scrape up
the interest or principal from somewhere before the pitiless first
of the month or else put up his hands like a prisoner of war
and listen to his creditor's 'Studies in History' with teeth on edge.
90 What if a friend in a tipsy moment wets the couch
or knocks off the table a bowl which must have been worn thin
by old Evander's fingers? Or say he is feeling hungry
and grabs a chicken that was served in my side of the dish,
shall I like him any the less for that? What would I do
if he stole, or went back on a pledge, or broke his word of honour?
Those who hold that sins are largely the same are floored
by real situations. Common sense and tradition say no,
and so does Expediency, the virtual mother of justice and fairness.

When living creatures crawled from the earth in its early days,
100 they were speechless and ugly beasts; they fought over lairs and
                                                                [acorns
with their nails and fists, and then with clubs, and so on
with the weapons which experience produced at each successive
                                                                [stage,
until they discovered nouns and verbs which gave a meaning
to their cries and feelings. Thereafter they began to avoid war,
to build towns, and to pass laws which made it a crime
for any person to engage in brigandage, theft, or adultery.
For Helen wasn't the first bitch to cause a war
by her foul behaviour, but men in those days died in obscurity;
making hurried and promiscuous love like beasts they were done
110 to death by a stronger rival, as happens with bulls in a herd.
If you're willing to read your way through the records of world
                                                                [history

you will have to admit that justice arose from the fear of its
                                                              [opposite.
Nature cannot distinguish between right and wrong as she does
in the case of desirable and undesirable, wholesome and harmful.
Reason will never prove that the man who breaks off a juicy
cabbage from someone's garden and the man who makes off at night
with sacred emblems are committing one and the same offence.
Let's have a fair penalty-scale for offences, or else
you may flay with the terrible cat something which merits the strap.
You might of course give a caning for a crime which called for the   120
                                                              [lash,
but that's not what I fear when you say theft's on a par
with armed robbery and threaten to use the same hook
for pruning every crime, great and small alike,
if you were given the crown.
                         But if the sage alone
is rich and handsome and a good cobbler and also a king,
why crave what you have?
                         'You don't understand,' he says,
'what the good Chrysippus means. The sage has never made
himself shoes or sandals, but the wise man's still a cobbler.'
                                                    How's that?
'Well even when silent, Hermogenes remains a first-rate singer
and composer; that smart fellow Alfenus, even after throwing   130
all the tools of his trade away and shutting up shop,
was still a cobbler; in the same way the sage alone
is master of every craft, and hence a king.'
                                        The cheeky
youngsters tug at your beard, and if you don't keep them at bay
with your stick they swarm around and mob you, while you, poor
                                                              [devil,
howl till you burst your lungs, O highest of Royal Highnesses!

So, not to labour the point, as you tread your kingly way
to a tenpenny bath without a single attendant to escort you,
except that ass Crispinus, my kind friends will forgive me
if, as a result of being a fool, I do something wrong.   140
I in turn will gladly overlook their lapses,
and, though a commoner, shall live a happier life than Your
                                                          [Majesty.

SATIRE 4

*In justifying his satire against the charge of malice Horace makes the
following points: 'the Greek comic writers and the Roman satirist
Lucilius branded criminals (1–7); unlike the wordy moralist Crispinus
I write very little (14–18); unlike the vain Fannius I do not seek
publicity (21–3); the innocent have nothing to fear (64–8); I do not
intend my poems to be sold, nor do I give public recitations (71–4);
real malice is quite different – it means backbiting one's friends and
spreading scandal (81–103); I was taught to notice wicked behaviour
by my father; he used individuals as examples of vice (103–131); I am
really quite a good-humoured fellow (91–2, 101–4); my observations
are for my own improvement (137–8); and my writings are just an
amusing pastime (138–9).'*

*In regard to style Horace says that Lucilius was harsh and careless
in his composition, and that he wrote too much (8–13). Later (39–
62) he argues that, unlike epic, satire is not really poetry; it is more in
the nature of metrical prose. Like New Comedy it remains close to
the level of everyday speech.*

*This is not a piece of dispassionate literary theory but a lively and
polemical statement of Horace's own conception of satire.*

Take the poets Cratínus, Eúpolis, and Aristophanes,
and the other men who go to make up the Old Comedy.
Whenever a person deserved to be publicly exposed for being
a crook and a thief, a lecher or a cut-throat, or for being notorious
in any other way, they would speak right out and brand him.

Lucilius derives entirely from them; he followed their lead
changing only their rhythms and metres – a witty fellow
with a keen nose, but harsh when it came to versification.
That's where his fault lay. As a *tour de force* he would often
10 dictate two hundred lines an hour standing on his head.
As he flowed muddily on, there were things you'd want to remove.
A man of many words, he disliked the effort of writing –
writing properly, that is; I don't care a hoot for quantity.

Here's Crispinus offering me long odds: 'Just take
your jotter if you please and I'll take mine. Let's fix a time
and a place and umpires; then see which of us can write the more.'

Thank God for giving me a timid mind with few ideas,
one which seldom speaks and then says practically nothing.
But you go ahead and give your version of a goat-skin bellows,
panting and puffing until the iron turns soft in the fire.   20

Fannius is happy to present his works unasked, complete
with a case to hold them and a bust of himself. But no one reads
what I write, for I shrink from giving public recitals –
there are certain people, you see, who detest this kind of writing,
for most *deserve* a scolding. Pick anyone you like
from a crowd: he's plagued with greed or else the curse of ambition.
One is obsessed with married women, another with boys.
One loves the glitter of silver; Albius stares at bronze.
One barters his wares from beneath the eastern sky
to lands warmed by the evening sun; he is swept along   30
through hardships, like dust raised by a whirlwind, in constant
                                                            [dread
of losing a penny of his capital or failing to make a profit.
All such men are afraid of verses and loathe poets.
   'There's hay on his horns! Give him a wide berth! For the sake
of raising a laugh he'll have no respect for himself or his friends.
And when he has smeared some dirt on his page, he is bursting to
                                                            [pass it
on to all the old women and servants on their way home
from tank and bake-house.'
                            Now let me say a few words in reply:
First, I'd exclude myself from those who can properly be called
poets. You would not consider it enough simply to turn   40
a metrical line. Nor, if a man wrote, as I do,
in a style rather close to prose, would you count him as a poet.
The honour of that name should be kept for someone with a natural
gift, an inspired soul, and a voice of mighty music.
That's why people have asked whether comedy is genuine poetry,
for in language and subject-matter it lacks the fire and force
of passion, and except that it differs from prose in the regularity
of its rhythm, it is prose pure and simple.
                                    'But you see the father
in a blazing temper with his wastrel of a son who dotes on a
                                                            [call-girl,
refuses to accept a wife who would bring him a fat dowry,   50

and causes dreadful embarrassment by parading drunkenly with
                                                            [torches
before dusk.'
                        But surely young Pomponius would get
just as severe a scolding from a father in real life?
So it isn't enough to write out a line in plain words
which, rearranged, could be spoken by any angry father
like the one in the play. As for the stuff that I'm writing now
and Lucilius wrote in earlier times, suppose you destroyed
the regular quantities and rhythm, reversing the order of words
and putting what is now at the end of a line right at the beginning,
60   it would not be the same as jumbling up 'when loathsome Discord
smashed apart the ironed posts and portals of war',
where you'd still find the remains of a poet, however dismembered.
But that's enough. Some other time we'll discuss whether this
type of writing is genuine poetry; at present I only ask
whether you're right to regard it with such suspicion. The zealous
Sulcius and Caprius prowl about with their hoarse indictments
causing a lot of anxiety to thugs, but anyone who lives
a decent life and has a clean record can dismiss them both.
And even supposing you were a thug like Caelius or Birrius,
70   I'd never be a Caprius or Sulcius. Why should you fear me?
No stall or pillar will offer my little books to be mauled
by the sweaty hands of Hermogenes Tigellius and the rest of the
                                                            [mob
and I never give readings except to friends – and then only
when pressed – not *anywhere* and to *any* audience. There are
                                                  [numerous people
who read their work in the middle of the square, or in the baths
(a lovely resonance comes from the vaulted space). It appeals
to empty heads, who never reflect whether their behaviour
is ill-timed or in bad taste.
                        'You like giving pain,'
says a voice, 'and you do it out of sheer malice.'
                                          Where did you get
80   that slander to throw at me? Is it endorsed by any
of my circle? The man who traduces a friend behind his back,
who won't stand up for him when someone else is running him
                                                            [down,
who looks for the big laugh and wants to be thought a wit,
the man who can invent what he never saw but can't keep a secret –
he's the blackguard; beware of *him*, O son of Rome!

Often, when four are dining on each of the three couches,
you will notice one who throws all kinds of dirt at the rest
except for the host – and at him too, later on, when he's drunk
and the truthful god of freedom unlocks his inner heart.
This is the fellow whom *you* think charming and civilized and   90
                                                    [forthright –
you, the enemy of blackguards!
                        If I laughed because the fatuous
Rufillus smells of sweet cachous, Gargonius of goat,
do you think I'm spiteful and vicious for that? If you were present
when someone happened to mention the theft carried out by Petillius
Capitolinus, you would defend him in your loyal way:
'I've known Capitolinus well and valued his friendship
since we were boys. He has done me many a favour (I had only
to ask him), and I'm glad that he's living in town as a free man.
Still – I'll never understand how he got away with that lawsuit!'
Now *there's* the essence of the black cuttlefish; *there's* the genuine   100
acid of malice. Such nastiness will never appear in my pages,
or even in my thoughts.
                        If for myself I can promise anything surely
I promise that.
                Yet if I'm a little outspoken or perhaps
too fond of a joke, I hope you'll grant me that privilege.
My good father gave me the habit; to warn me off
he used to point out various vices by citing examples.
When urging me to practise thrift and economy and to be content
with what he himself had managed to save he used to say:
'Notice what a miserable life young Albius leads and how Baius
is down and out – a salutary warning not to squander   110
the family's money.' Steering me away from a squalid attachment
to a whore he would say: 'Don't be like Scetanus!' To stop me
chasing another man's wife when legitimate sex was available:
'It isn't nice to get a name like that of Trebonius – he
was caught in the act.' He would add: 'A philosopher will give you
                                                    [reasons
why this is desirable and that is better avoided. For me
it's enough to preserve the ways which our forefathers handed
                                                    [down,
to look after your physical safety and keep your name untarnished
while you need a guardian. When time has toughened your body and
                                                    [mind
you'll be able to swim without a ring.' And so by his talk   120

he would form my young character. Recommending something he'd
                                                                    [say:
'You've a good precedent for that,' and point to one of the judges
selected by the Praetor; or by way of dissuading me: 'How can you
                                                                    [doubt,'
he'd say, 'whether this is a wrong and foolish thing to do
when X and Y are the centre of a blazing scandal?'
                                                            The sick
who are tempted to over-eat are given a fright by the funeral
of the man next door, and the terror of death compels them to go
                                                                    [easy;
young folk too are often deterred from doing wrong
by the ill repute of other people. That is the reason
130   why I am free from the graver vices and have to cope
only with milder, more venial, faults.
                                                    Perhaps even these
may be largely removed by the lapse of time or the straight talk
of a friend, or my own reflection. For when I go off to my sofa
or the colonnade, I'm not idle: 'This is more honest;
this will help to improve my life; this will endear me
to my friends; that was a dirty trick so and so did; could I
ever be so thoughtless as to act like that?' Such is the discourse
that I hold behind closed lips. When I get any free time
I amuse myself on paper. That's one of the milder faults
140   I mentioned above. If you aren't prepared to fall in with this habit
a mighty company of poets will rally round to bring me
assistance (for we are by far the larger group in numbers)
and, like the Jews, we shall make you fall in with our happy band.

SATIRE 5

*This is an account of the journey which Horace took in the company
of Maecenas to a summit conference – probably that which was held
in Tarentum in the spring of 37 BC. As a result of this conference the
final clash between Antony and Octavian was postponed for another
six years. Apart from his value as a travelling companion Horace may
have had some secretarial duties to perform, but this is never stated
and the serious purpose of the trip is not allowed to obtrude.*

*The sketch-map opposite shows the route taken. I have added
Venusia (Horace's birthplace) and Tarentum, even though they are*

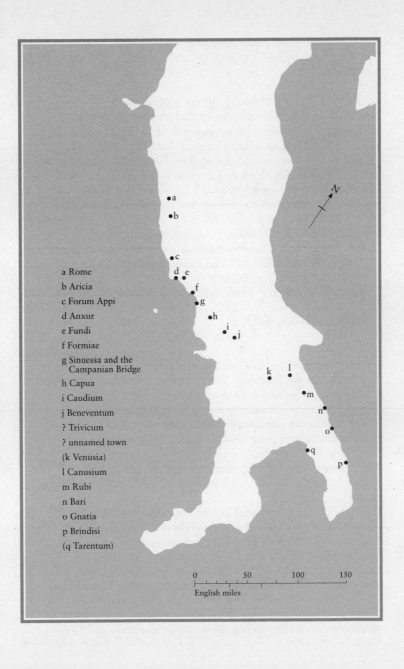

a Rome

b Aricia

c Forum Appi

d Anxur

e Fundi

f Formiae

g Sinuessa and the
  Campanian Bridge

h Capua

i Caudium

j Beneventum

? Trivicum

? unnamed town

(k Venusia)

l Canusium

m Rubi

n Bari

o Gnatia

p Brindisi

(q Tarentum)

0   50   100   150

English miles

not mentioned in the poem. The total distance from Rome to Brindisi
was about 340 miles. The journey as described by Horace took just
under a fortnight.

Leaving the big city, I found lodgings at Aricia
in a smallish pub. With me was Heliodorus, the professor
of rhetoric, the greatest scholar in the land of Greece. From there
to Forum Appi crammed with bargees and stingy landlords.
Being lazy types we divided this stretch, though speedier travellers
do it in one. The Appian is easier when taken slowly.
Here I declared war on my stomach because of the water
which was quite appalling, and waited impatiently as the other
                                                                    [travellers
enjoyed their dinner.
                          Night was preparing to draw her shadows
10 over the earth and to sprinkle the heavens with glimmering lights
when the lads started to shout at the boatmen, who replied in kind.
   'Bring her over here!' 'How many hundred are you going to
                                                                    [pack in?'
   'Whoah, that's enough!'
                          While the fares are collected and the mule
                                                    [harnessed,
a whole hour goes by. The blasted mosquitoes and the marsh
frogs make sleep impossible. The boatman, who has had a skinful
of sour wine, sings of his distant loved one, and a traveller
tries to outdo him. At last the weary traveller begins
to nod. The lazy boatman allows the mule to graze;
he ties the rope to a stone and lies on his back snoring.
20 When day dawns we find the barge is making no progress.
This is remedied when a furious passenger jumps ashore,
seizes a branch of willow, and wallops the mule and the boatman
on the head and back.
                          It was almost ten before we landed.
We washed our hands and face in Feronia's holy spring.
Then after breakfast we crawled three miles up to Anxur
perched on its shining rocks which are visible far and wide.
This was where the excellent Maecenas was due to come,
along with Cocceius – envoys on a mission of huge importance;
both were adept at reconciling friends who had quarrelled.
30 I went in to smear some black salve on my eyes,
which were rather bloodshot. Meanwhile Maecenas and Cocceius
                                                                    [arrived,

and also Fonteius Capito, a man of consummate charm
and tact, who held a unique place in Antony's affections.

We left Fundi with relief in the Praetorship of Aufidius Luscus,
laughing at the gear of that fatuous official – the toga complete
with border, the broad-striped tunic, and the pan of glowing
                                                          [charcoal.
After a weary journey, we stopped at the Mamurras' city.
Murena lent us his home, Capito provided the food.

Dawn the next day found us in a state of high
excitement, for on reaching Sinuessa we were joined by Plotius,   40
                                                          [Varius,
and Virgil. No finer men have ever walked the face
of the earth; and no one is more dearly attached to them all than I am.
Imagine how pleased we were and how warmly we greeted each
                                                          [other!
For me there's nothing in life to compare with the joy of friendship.
Near the Campanian Bridge accommodation was provided
by a small house, fuel and salt by official caterers.
Then, at Capua, the mules laid down their packs early.
Maecenas went off to take exercise; Virgil and I had a sleep,
for ball-games are bad for inflamed eyes and dyspeptic stomachs.

Next we put up at a well-stocked villa belonging to Cocceius,   50
which overlooks the inns of Caudium. Now, O Muse,
recount in brief, I pray thee, the clash of Sarmentus the clown
with Messius Cicirrus, and from what lineage each entered
the fray. Messius comes of glorious stock – Oscans!
Sarmentus' lady owner is still alive. With such
pedigrees they joined battle. Sarmentus was the first to strike:
'I declare you're the image of a wild horse!'
                                        'Right!' says Messius,
amid general laughter, and tosses his head.
                                        'Hey,' says the other,
'If you scare us like that when your horn's cut off, what would
                                                          [you do
with it still on your head?' (The point being that the left side   60
of his hairy brow was in fact disfigured by an ugly scar.)
After many jokes about Messius' face and 'Campanian disease'
he pleaded with him to do the dance of the shepherd Cyclops,
swearing he would have no need of a mask or tragic buskins.

Cicirrus wasn't lost for an answer. Had Sarmentus got round to
                                                    [offering
his chain, as promised, to the household gods? His status of clerk
in no way diminished his mistress's claim on him. Finally, why
had he bothered to run away when a single pound of meal
would have been enough for a tiny miserable scrap like him?

70   We had great fun as the party continued into the night.

From there straight on to Beneventum, where the fussy host very
                                                    [nearly
burnt his house down while turning some skinny thrushes on the
                                                    [fire.
For Vulcan fell out sideways through the old stove, and his darting
flame instantly shot up to lick the roof overhead.
Then, what a sight! greedy guests and frightened servants
snatching up the dinner and all struggling to put out the blaze.

From that point on Apulia began to bring into view
her familiar hills. They were scorched as usual by the Scirocco,
and we'd never have crawled across them had it not been for a villa
80   close to Trivícum which provided shelter – and weepy smoke.
(Damp branches were burning in the stove, leaves and all.)
Here, like an utter fool, I stayed awake till midnight
waiting for a girl who broke her promise. Sleep in the end
overtook me, still keyed up for sex. Then scenes from a dirty
dream spattered my nightshirt and stomach as I lay on my back.

From there we bowled along in waggons for twenty-four miles
putting up at a little town which can't be named in verse,
though easily placed by its features: there they sell the most common
of all commodities – water, but their bread is quite the finest,
90   and a traveller, if wise, usually carries some with him on his journey;
for the sort you get at Canusium (founded by bold Diomédes
of yore) is gritty, and your jug is no better off for water.
Varius here said a sad good-bye to his tearful friends.

The following night we arrived at Rubi, utterly jaded
from covering a long stretch of road damaged by heavy rain.
On the next day the weather was better but the road worse
all the way to the walls of Bari, renowned for fish.

Then Gnatia, on whose construction the water-nymphs scowled,
provided fun and amusement by trying to persuade us that incense
melts without fire on the temple steps; Apella the Jew   100
may believe it – not me, for I have learned that the gods live a life
of calm, and that if nature performs a miracle, it's not
sent down by the gods in anger from their high home in the sky.

Brindisi marks the end of this long tale and journey.

SATIRE 6

*'In spite of your distinguished ancestry, Maecenas, you don't look
down on people of humble birth. But snobbery is very prevalent, and
it's hard for ordinary men to reach high positions. Yet perhaps such
men are happier without political power. Certainly I have no ambition
for myself, in spite of what people think. The position which I enjoy
as your friend is a private matter. I gained it through personal qualities,
for which I have to thank my father. He was responsible for my
upbringing and education. The kind of life which I now enjoy would
be impossible if I ever entered on a public career.'*

*A well-to-do young Roman with political ambition would first do
a period of military service. Then, in his late twenties, after holding
some minor civil magistracy, he would stand for the Quaestorship.
This office, which dealt with finance, carried with it admission to the
Senate. After that, he might do a spell of civil administration as an
Aedile before becoming a candidate for the Praetorship – an important
office concerned with the administration of justice. Finally, at about
the age of forty-two, he would be eligible for the Consulship.*

*Horace did not wish to embark on this career himself, and he
thought little of those who were now competing for positions of
power. Yet he felt that such positions ought to be open to men of
ability and not be restricted, as they had been in the past, to members
of the upper class. These mixed emotions make the satire a rather
complex poem.*

Although of all the Lydians settled on Tuscan soil
none is of more exalted birth than you, Maecenas,
and though you had forebears on both your mother's and father's
                                                          [side
who held command over mighty legions in days gone by,

you don't on that account curl your nostril, as most people do,
at men with unknown or (like myself) with freedmen fathers.
When you assert that a man's parentage makes no difference
provided he himself is a gentleman, you rightly acknowledge
that before Tullius held sway with his undistinguished monarchy
10   many a man of no pedigree succeeded in living
an upright life and was often honoured with high office;
whereas Laevinus, a descendant of that Valerius who hurled
Tarquin the Proud from his throne and drove him into exile, was
                                                              [never
rated a penny the higher, even by the verdict of the people
(that judge whom you know so well), who often foolishly confer
office on worthless candidates and are stupidly enthralled by fame,
gaping entranced at inscriptions and busts. So what is the right
course for us who live in a different world from the masses?

For granted the people would have liked to put a Laevinus in office
20   rather than a self-made Decius, and Appius the Censor would have
                                                              [struck
me off the roll because my father wasn't a gentleman –
and rightly, for I ought to have rested content in my own skin.
Yet Glory drags in chains behind her dazzling car
the obscure no less than the noble. What did it do for Tillius
to resume the broad stripe he had shed and become a Tribune?
Resentment increased. (It would have been less had he stayed out of
                                                              [politics.)

When a man is silly enough to wind those black straps
around his calves and have a broad stripe going down his chest
he immediately hears 'Who *is* this fellow? What was his father?'
30   Anyone who suffered from Barrus' complaint and was eager to win
fame for his beauty would, wherever he went, arouse
the girls' anxious concern about personal details: 'What sort of
face and legs and feet and teeth and hair does he have?'

So anyone who claims that *he* will take charge of the citizen body,
capital, Italy, empire, and the holy shrines of the gods,
inevitably causes the whole world to take notice and ask
who his father was and whether he's stained by a low-born mother.
   'Do you, the son of Syrus, Dionysius or Dama, presume
to hurl Romans from the rock or hand them over to Cadmus?'
40   'Why not? My colleague Newman sits in the row behind me.

He is now what my father was.'
                        'Do you think that *that*
makes *you* a Paulus or Messalla? If a couple of hundred waggons
crashed into three big funerals in the Forum, Newman could
                                                  [drown
the horns and trumpets with his voice; at least he has that in his
                                                    [favour.'

I now revert to myself – only a freedman's son,
run down by all as only a freedman's son,
now because I'm a friend of yours, Maecenas, before
because as a military tribune I commanded a Roman legion.
The two factors are different; a person might have reason
to grudge me that rank, but he shouldn't grudge me your friendship   50
                                                  [too,
especially as you are so careful to choose suitable people,
and to hold aloof from rogues on the make. I could never say
I was lucky in the sense that I *just happened* to win your friendship.
It wasn't chance that brought you into my life. In the first place
the admirable Virgil and then Varius told you what I was.
When I met you in person I simply gulped out a few words,
for diffidence tied my tongue and stopped me from saying more.
I didn't pretend I had a distinguished father or owned
estates outside Tarentum which I rode around on a horse.
I told you what I was. As usual, you answered briefly. I left.   60
Nine months later you asked me back and bade me to join
your group of friends. For me the great thing is that I won
the regard of a discriminating man like you, not by having
a highly distinguished father but by decency of heart and character.

Yet if my faults are not too serious and not too many,
if my nature, apart from such blemishes, in other respects is sound
(just as on a handsome body you might notice a few moles),
if no one can fairly accuse me of greed or meanness or frequenting
brothels, if (to blow my own trumpet) my life is clean
and above reproach, and my friends are fond of me, then the credit   70
is due to my father.
                         He was a poor man with a few
scraggy acres, yet he wouldn't send me to Flavius' school
where important boys, the sons of important sergeant-majors,
would go, with satchel and slate swinging from the left arm,
clutching their tenpenny fee on the Ides of every month.

Instead he courageously took his boy to Rome, to be taught
the skills which any knight or senator would have his own
progeny taught. Anyone who noticed my clothes and the servants
in attendance (a feature of city life) would have assumed
80 that the money for these items came from the family coffers.
My father himself, who was the most impeccable guardian,
went with me to all my classes. In short he preserved my innocence
(the basic feature of a good character), and therefore saved me
not only from nasty behaviour but from nasty imputations.
He wasn't worried that someone might fault him later on
if I became an auctioneer or, like himself, a broker,
and didn't make much money; nor would I have complained.
As it is, I owe him all the more respect and gratitude.

I would never dream of complaining of such a father, and so
90 while people often protest that it's no fault of theirs
that they don't happen to possess noble and famous parents,
I shan't adopt that line. What *I* say and think is entirely
different. If, at a certain point in our lives, nature
ordered us all to travel again the way we had come
and to choose, in keeping with our self-esteem, whatever parents
we each thought best, I should be happy with the ones I had;
I should not choose people whose honour was officially attested by
                                                                   [rods
and thrones. The masses would think me crazy, but you might think
I was wise to avoid a load of trouble which I've never been used to.

100 For then I should immediately have to acquire a large establishment,
greet more visitors, take one or two companions with me
to avoid being on my own when going off to the country
or travelling abroad; I should have to maintain more grooms and
                                                                   [horses
and take a convoy of waggons. As things are, I can
if I wish go all the way to Tarentum on a gelded mule
with his flanks chafed by the heavy pack and his withers by the
                                                                   [rider.
No one will call me stingy as they do you, Tillius,
when though a Praetor you have only five servants behind you
carrying a commode and a wine-cask along the road to Tivoli.
110 In this and a thousand other ways I've an easier life
than you, my eminent senator.
                              I wander wherever I please

on my own; I ask what price they're charging for greens and flour;
often in the evenings I stroll around the Circus and Forum,
those haunts of trickery; I loiter by the fortune-tellers; and then
I make my way home to a plate of minestrone with leeks and peas.
My supper is served by three boys; on a white slab
stand two cups and a ladle, beside them a common cruet,
a flask of oil, and a saucer – all of Campanian ware.
Then I go off to bed with no worries about having
to be up early in the morning and appear in front of Mársyas   120
who shows that he can't abide the face of Newman junior.

I stay in bed till ten, then walk; or else after reading
or writing something for my private pleasure I have a massage,
but not, like that filthy Natta, with oil pinched from the lamps.
When I'm feeling tired and the sun grows fiercer, showing it's time
for the baths, I finish my game of triangle and leave the Park.
A light lunch – enough to save me from having to go
through the day on an empty stomach; then I laze about at home.

That's what life is like when you're free from the cruel compulsion
to get to the top. So I comfort myself that I'll live more happily   130
than if my grandfather, father, and uncle had all been Quaestors.

SATIRE 7

The setting for this piece of repartee is Clazomenae, a town on the
coast of Asia Minor. The dramatic date is 43 BC when Brutus was in
charge of the province. Brutus' distant ancestor had driven King Tar-
quin out of Rome, and in 44 BC he himself had got rid of Julius Caesar
whose regal pretensions had alienated the republican nobility. The
satire is justified by its mock-heroic presentation rather than by the
concluding pun.

The story of how the half-breed Persius repaid the foul
and venomous outlaw Rupilius King is known, I imagine,
to every barber in town and everyone with sore eyes.
Now Persius was a wealthy man engaged in very big business–
concerns at Clazómenae *and* in a troublesome lawsuit with King.
He was a tough customer, who had the beating of King in rudeness.
Arrogant, loud, and blustering, when it came to scathing abuse

he could leave men like Sisenna and Barrus standing at the post.
Reverting to King: when the two had failed to reach agreement –
10 (for those who meet in warfare face to face are ever
found to be no less stubborn than valiant; the wrath between Hector
son of Priam and the fierce Achilles was murderous, so that
only death in the end could part them, for this very reason
that both possessed the utmost courage, but if two cowards
became embroiled in a quarrel, or if strife arose between men
of unequal might – Diomedes, say, and the Lycian Glaucus –
the more faint-hearted would withdraw from battle and even proffer
gifts of appeasement) – when Brutus was Praetor in charge of Asia
and all its wealth, a clash took place between Persius and King,
20 a pair just as evenly matched as Bacchius and Bithus.
They rush fiercely into court, each a memorable sight.
Persius states his case amid general laughter; he praises
Brutus, calling him 'the sun of Asia', and he praises his staff,
calling them all 'stars of health', except for King,
who, he says, has come like the infamous Dog – that star
which is so detested by farmers. He rushes on like a wintry
torrent in a wild ravine where an axe but seldom reaches.

Faced with that mighty flood of wit the man from Praeneste
at once proceeds to hurl back the sort of abuse
30 that is squeezed from the vineyard, like a tough vine-dresser used
                                                              [to victory
who routs any passer-by that shouts a loud 'Cuckoo!'
Thereupon Persius the Greek, drenched as he is in Italian
vinegar, roars 'For god's sake Brutus! You are used to
disposing of kings. Why don't you cut *this* King's throat?
Believe me, we badly need your special skill!'

SATIRE 8

An old burial-ground on the Esquiline Hill is being converted by
Maecenas into pleasant gardens. Watching over the gardens is a
wooden statue of the vegetation god Priapus which has a large crack
in its posterior. The reason for this becomes clear at the end of Priapus'
story of triumphant if involuntary revenge.

Once I was the trunk of a fig-tree, a useless lump of wood.
Then the carpenter, wondering whether to make a bench or a
                                                    [Priapus,
preferred me to be a god. So a god I am, the terror
of thieves and birds. Thieves are deterred by the weapon in my hand
and also by the red stake projecting obscenely from my crotch.
The birds are an absolute pest, but the reed stuck in my head
frightens them off and stops them settling on the renovated gardens.

Before, the corpses of slaves, pitched from their narrow cells,
would be carried here in a cheap box at a friend's expense.
This too was the common graveyard of destitute citizens –   10
men like Grab-all the sponger and the waster Nomentanus.
Here a pillar assigned a frontage of a thousand feet
and a depth of three hundred: THIS MONUMENT NOT TO DESCEND
TO HEIRS. But now the Esquiline Hill is a healthy place
to live in; you can stroll along the wall in the sunshine where lately
you had a grim view of white bones strewn on the ground.

For myself, however, I'm not so worried and annoyed by the thieves
and wild animals that still come and infest the place
as by those hags, who are for ever plaguing the souls of men
with their spells and potions. I can't get rid of them, whatever I do,   20
or manage to stop them gathering bones and deadly plants
when once the wandering moon has shown her lovely face.
With my own eyes I saw Canidia walking barefoot,
her black robe tucked up and her hair streaming free,
shrieking with the elder Ságana; their faces were both made hideous
by a deathly pallor. They scraped away the earth with their nails.
Then taking a black lamb they set about tearing it to pieces
with their teeth, letting the blood trickle into the trench, from where
they meant to summon the spirits of the dead to answer their
                                                    [questions.
There was also a woollen doll, and another of wax – the woollen   30
was larger so as to dominate and punish the smaller. The latter
stood in an attitude of supplication as if expecting
a slave's death. One of the women called on Hécate,
the other on cruel Tisíphone. You could see snakes and hell-hounds
roaming at large, and the moon blushing with shame as she hid
behind the high tombs to avoid seeing such horrors.

If any of this is untrue may I have my head fouled white
by the droppings of crows, and may Julius and the mincing Miss
                                                                                [Pediatius
and Voranus the thief all come and piss and shit against me.
40   But why repeat each detail – how the spirits sounded mournful
and shrill as they answered Ságana's questions, how the two witches
stealthily buried a wolf's beard along with the fang
of a spotted snake, how the flame flared up as the wax image
melted, and how I wreaked vengeance for having to witness
in terror all that was said and done by the two Furies?
With a sudden report like a burst balloon I let a fart
which split my fig-wood buttocks; the hags scurried off down town;
Canidia dropped her false teeth, the high wig
tumbled from Ságana's head, and herbs and enchanted love-knots
50   fell off their arms. If only you'd seen it! You'd have laughed and
                                                                                [cheered.

SATIRE 9

*A description of how Horace on his morning walk encountered a pest
who claimed to know him and tried to engineer an introduction to
Maecenas. The account may be based on an incident in the poet's
experience, but the pest has no individual features and attempts to
identify him are futile.*

I happened to be strolling on Sacred Way, going over in my mind
some piece of nonsense, as I often do, and completely absorbed,
when suddenly a fellow whom I knew only by name dashed up
and seized me by the hand.
                                        'My dear chap,' he said, 'how are
                                                                                [things?'
     'Fine at the moment, thank you,' I said. 'Well, all the best!'
He remained in pursuit, so I nipped in quickly: 'Was there
                                                                                [something else?'
     'Yes,' he said. 'You should get to know me. I'm a man of letters.'
     'Good for you!' I said.
                                        Desperately trying to escape,
I now quickened my pace, now halted abruptly,
10   then whispered something in my servant's ear, sweating from head
to foot. As he rattled on, praising street after street

and finally the entire city, I kept breathing to myself
'Ah Bolanus, how I envy that fiery temper!'

As I still ignored him he said 'You're desperately keen to be off;
I've noticed that. But it's no use; I'll stick with you.
Wherever you're going I'll dog your steps!'
                                              'No need to take you
out of your way. I'm visiting someone you don't know.
He's ill in bed, away across the Tiber, near Caesar's Gardens.'
    'I've nothing to do and I'm pretty fit – I'll go all the way.'

I dropped my ears like a sullen donkey when he feels too heavy   20
a load on his back. Our friend began: 'If I'm any judge
you'll value my friendship just as highly as that of Viscus
and Varius. No one can write as many verses as I can –
and in so short a time. I'm the smoothest dancer in town,
and even Hermogenes might well envy my singing voice.'
Here was my chance: 'Have you a mother or next of kin
expecting you home?'
                    'No, not one. I've buried them all.'
Lucky for them! That leaves me. So finish me off!
A sinister doom is approaching which a Sabine crone predicted
when I was a boy. Shaking her urn the soothsayer chanted: 30
    'No deadly poison or foeman's blade shall work his fate;
no ailing lungs or hacking cough or slow-foot gout;
whene'er it be, a chatterbox shall wear him out;
let him avoid all gasbags on reaching man's estate.'

When we got to Vesta's temple it was after nine – the time
at which, as it happened, he was due to appear in court; if he didn't,
he would lose his case. 'Be a decent chap,' he said, 'and give me
a hand in here for a while.'
                            'My god, I could never manage
to stand in the box, and I haven't a clue about the law! Besides,
I'm in a hurry – you know where.'   40
                                'I can't make my mind up.
Do I abandon you or my case?'
                            'Oh me, please!'
                                            'No I shan't!'
he said, and strode out in front. It's hard to fight when you're beaten,
so I duly followed.
                    'How do you get on with Maecenas?' he resumed,

'He's a man of sound judgement and he chooses his friends with
                                                          [care.
No one has turned his luck to better account. Now if
you would introduce yours truly you'd have a powerful helper
to back you up. Why dammit you'd have beaten the lot by now!'

    'We don't behave up there in the way you imagine. Why nowhere
is cleaner and more remote from that kind of corruption.
50 I'm not worried, I assure you, that so and so is better read
and better off than I am. We each have our own position.'
    'That's fantastic! I can hardly believe it!'
                                        'It's true all the same.'
'That fires my resolve to be on close terms with him.' 'Well then,
you've only to make the wish. With your sterling qualities
you'll take him by storm. He's the sort that is open to conquest –
                                              [and that's why
he makes the outer approaches difficult.'
                            'I shan't be found wanting.
I'll bribe his servants; and if today they shut me out,
I'll persevere, bide my time, meet him in the street,
escort him home. "Not without unremitting toil
60 are mortal prizes won."'
                        In the middle of this performance
who should appear but my friend Aristius Fuscus, who knew him
all too well. We stopped. 'Hello,' he said, 'where are you off to?'
I told him and he did the same. I began tugging at his sleeve,
squeezing his arm (which was quite nerveless), nodding my head,
and glancing sideways 'Get me *out* of here!' But he chose this
                                  [moment to be funny,
and smilingly turned a blind eye. My temper flared:
    'I'm sure you said there was something private you wanted to
                                          [discuss.'
    'Ah yes, I remember. But I'll tell you another time –
when it's more convenient. Today is the thirtieth – the Sabbath,
                                          [you know.
70 Do you want to affront the circumcised Jews?'
                                    'I have no religious
objections.'
                'But I have. I'm a somewhat weaker brother –
one of the multitude. Sorry. I'll tell you again.'
                                    To think
I should ever have seen so black a day! The wretch ran off

and left me with the knife at my throat. Suddenly the fellow's
                                                    [opponent
ran into him. 'Where are you off to, you crook?' he roared. And
                                                    [to me:
'Will you act as a witness?' I allowed him to touch my ear.
He hustled him off to court. There were shouts all round, and
                                                    [people
came running from every side. Thus did Apollo save me.

SATIRE 10

*The admirers of Lucilius must have shown their annoyance at what
Horace had said in I. 4 about the older poet's stylistic shortcomings.
As a result Horace now amplifies and, where necessary, modifies his
earlier statement. In doing so he provides the fullest account of his
own, classical, theory of satire.*

True, I did say that Lucilius' verses lurched
awkwardly along. Which of his admirers is so perverse
as not to admit it? But he is also praised on the same page
for scouring the city with caustic wit. While granting him this,
however, I cannot allow the rest as well, for then
I should have to admire Laberius' mimes for their poetic beauty.

So it's not enough to make your listener bare his teeth
in a grin – though I grant there's some virtue even in that.
You need terseness, to let the thought run freely on
without becoming entangled in a mass of words that will hang   10
heavy on the ear. You need a style which is sometimes severe,
sometimes gay, now suiting the role of an orator or poet
now that of a clever talker who keeps his strength in reserve
and carefully rations it out. Humour is often stronger
and more effective than sharpness in cutting knotty issues.
Humour was the mainstay of those who wrote the Old Comedy;
that's the respect in which they ought to be followed – men
who have never been read by the pretty Hermogenes or by that ape
whose only artistic achievement is to croon Calvus and Catullus.

  'It was a great feat, however, to blend Latin with Greek!'   20
You've just caught up with yesterday's fashion! Do you really think

there is something marvellous and difficult in what Pitholeon of
                                                          [Rhodes
achieved?
            'But we get a more pleasant style when one of the tongues
is mixed with the other, as when we blend Falernian with Chian.'

Is it just when you are writing verses (I'm asking you yourself)
or does the same apply when you have to plead an awkward
case in defence of Petillius? No doubt while Pedius Publicola
and Corvinus sweat out their cases, you would rather forget
your fatherland and father Latinus and interlard
30 your fathers' speech with foreign importations, like a hybrid
                                                          [Canusian.
I myself once tried to compose a piece in Greek,
in spite of being born this side of the water; but after midnight,
when dreams are true, Quirinus appeared and stopped me. He said:
    'For you to aspire to swell the mighty ranks of the Greeks
is just as silly as carrying a load of wood to the forest.'

So while the turgid Alpman murders Memnon and plasters
the head of the Rhine with mud, I write these entertainments
which will never ring out in the hall where Tarpa judges contestants
nor be revived again and again for a theatre audience.

40 In constructing chatty comedies where Davus and a crafty mistress
outwit old Chremes, you, Fundanius, delight us more
than anyone living. Pollio praises the deeds of kings
with triple beat. Varius marshals heroic epic
with a fiery spirit no one can match. To Virgil the Muses
who love the country have given a light and charming touch.
This form had been tried by Varro of Atax and others
without success and was therefore one which I could perhaps
develop – though always below its inventor. I wouldn't presume
to snatch from his head the crown which he wears with such
                                                          [distinction.

50 But I said he flowed muddily on, and that in the stuff he brought
                                                          [down
there was often more to be removed than retained. Well now, do
                                                          [you
with all your learning find nothing to fault in mighty Homer?

Does your charming Lucilius let Accius' tragedies pass without
                                                              [change?
Does he not laugh at those lines of Ennius which fail in dignity,
without speaking of himself as superior to the men he faults?
So why shouldn't we inquire as we read Lucilius' writings
whether it was his own harsh nature or that of his times
which prevented his verses from being more finished and smoothly
                                                              [flowing
than those of a man whose only concern is to force his matter
into a framework of six feet, and who gaily produces   60
two hundred lines before dinner and as many after –
just like the Etruscan Cassius whose creative power was fiercer
than a raging river and who, we are told, was burnt on a pyre
made of his own books, cases and all?
                                    Very well,
let us grant Lucilius had a charming and civilized wit; let us grant
he was also more polished than the author of a crude verse never
                                                              [handled
by the Greeks *and* than the older crowd of Roman poets;
still, if fate had postponed his birth till our own day,
he would file his work drastically down and prune whatever
rambled beyond the proper limit, and in shaping his verses   70
he would often scratch his head and nibble his nails to the quick.

If you hope to deserve a second reading you must often employ
the rubber at the end of your pencil. Don't seek mass adulation.
Be content with a few readers – or are you so mad
as to want your poems dictated in shabby schools? Not me.
'I'm happy if the better classes applaud me,' as the dauntless Miss
                                                              [Tree
remarked when hissed off the stage – she had only contempt for the
                                                              [rest.
Should I be worried by that louse Carper, or suffer agonies
because Demetrius sneers behind my back or the silly
Fannius (toady of Hermogenes Tigellius) runs me down?   80
I should like these poems to win the approval of Plotius and Varius,
Maecenas and Virgil, Valgius, Octavius, and the excellent Fuscus;
and I hope the Viscus brothers will enjoy them; I can also mention
you, Pollio, without incurring any suspicion
of flattery, you, Messalla, and your brother, and also you,
Bibulus and Servius, and with them you, my candid Furnius,

and several others whom I knowingly omit, though friends and
                                                              [men of
letters. I should like *them* to find my work attractive,
such as it is; I'd be sorry if it caused *them* disappointment.
90 But you, Demetrius and you, Tigellius, do me a favour –
go and wail to your lady pupils in their easy chairs.

Off with you, boy; add this at once to my little volume.

BOOK II

SATIRE I

*Although this poem serves as an introduction to the second book it
was probably written later than the other pieces. It purports to explain
why Horace continues to write satire – he can't sleep, he is committed
to writing, he comes from a long line of fighting men, he has an
irresistible inner impulse, he is following the example of Lucilius, he
is confident of avoiding prosecution. But the explanation is not quite
what it appears to be, for each assertion is a subtle evasion of the
point. Horace never actually says that his satire will be fearless and
aggressive – naturally enough, for the other seven pieces are for the
most part inoffensive. This poem, which is cast in the form of a
dialogue with a distinguished legal expert, is therefore in essence a
humorous charade, though it does contain some genuine information
about Horace's outlook on life and literature.*

To some I am too sharp in my satire and seem to be stretching
the form beyond its legitimate limits; the rest maintain
that whatever I write is slack and that a thousand verses like mine
could be wound off every day. Please advise me, Trebatius;
what am I to do?
        'Take a rest.'
                        Not write verses at all,
you mean?
    'I do.'
                Dammit you're right; that *would* be the best thing.
But I can't get to sleep.
                  'For sound sleep: take an oil massage;
swim the Tiber three times; before retiring
ensure that the system is thoroughly soaked in strong wine.
Or, if you're so carried away by this passion for writing,
try your hand at recounting the triumphs of Caesar. Your trouble

will be most handsomely rewarded.'
                                    I only wish I could, sir;
but I lack the power. Not everyone, after all, can portray
lines of battle bristling with lances, Gauls dying
with their spears splintered, or the wounded Parthian slipping from
                                                              [his steed.
   'But you could depict his fairness and courage, as Lucilius wisely
did with Scipio.
                        'I shan't be found wanting when the chance occurs.
If the moment isn't right, then Floppy's words won't penetrate
Caesar's pricked-up ear. Rub him the wrong way
20 and he'll lash out right and left with his hooves in self-defence.
   'That would be infinitely better than writing acid verse
which hurts Grab-all the sponger and the waster Nomentanus,
and makes everyone, though quite unscathed, nervous and hostile.'

What am I to do? Milonius dances when the heat mounts
to his reeling brain, bringing a vision of double lights.
Riding is Castor's passion; boxing that of the twin
born of the self-same egg. Take a thousand men, you'll find
a thousand hobbies. Mine is enclosing words in metre,
as Lucilius did – a better man than either of us.
30 He in the past would confide his secrets to his books, which he
                                                              [trusted
like friends; and whether things went well or badly he'd always
turn to them; in consequence, the whole of the old man's life
is laid before us, as if it were painted on a votive tablet.

I follow him, as a son of Lucania – or is it Apulia?
Because the Venusian settler ploughs on the border of both.
He was sent out, as the story has it, after the Samnites
were expelled, so that if the wild Apulian or Lucanian folk
unleashed a war they might be prevented from dashing on Rome
across the open space. But this steely point
40 will never attack a living soul, unless provoked.
I'll carry it for self-defence, like a sword in its scabbard. Why bother
to draw it so long as I'm safe from lawless attack? O Jupiter,
father and king, grant that my weapon may hang there, corroding
with rust, and that no one may injure a peace-loving man like me.
But whoever stirs me up (better keep your distance, I'm telling you!)
will be sorry; he'll become a thing of derision throughout the city.
When angry, Cervius points to the ballot-box and the laws;

Canidia cows her opponents with the poison that did for Albucius;
Turius threatens a heavy fine if you come before him;
everyone uses his strongest weapon to frighten potential   50
enemies. That is Nature's royal decree. For consider:
the wolf attacks with his fangs, the bull with his horns – why,
if not impelled by instinct? Trust a waster like Hand
with his elderly mother; the affectionate lad won't lay a finger on her.
Surprising? But then a wolf doesn't kick or an ox bite.
A cocktail of honey and hemlock will finish the old girl off.
In short, whether a serene old age awaits me or whether
death is already hovering near on sable wing,
in Rome or if fortune so ordains in exile – whatever
the complexion of my life, I'll continue to write.   60
                                        'My lad, I'm afraid
you may not be long for this world. One of your powerful friends
may freeze you stiff.'
                        But why? When Lucilius first had the courage
to write this kind of poetry and remove the glossy skin
in which people were parading before the world and concealing
their ugliness, was Laelius offended by his wit or the man who
                                                            [rightly
took on the name of the African city which he overthrew?
Or did they feel any pain when Metellus was wounded and Lupus
was smothered in a shower of abusive verse? And yet Lucilius
indicted the foremost citizens and the whole populace, tribe
by tribe, showing indulgence only to Worth and her friends.   70
Why, when the worthy Scipio and the wise and gentle Laelius
left the stage of public life for the privacy of home,
they would let their hair down and join the poet in a bit of
                                                            [horseplay,
as they waited for the greens to cook. Whatever I am, and however
inferior to Lucilius in rank and talent, Envy will have
to admit, like it or not, that I've moved in important circles.
She may think I'm fragile, but she'll find me a tough nut
to crack. But perhaps, my learned Trebatius, you hold a different
opinion?
            'No, I find that argument entirely solid.
I must warn you, notwithstanding, to beware of trouble arising   80
from ignorance of the majesty of the law: if a party compose
foul verses to another's hurt, a hearing and trial
ensue.'
        Foul verses, yes; but what if a party compose

fine verses which win a favourable verdict from Caesar?
Or snarl at a public menace when he himself is blameless?
   'The charge will be dissolved in laughter, and you'll go free.'

SATIRE 2

*This sermon on the virtues of simple living is put into the mouth of
Ofellus, a peasant whom Horace knew in his boyhood days. 'Pleasure
in eating depends more on one's appetite than on the price of the food.
So-called epicures often admire a bird or a fish for quite irrelevant
reasons. Enjoyment is diminished by excess; it can also be prevented
by meanness. Unlike the wise man the glutton ruins his health, his
reputation, and his fortune.' The closing section describes how Ofellus
lived according to his philosophy.*

My friends, I want you to hear the virtues of plain living.
(This talk isn't mine but the teaching of the farmer Ofellus,
an unprofessional philosopher of sturdy common sense.)
Let's consider it, not surrounded by shining tables
and plate, when the eye is dazzled by senseless glitter and the mind
swings in favour of the sham rejecting better things,
but right here, before we have breakfast.
                              'What's the point?'
I'll try to explain. No judge that has been corrupted
can properly weigh the truth. When you're tired from hunting hare
10 or breaking a horse – or if Roman army sports are too tough
for someone with Greek habits, perhaps a fast game of ball
appeals to you (the harsh exertion is sweetened and disguised by the
                                         [fun)
or throwing a discus: if so, scatter the air with a discus –
when exertion has knocked the choosiness out of you, and you're
                                    [hungry and thirsty,
turn up your nose at plain food: refuse to drink mead
unless the wine is Falernian and the honey from Hymettus! The
                                       [butler
is out, the fish are protected by a dark and wintry sea;
well, bread and salt will do to appease your growling stomach.
Why do you think that's so? The highest pleasure lies
20 not in the rich savoury smell but in you. So get

your sauce by sweat. The man who is pale and bloated from
                                                            [gluttony
will never enjoy his oysters and wrasse and imported grouse.

And yet you've a deep-rooted inclination, when a peacock is served,
to caress your palate with it rather than a chicken. Your judgement
is impaired by what doesn't count: the bird is hard to come by,
it costs a packet, and its spreading tail is a colourful sight –
as if that mattered a damn! Do you actually eat those feathers
which you find so gorgeous? Does the thing look equally splendid
                                                            [when cooked?
In the meat there's nothing to choose between them. And yet you go
for the peacock, deluded by the difference in looks! Well, let it pass.   30

By what process can you tell whether that gaping bass
was caught in the Tiber or the sea, in the current between
                                                            [the bridges
or near the mouth of the Tuscan river? Like a fool, you admire
a three-pound mullet which you have to cut into separate helpings.
I know, it's the appearance that attracts you; but then why dislike
long bass? Because, no doubt, in the course of nature
bass reach a substantial size whereas mullet are small.
A hungry stomach rarely despises common food.

'I'd love to see something huge stretched out on a huge dish!'
So says a gullet which for sheer greed would do credit to a Harpy.   40
Ye warm south winds, come and 'cook' their viands! And yet
                                                            [the boar
and turbot, however fresh, are already rotten, for the queasy
stomach is upset by too much food; gorged to repletion
it prefers radishes and sharp pickles.
                            Yet poverty hasn't
entirely vanished from our barons' menus; cheap eggs
and black olives still hold their place. It's not so long
since the auctioneer Gallonius caused a scandal by serving
a sturgeon. Why? Did the sea breed fewer turbots then?
The turbot was safe and the stork safe in its nest before
the Praetor taught you his lesson. So now, if someone proclaimed   50
in an edict that roast seagull was nice, the youth of Rome
would accept it – always amenable to any perverse suggestion.
Ofellus maintains that a simple diet will be quite distinct

from a stingy one; for there's no point in avoiding extravagance
if you then swerve off to the opposite vice. Avidienus,
who is called 'the Dog' (a name which has stuck for excellent
                                                        [reasons),
eats olives which are five years old and cornels from the woods.
He's too mean to open his wine until it's gone sour.
The smell of his oil is unbearable, and even when holding a wedding
60 or a birthday or some other celebration, dressed up in a clean toga,
he lets the oil drop onto the cabbage from a two-pound horn
which he holds himself, though he's lavish enough with his nasty old
                                                        [vinegar.

So what standard should the wise man adopt, and which of these
will he imitate? Here's the wolf, as they say, and here's the dog.
He'll be smart enough not to be branded as mean, and in his style
of living he will not come to grief in either way. He will not
be brutal to his servants when giving them orders, like old Albucius,
nor, like Naevius, be so informal as to offer his guests
greasy water (that, too, is a serious blunder).

70 Now I come to the great benefits which accrue from simple
living. First, you have decent health. Think of the harm that
a conglomeration of stuff does to a man. Remember
the plain food that once agreed with you so well. But as soon
as you mix boiled with roast, and oysters with thrushes, the sweet
juices will turn to acid, and sticky phlegm will raise
a revolt in the interior. Notice how green they all look
as they come away from the 'problem meal'! Worse still, the body,
heavy from yesterday's guzzling, drags down the soul
and nails to the earth a particle of the divine spirit.

80 The other man, after a light supper, falls asleep
as his head hits the pillow, and gets up fresh for the work of the day.
And yet from time to time he can switch to a better diet
when, in the course of the year, some holiday comes around,
or when he is undernourished and in need of a treat, or when
with the advancing years his ageing body asks for some extra
comfort. But what have *you* to fall back on when you're forced to
                                                        [bear
the strains of illness and of old age with its shuffling steps?
You've grabbed your comforts already, while you're still young and
                                                        [healthy!

Our ancestors used to say that boar should be eaten high,
not because they had no noses; they meant, I assume,   90
that it should be kept for a guest who was late – though it might go
                                                                [off –
rather than gobbled up fresh by the head of the house. If only
I could have lived with that race of heroes, when the world was
                                                                [young!

Do you like to be well thought of? (No songs are sweeter to the ear
than songs of praise.) But the bigger the turbot and dish the bigger
the scandal, not to mention the waste of money. Also your uncle
and the neighbours will be furious; you'll lose your self-respect and
                                                                [resolve
on suicide – except you'll be so broke that you won't have a penny
for a rope.
              'You can talk like that to Trausius,' he says. 'For he
deserves it. But I have a large income and a bigger fortune   100
than three kings put together.'
                                  Well then, can't you think of a better
                                                                [way
to get rid of your surplus? Why should any decent man
be in need when you are rich? Why are the ancient temples
of the gods falling down? Why, if you've any conscience,
don't you give something from that pile you've made to the land of
                                                                [your birth?
For you alone, I suppose, nothing will ever go wrong.
What a whale of a laugh you'll give your enemies! In times of crisis
which of the two will have greater confidence – the man who has led
his mind and body to expect affluence as of right,
or the man with few needs who is apprehensive of the future   110
and who in peacetime has wisely made preparations for war?

To bring this home, as a boy I knew Ofellus well,
and when he had all his money he lived as simply as he does
now that he's poor. He is still to be seen with his sons and livestock
working undaunted as a tenant on the farm now re-assigned.
'As a rule,' he says, 'on a working day I would never eat
any more than a shank of smoked ham and a plate of greens.
But if friends arrived whom I hadn't seen for a long time
or a neighbour dropped in for a friendly visit on a wet day
when I was idle, we used to celebrate, not with fish   120
sent out from town, but a chicken or a kid, followed by dessert –

raisins taken down from the rafters with nuts and figs.
Then we had drinking games where a failure meant a forfeit,
and Ceres, receiving our prayer that she'd rise high on the stalk,
allowed the wine to smooth away our worried wrinkles.
Whatever new horrors and upheavals Fortune brings
she can't take much away from that. How many of our comforts
have we had to give up, my lads, since the new occupant came?
I say "occupant", for by nature's decree possession of the land
130   isn't his or mine or anyone else's. *He* turned *us* out,
and he'll be turned out by his own improvidence, his inability
to cope with the law's cunning, or at last by the heir who outlives
                                                                  [him.
The farm is now in Umbrenus' name; not long ago
it was called Ofellus'; no one will own it, but its use will still
be enjoyed – now by me, in time by another. So be brave
and bravely throw out your chest to meet the force of fate!'

SATIRE 3

*Horace is spending the Saturnalia (17–19 December) on his Sabine
farm. Damasippus enters and immediately takes him to task for his
laziness. As the dialogue develops Damasippus tells how Stertinius
converted him to Stoicism by preaching on the text 'Everyone is mad
except the sage.' The sermon deals in turn with avarice, ambition,
self-indulgence, and superstition, all of which are regarded as types of
madness. The piece concludes with an epilogue in which Damasippus
explains how the sermon is relevant to Horace's condition.*

You write so little that you get to the point of asking for parchment
less than four times a year. You unravel what's written, annoyed
that with plenty of wine and sleep you produce nothing to speak of.
What's going to happen? As soon as the Saturnalia came,
you fled out here like a sober man. So don't disappoint us.
Give us a word or two, starting now . . . nothing forthcoming.
No use blaming your pen or battering the innocent wall,
screaming that its very existence is an insult to gods and poets.
And yet you had a face which promised lots of splendid things
10   when you got away to the peace and warmth of your little villa.
What was the point of bringing out such weighty companions,
packing Archilochus, Eupolis, and Plato along with Menander?

Will people begin to like you if you stop attacking vice?
You pathetic creature! They'll merely despise you. Avoid Sloth,
that seductive Siren, or else make up your mind to relinquish
all you've achieved in better days.
                                'That's good advice,
Damasippus, and as a reward may heaven send you – a barber.
But how do you know me so well?'
                                Since my entire fortune
crashed on the floor of the Stock Exchange, pitching me out of my
                                                                [business,
I've been minding other people's. I used to enjoy deciding   20
which was the bronze that wily old Sisyphus washed his feet in,
what was crudely carved and what was roughly cast.
I would shrewdly invest a hundred thousand in a given statue.
Nobody else had my knack of making a profit
from deals in luxurious houses and grounds. That's why the people
at auctions gave me the nickname 'Lucre's lad'.
                                'I know,
and I'm surprised you've been cured of that obsession. But the odd
                                                                [thing is
that a new disorder has taken the place of the old, as happens
in the body when a headache or a pain in the side shifts to the
                                                                [stomach,
or a patient wakes from a coma and starts to punch his doctor.   30
Short of that, do as you please!'
                                Now let's get this clear.
You're mad too, and so are pretty well all fools,
if there's any truth in Stertinius' guff. Like a faithful pupil
I took this marvellous message down from him on the day
when he gave me comfort, and bade me grow the beard of wisdom,
and sent me home from the Fabrician bridge with joy in my heart.
After my business collapsed, I intended to cover my head
and jump in the river. But there he was at my side. 'Now don't
do anything rash,' he said. 'Your feelings of guilt are misplaced.
You're afraid of being thought mad by folks who are mad   40
                                                                [themselves!
First let me ask what madness is. If it proves to be something
peculiar to you, I'll leave you free to die like a man.

'Chrysippus and his flock in the Porch maintain that a madman
                                                                [is one
who is driven blindly on by the curse of folly, in ignorance

of the truth. That definition embraces mighty monarchs
and people – everyone, in fact, but the sage.

                                Now this is the reason
why those who call you mad are every bit as crazy
as you are: You know how people lose their way in the woods –
one goes wandering off to the left, another to the right;

50   both are equally wrong, though each has strayed in a different
direction. So you may rest assured that if you're to be counted
mad the fellow who laughs at you is no saner himself.
He too has straw in his hair.

                        One sort of idiot
is plagued by imaginary fears; though standing on level ground
he insists that fires, rocks, and rivers are blocking his path.
Another, with the opposite kink but no less dotty, goes charging
into the middle of a fire or river. His beloved mother
and worthy sister, his father, wife, and relatives shout
"Look out! There's a big ditch in front of you! Now there's a
                                       [boulder!"

60   but he'll pay no more attention than the drunken Fufius did
when he over-played the sleeping Ilíona and a thousand voices
joined Catiénus in shouting "Mother, I'm calling you!"

                                    I'll show
that people in the mass are crazy in just this kind of way.
Damasippus has a mania for buying old statues. But the man
who lends Damasippus money – is he normal? Very well.
If I said to you "Here's some money; don't bother to return it",
would you be mad to take it? Or would it be more insane
to reject a bonus so kindly offered by the Lord of Luck?
Write ten of Nerius' I.O.U.s – no good; add a hundred

70   of Hemlock's tightly drafted bonds; add a thousand chains.
He'll still wriggle out; that rascally Proteus can't be tied down.
When you take him to court he'll proceed to laugh at your expense,
becoming a hog or a bird at will, or a stone or a tree.
If bungling in business is a sign of lunacy, and vice versa,
I assure you Perellius is far more soft in the head for stating
the terms of a loan which you can never hope to repay.

'Settle down then please and pay attention. I'm talking to all
who are plagued by the curse of ambition or a morbid craving for
                                     [money,
all who are obsessed with self-indulgence or gloomy superstition,

80   or any other fever of the soul; come here to me

and I'll convince you, one by one, that you're all mad.
By far the biggest dose of hellebore should go to the greedy;
they ought, in fact, to receive all Antícyra's output.
Staberius' heirs engraved the sum of his estate on his tombstone.
Had they failed to do so, they were bound by his will to regale the
                                                    [public
with a hundred pairs of gladiators, a banquet (arranged by Arrius),
and all the corn in Egypt. "Whether I'm right or wrong
in issuing these instructions, you are not to scold me."
Staberius, I take it, had enough sense to foresee their reaction.
So what did he mean by insisting that his heirs should carve on   90
                                                    [stone
the full amount of his estate? Well, he had a lifelong conviction
that poverty was a dreadful sin. He shunned it with horror. And so,
if he'd died a penny poorer, he would in his own estimation
have been that much more depraved. The fact is that goodness,
honour, reputation – everything human and divine – gives way
to the charm of money. The man who has made a pile – the same
is famous, brave, and upright.'
                              'And wise?'
                                        'Yes, and a king
and whatever he likes. Staberius thought that his wealth would
                                                    [establish
his probity and would win him respect.
                              What had he in common
with the Greek Aristippus who, when crossing the Libyan desert,   100
ordered his servants to throw all his gold away – its weight,
he said, was hampering their progress. Which of these was the
                                                    [madder?

'A case doesn't help that replaces one issue with another.
If a man, after buying guitars, placed them all together,
without any love of guitars or any branch of music,
if a non-shoemaker hoarded knives and lasts, or a man
who disliked trading collected sails, he would rightly be thought
a crazy idiot by everyone else. But is *he* any different,
who amasses coins and gold unaware of how to use them,
who dreads to touch his treasure as if it were something holy?   110
'Suppose a man took a big stick and lay on the floor,
keeping a constant watch on a large corn-heap, refusing
however hungry to touch a grain of it, although it was his,
and existing instead on a miserly diet of bitter leaves.

If in spite of having in his cellar a thousand – that's nothing, let's say
three hundred thousand bottles of old Falernian and Chian,
he opted for sour vinegar. And if, when pushing eighty,
he slept on a straw mattress although expensive bedclothes
were rotting in a chest, providing moths with a royal banquet,
120   no doubt he'd be judged insane – by a few, the reason being
that most men toss and turn in the grip of the same fever.
You wretched old man! Are you saving this for your son or
                                                                    [freedman
to swallow when you're dead? Or is it in case you run short?
Think of how little would be docked from your capital every day
if you started to use a decent oil for dressing your salad
and for your hair. Look at it! Matted and thick with dandruff!
If "anything goes" why do you lie and cheat and pilfer
right and left? You sane! If you pelted with stones
people in the street or slaves whom you'd bought with hard cash,
130   everyone, male and female, would shout "The man is mad!"
When you strangle your wife or poison your mother you are, I
                                                                    [suppose,
of sound mind. After all, you're not doing it in Argos,
nor are you killing your mother with a sword like the mad Orestes!
Or perhaps you think it was only *after* murdering his parent
that he went insane, and that he wasn't maddened by the evil Furies
before he warmed the sharp blade in his mother's throat.
The truth is quite the reverse. From the moment when Orestes was
                                                                    [held
to be mentally deranged his conduct was wholly above reproach.
He refrained from slashing at Pýlades, his friend, and his sister
                                                                    [Electra;
140   he merely abused them both; she, he said, was a Fury,
he some other creature that his mad condition dictated.
'Richman, a pauper in spite of his hoard of gold and silver,
when holidays came around would drink Veientine wine
from a Capuan mug; his normal drink was fermented must.
Once he was sunk in so deep a coma that his heir had already
grabbed the keys and was prancing around his coffers in jubilant
excitement. The doctor, a quick thinker and a loyal friend,
revived him so: he had a table brought in and some bags of coins
poured out on top of it; then he asked some people to come
150   and count them. On bringing the patient to, he added "If you don't
look after your property, your greedy heir will make off with the
                                                                    [lot!"

"Over my dead body!"
                              "Wake up then and live. Now here – "
"What's this?"
                    "You're weak. Your pulse is low, and your whole
                                                                    [system
will collapse if it's not sustained by food and a strong tonic.
What are you waiting for? Come on, take a sip of this rice gruel."
"How much was it?"
                         "Not much."
                                        "Well *how* much?"
                                                            "Tuppence."
                                                                ["Ah dear!
What matter whether I die from illness or from theft and pillage?" '
'Well who is sane?'
                         'The man who isn't a fool.'
                                                        'And the greedy?'
'Fools and madmen.'
                         'But suppose a person isn't greedy,
is he therefore sane?'   160
                         'Not at all.'
                                    'Why, my good Stoic?'
                                                            'I'll tell you.
Suppose that, according to Cráterus, a patient has nothing wrong
with his stomach. Does that mean he's well enough to get up?
No, for he's got a severe infection of the lungs or kidneys.
Here's a man who is neither liar nor miser. He may thank
his lucky stars for that. But he is ambitious and reckless.
Put him on board for Antícyra! What matter whether you throw
your possessions into a pit or never use your savings?

'There's a story that Servius Oppidius, a rich man by the standards
of an earlier day, made over his two farms at Canusium
to his two sons. When dying, he called the lads to his bedside: 170
"Ever since I saw you, Aulus, carrying your dice
and marbles in an unsafe pocket, giving and gambling them away,
and you, Tiberius, counting them sourly and hiding them in crannies,
I have worried that you might develop opposite forms of obsession,
you imitating Nomentanus and you Hemlock.
And so, here, in our old home, I appeal to you both:
you mustn't reduce, and *you* mustn't increase
what your father considers enough and what falls within nature's
                                                                    [limits.

Moreover, in case you are excited by the charms of public life,
180 I shall have you swear an oath: if either becomes an Aedile
or Praetor he shall forfeit his legal powers and be cursed of heaven.
Would you waste your money like an idiot on vetches, beans, and
                                                                    [lupines
simply to strut and swagger in the Circus or stand in bronze,
stripped of the land your father left you and stripped of his money?
I suppose you want to win the applause that Agrippa wins –
like the cunning fox that masqueraded as a noble lion!''

' ''You forbid us, son of Atreus, to bury Ajax. Why?''
''I am king.''
                ''As a commoner I inquire no further.''
                                                    ''Also
it's a fair order. If anyone thinks I'm being unjust
190 he has my permission to speak his mind.''
                                        ''Most royal highness,
God grant you may capture Troy and bring the army home.
Is it therefore in order to hold an exchange of question and
                                                        [answer?''
''Go ahead.''
            ''Then why does Ajax, the hero next to Achilles,
who so often won distinction by saving Achaean lives,
lie rotting? Is it so that Priam and his people may enjoy the exposure
of one who deprived so many lads of a family grave?''
    ''He was mad. He slaughtered a thousand sheep, and in doing so
                                                        [roared
he was killing the famous Ulysses, and Menelaus, and me.''
    ''But when *you* do a frightful thing like making your darling
                                                        [daughter
200 stand at the altar instead of a calf, sprinkling her head
with salt meal, are you in your right mind? What harm
was done by the mad Ajax when he slew the flock? He spared
his wife and child. He hurled abuse at the sons of Atreus
but he did no act of violence to Teucer or even Ulysses.''
''My ships were moored on a lee shore. To get them away,
after full deliberation I secured the favour of heaven with blood.''
    ''Yes, your own, you maniac!''
                                ''My own, but I wasn't a maniac.''

'A man who gets hold of wrong ideas – ideas confused
by the turmoil arising from his own guilt – is held to be crazy,

no matter whether his illusions are caused by folly or anger.   210
When Ajax kills inoffensive lambs he's deranged. When you
"after full deliberation" commit a crime for a pompous inscription,
are you stable? Does a swollen head make sound decisions?
If a man took to dressing up a lamb and carrying it round
in a litter, providing (as if it were his daughter) clothes, and maids,
and jewellery, calling it Ruby or Babs, and planning to marry it
to a dashing husband, the Praetor would issue an injunction to
                                                          [bar him
from control of his property and commit him to the care of his sane
                                                          [relations.
Well if someone slays his daughter instead of a dumb lamb,
you needn't tell me he's mentally balanced. The worst insanity   220
is found in conjunction with wicked folly. A criminal is always
mad, and whoever is entranced by Fame's glassy glitter
hears all around him the thunder of Bellona revelling in blood.

'Join me now in denouncing extravagance and Nomentanus.
It's easy to prove that spendthrifts are fools and therefore madmen.
One, on receiving a legacy of a million pounds from his father,
issued a proclamation: fishermen, fruitgrowers, fowlers,
perfumers and all the unholy gang from Tuscan Lane,
poulterers and parasites, the whole Market including the Velabrum
were to call at his house next morning. Of course, they came in   230
                                                          [droves.
A pimp acted as spokesman: "Whatever my colleagues and I
have in stock is as good as yours. You may order now or
                                                          [tomorrow."
Here's what the fair-minded fellow replied: "You there sleep
with your leggings on in the snow of Lucania to supply me
with a boar for my dinner; you sweep fish from a wintry sea.
I'm a layabout; I don't deserve all this money. So here –
fifty thousand for you – and you – and three times that
for you with the wife who comes so quickly when called at
                                                          [midnight."

'Aesop's son, with the object, I take it, of polishing off
a lump sum of a million, took from Metella's ear   240
a magnificent pearl which he melted in vinegar. Could he have been
                                                          [madder
if he'd flung it into a fast-flowing river or an open sewer?
The sons of Quintus Arrius, a famous pair of brothers,

twins in vice and frivolity and in their decadent tastes,
lunched on nightingales, buying them up at vast expense.
Where should *they* go? Do we check them as sound or mark them
[cracked?

'If someone old enough to shave enjoyed playing odds and evens,
building dolls' houses, riding a big cock-horse,
and harnessing mice to a tiny cart, he'd have to be simple.
250 Well if I can prove that being in love is more infantile still,
that there's nothing to choose between playing with bucket and
[spade, as you did
at the age of three, and getting upset and weeping with love
for a piece of skirt, would you then do what Polemon did
on being converted? Get rid of the invalid's paraphernalia –
leg-bands, pillow and muffler – just as he, we are told,
quietly removed the garlands from his neck after being stopped
on his way home from a binge by his teacher's sober voice?
When you press an apple on a sulky child he won't have it.
"Take it, pet!" He says "No." If it wasn't offered, he'd want it.
260 In the same way the lover, who has been shut out, debates
whether or not to call at the place he had meant to revisit
until he was asked. He dithers at the door he hates. "Should I go
now that she invites me? Or make an effort to stop this misery?
She snubbed me; she calls me back; should I go? Not if she begged
[me!"
Here's a servant with a lot more sense: "Now sir, a thing
which doesn't admit of method or system can't be handled
by rules and logic. There are always two troubles in love:
war and peace – things which change much as the weather.
They come and go by blind chance; so if anyone sweated
270 to give an account of their movements he'd make no better sense
than if he tried to go mad with the aid of rules and logic.
When you pick the pips from a Cox's apple and go into transports
if you manage to hit the ceiling, are you in command of your senses?
When you let a stream of baby-talk trip from your silly old palate,
have you more sense than the child with its doll's house? And
[remember:
folly can lead to bloodshed; passion is playing with fire.
The other day when Marius stabbed Miss Hellas and then
jumped to his death, was he deranged? Or would you acquit him
of having an unsound mind and find him guilty of a crime,
280 describing things, as one often does, in related terms?"

'There used to be an old freedman who would wash his hands
                                              [every morning
and run, cold sober, from shrine to shrine, praying aloud:
"Save me, just me, from death!" "I don't ask much," he would add.
"With the gods all things are possible." His sight and hearing were
                                              [sound,
but as for his brain – his owner would never have guaranteed *that*
when selling him, unless he wanted to be sued. That sort of person
belongs, according to Chrysippus, to Menenius' flourishing family.

' "O Lord who givest and takest away our heaviest sorrows"
(a mother is praying for her son, who has been five months in bed)
"If my boy succeeds in shaking off the quartan fever   290
he will stand naked in the Tiber on the morning of the day which
                                              [thou
dost appoint for fasting." If thanks to luck or the doctor the patient
is saved from his critical condition, the crazy mother will hold him
in the freezing water and kill him by bringing back his fever.
And what destroyed her reason? Superstition, pure and simple.'

Those are the weapons Stertinius, the eighth wise man, supplied
for his friend, so that if abused I'd never fail to get even.
The man who calls me insane will get just as many brickbats
in return – which will help to remind him that he lives in a glass
                                              [house.

'My dear Stoic, to make up for your losses may you sell everything   300
at a profit! But in what folly (there are several forms) do you think
my madness consists? For *I* believe I'm sane.'
     What of it? When Agave tears the head off her luckless son
and carries it round, does *she* believe she's out of her mind?
     'All right, I'm a fool – one must acknowledge the truth –
even a lunatic; but do make one point clear: from what
mental defect do you think I'm suffering?'
                                 I'll tell you. First,
you're putting up buildings; which means you're copying tall men,
though you measure no more than two foot from head to toe.
You laugh at Turbo in his armour, saying his pluck and swagger   310
are too big for his body. Well you're just as funny yourself.
Or are you entitled to do whatever Maecenas does,
though you're so unlike him and so unfit to challenge comparison?

When a mother frog was away from home, a calf trod on
her family. One escaped and told her the whole story –
how a huge beast had squashed his brothers.

'How big *was* it,'
she said, as she puffed herself up, 'hardly as big as this?'
'Half as big again.'

'Well what about this?' She continued
to pump herself up and up.

'You can blow till you burst,' he
[answered,
320   'but you'll never be as big.'

That picture is not so unlike yourself.
And don't forget your poems (just to add fuel to the flames).
If there's any such thing as a sane poet, you're sane!
Not to speak of your mad outbursts of rage –

'Now stop it!'

You're
[living
beyond your means –

'Damasippus! Would you please mind your
[own business!'
Your infatuation with hundreds of girls and hundreds of boys –
  'For heaven's sake, have mercy as a greater to a lesser madman!'

SATIRE 4

*Horace is treated to a disquisition on gastronomy by Catius who has
just been attending a lecture on the subject.*

Catius! Where are you off to?

'. . . No time to stop, for I must
jot down these new philosophical rules which are going to eclipse
Pythagoras and the condemned Athenian and Plato's genius.'

I know I shouldn't delay you at such an awkward time;
you will forgive me, won't you? But if anything slips your mind
you'll soon recall it with that memory of yours, which is quite
[amazing
whether it's a natural gift or something acquired by practice.

'Well I *was* anxious to make sure of remembering the whole lecture,
for it was all subtle material presented in a subtle style.'

Can you reveal the man's name? Was he a Roman or a stranger?   10

'I'll repeat the rules from memory; the source must remain a secret.
When serving eggs remember to choose the long variety,
for they are superior in flavour to the round, and their whites are
                                                          [whiter;
(the shells, you see, are harder and contain a male yolk).
Cabbage grown in a dry soil is sweeter than what comes
from the suburbs – stuff from a watered garden has the taste washed
                                                          [out of it.

'If a visitor suddenly descends on you late in the day, and you want
to save his jaws from having to struggle with a tough fowl,
you'd be well advised to plunge it alive in Falernian juice.
That will make it tender. The best quality mushrooms   20
come from the meadows; the others are risky; you'll get through
                                                          [the summer
without sickness if you finish your lunch with black mulberries
picked from the tree before the sun is unpleasantly hot.

'Aufidius always mixed his honey with strong Falernian –
a bad idea; when the veins are empty it doesn't do
to fill them with anything that isn't mild. So a mild type of mead
is better for moistening the lining of the stomach. If the bowels
                                                          [are sluggish,
mussels and ordinary shellfish and tiny sorrel leaves
will remove the blockage – all to be taken with white Coan.
Slippery shellfish begin to swell as the moon waxes,   30
but the finest varieties aren't found growing in every sea.
The large Lucrine cockle is better than the one from Baiae;
Circeii is the place for oysters; urchins come from Misenum.
Tarentum, the home of luxury, is proud of her broad scallops.

'The average person cannot lay claim to the art of dining.
First there is a complex science of flavours which has to be mastered.
And it isn't enough to sweep fish from a high-priced slab
unaware of which are better with sauce and which should be grilled
in order to tempt the flagging guest to resume eating.

40   'If you like your meat tasty make sure that the boar which bends
     the big round dish is an Umbrian fed on acorns of ilex;
     the Laurentian is poor, because he has been fattened on sedge and
                                                              [reeds.

     'Roes from the vineyard don't invariably make good eating.
     The expert on hare will go for the wings of the fertile female.
     The optimum age of fish and fowl and their natural properties
     eluded every researcher's palate before mine.

     'Some talents are confined to devising new pastries,
     but to overspecialize in one department is unsatisfactory.
     Imagine someone whose sole concern was decent wine
50   and who didn't care about what kind of oil his fish were cooked in!
     'If you put Massic wine out of doors in fine weather,
     any thickness it may have will be cleared by the night air,
     and the aroma which causes giddiness will pass away; whereas
     straining it through linen spoils it by removing the full flavour.
     With Surrentine, a connoisseur adds Falernian lees,
     then cleverly uses a pigeon's egg to collect the sediment.
     (Impurities stick to the yolk, you see, as it sinks to the bottom.)

     'When a drinker is flagging, fried prawns and African snails
     will renew his zest. Lettuce won't, for it floats on the stomach,
60   which is sour after all the wine and craves to be re-awakened
     rather by the tang of ham and sausages – in fact it enjoys
     any savouries that come in hot from the messy stall.
     It is worth while to become thoroughly versed in the contents
     of double sauce. The simple consists of fresh olive oil,
     which has to be mixed with a heavy wine and also with brine.
     (Make sure the brine comes from a stinking Byzantine jar.)
     Stir in some chopped herbs, bring to the boil, and sprinkle
     with saffron from Córycus. Let it stand; then add in conclusion
     the oil obtained by squeezing the choice Venafran olive.

70   'Apples from Tivoli are inferior in taste to those of Picenum,
     which is odd, for they look nicer. Venuculan grapes should go
     to the preserving jar; the Alban are better for drying in smoke.
     You'll find I was the first to serve these with apples;
     I was the first to provide wine-lees and tartar, and to sift
     white pepper and black salt into clean little dishes.

'It's a dreadful mistake to pay three thousand for fish at the market
and then to squeeze the sprawling creatures in a narrow dish.
How utterly sickening when a servant hands you a cup with fingers
covered in grease from the stolen pickings he has just been nibbling,
or an old bowl is encrusted with a layer of nasty fuzz!   80
Ordinary brushes, dusters, sawdust – think how little
expense they involve; but when they're forgotten the disgrace is
                                                          [enormous.
Imagine sweeping a mosaic pavement with a dirty broom
of palm-leaves, or keeping grubby covers on Tyrian upholstery,
forgetting that, as these items cost little trouble and money,
failure to provide them is less excusable than it is in the case
of things that only the rich can expect to have in their dining-rooms.'

What expertise! For god's sake, Catius, look, we're friends,
so be sure to take me to the next lecture, wherever it is.
For even if you told me his entire doctrine, word for word,   90
it wouldn't mean the same secondhand. And apart from that,
there's the man's face and presence. *You* don't think it important
to see him because you have happily had that privilege, but I
have a passionate longing to find my way to that far-off fountain
and from there to draw instructions for a truly happy life.

                              SATIRE 5

Like its famous prototype in the Odyssey Book XI, *this dialogue is
set in Hades. Ulysses faces the prospect of returning home penni-
less, and so he asks the prophet Tiresias how he can restore his
fortunes.*

'Answer me one more question, Tiresias, besides what you've
                                                          [told me.
Can you suggest ways and means of recovering the property
I've lost . . . What are you laughing at?'
                                        'So the man of many wiles
is not content to return to Ithaca and see the gods
of his homestead!'
                        'You, sir, have never told a lie. You see
how, as you foretold, I'm returning home naked and destitute;

there both my cellar and livestock have suffered at the suitors'
                                                              [hands.
Yet breeding and character, without assets, aren't worth tuppence.'

'Let's not mince words. Poverty is what you're afraid of.
10   So here's the way to get rich. Suppose you're given a thrush
or something else for yourself, let it fly away to the glitter
of a great household with an aged master. Your sweetest apples
and the various glories that come to you from your tidy farm –
let the rich man taste them before the god of your hearth, for he
is more worthy of honour. He may be a liar and a man of no family,
an escaped convict stained with his brother's blood; no matter.
If he asks you to go for a walk, be sure to keep outside him.'

'What? Defer to some filthy menial? I did not behave
like that at Troy, where I always strove with my betters!'
                                                              'All right,
20   you'll be a pauper.'
                          'I shall brace my heart to bear what you spoke of.
I have endured even greater ills e'er now. So tell me, sir,
with your prophet's insight, how to rake in piles of cash.'

'I've told you and I'll tell you again. You must fish cunningly
                                                              [around
for old men's wills. If one or two are clever enough
to nibble the bait off the hook and escape your clutches, you mustn't
be so disappointed as to give up hope and abandon your craft.
If a case, of whatever size, comes up, discover which party
is rich and childless; then, although he's a crook and even
has the gall to indict a better man, you take his side.
30   As for the citizen who has the sounder case and character,
despise him, if there's a son at home or a fertile wife.
Say "Peter", for instance, or "Paul" (susceptible ears enjoy
their own first names), "Your manly integrity has made me your
                                                              [friend.

I know the ins and outs of the law and how to conduct
a defence. I'd lose a leg rather than see you insulted
or robbed of a penny. My sole concern is to watch that no one
swindles or deceives you in any way." Tell him to go home
and look after his health. You yourself become his attorney.
Carry on and stick at it, even if "The glowing Dog-star

the dumb statues splits', or Furius distended with greasy   40
tripe "Bespews the wintry Alps with hoary snow".
"Look," someone will say, nudging the man beside him,
"how patient he is! How helpful to his friends! How very keen!"
More tunnies will come swimming up and your fish-ponds will
                                                              [grow.

'Again, if you risk detection by paying open respect
to a bachelor, find a man who is rearing a delicate son
in an opulent style. Then, by your constant attentions, creep
softly towards your goal – to be named as second heir.
If an accident sends the boy to his grave, *you* can move into
the vacant place. That's a gamble which rarely fails.   50

When someone hands you his will to read, be sure to decline
and wave the document aside – contriving, however, to catch
with the corner of your eye the instructions on the second line of
                                                        [page one.
Glance at it quickly to see if you are the sole heir
or one of several. Frequently a raven with open beak
will be fooled by a civil servant cooked up from a minor official
and Coránus will have the laugh on Nasíca the fortune-hunter.'
     'Are you raving? Or purposely teasing me with this involved
                                                    [prediction?'
     'Son of Laertes, what I say will, or will not, come to pass,
for mighty Apollo has granted me the gift of second sight.'   60
     'Well anyway, if you don't mind, would you tell me the point of
                                                    [the story?'

     'In the days when a young hero, the scourge of the Parthian race,
born of Aeneas' noble line shall rule over land
and sea, the gallant Coránus shall take in marriage the queenly
daughter of Nasíca who hates paying his debts in full.
Then the aged groom shall act as follows: handing his father-in-law
a copy of his will he shall beg him to read it; with many protests
Nasíca shall take it and read it in silence, to find that nothing
has been left to him and his but wailing and gnashing of teeth.

'A further point: if the old dotard happens to be under   70
the thumb of some scheming woman or freedman, make a deal:
you praise them, they praise you when you're not there.
That helps too. But much the best device is to storm

the main objective. If the idiot churns out doggerel – praise it.
Is he a lecher? Don't wait to be asked – do the decent thing
and hand Penelope over to your more deserving rival.'
    'Do you think she can be prevailed on, a lady so pure and proper,
a lady whom the suitors have failed to tempt from the straight and
                                                        [narrow?'
    'Of course! When those lads came, they were rather mean with
                                                        [their presents;
80 it wasn't sex that enticed them so much as the palace cooking.
That's why your Penelope is pure. But if you make her a partner
and let her taste some cash at an old fellow's expense,
there'll be no holding her. She'll be like a dog with a juicy bone.

    'I'll tell you something that happened in my later years. An ancient
bitch in Thebes left some odd instructions for her funeral: her body
was soaked in oil, then carried by her heir on his bare shoulders.
No doubt she hoped on her death to slip out of his clutches.
                                                        [I suppose
he'd been over-insistent in her lifetime.
                                    Watch how you make your
                                                        [approach.
You mustn't let things slide, nor yet be too attentive.
90 A peevish and moody man will be irked by chatter. Apart from
"Yes" and "No" keep quiet. Be like Davus in the comedies,
standing with head bowed, as if you'd something to fear.
Solicitude should be your plan of attack: if the breeze freshens,
tell him to be careful and cover his precious head. Make a pathway
through the crowd with your shoulders. Cock an ear to his chatter.
If his constant conceit gets on your nerves, keep on blowing
and inflate the old balloon with windy praises, until
he throws up his hands to the skies and exclaims "Oh, steady on!"
    'When you are released from your long term of trouble and
                                                        [service,
100 and you hear the words "A fourth part of my estate is to go
to Ulysses," then, after making sure you're awake, let fall
here and there "So my old friend Jack is no more! Where shall I find
another so staunch and loyal?" Squeeze a tear if you can.
If your face betrays your delight, you can always hide it. The tomb
may be left to your discretion; if so, spare no expense
on its building. Put on a splendid funeral for the neighbours to
                                                        [admire.
If a co-heir is getting on in years and has a church-yard cough,

tell him if he'd like to buy an estate or a house that is part of
your share, you'll let him have it for a song. But Queen
Proserpine calls. Good-bye then, and don't let life get you down!'   110

SATIRE 6

*This poem was written late in 31 BC, three or four years after Maecenas
had presented Horace with the Sabine farm. It contrasts the pleasures
of the country with the strain of city life. It was imitated by Pope and
Swift.*

This is what I prayed for. A piece of land – not so very big,
with a garden and, near the house, a spring that never fails,
and a bit of wood to round it off. All this and more
the gods have granted. So be it. I ask for nothing else,
O son of Maia, except that you make these blessings last.

If I haven't increased my assets by any dishonest trick
and don't intend to fritter them away by waste or neglect,
if I'm not such a fool as to pray: 'I wish my little farm
could take in that corner of my neighbour's, which at present
                                                       [spoils its shape;
I wish I could stumble on a pot of silver and be like the fellow   10
who on finding some treasure bought and ploughed the very field
in which he had worked as a hired hand; it was Hercules' favour
that made him rich'; if I'm pleased and content with my lot, then this
is my prayer: 'make fat the flocks I own and everything else
except my head, and remain as ever my chief protector.'

Well then, now that I've left town for my castle in the hills
what can I better praise in the satires of my lowland muse?
I'm spared the accursed struggle for status, and the leaden sirocco,
which in the tainted autumn enriches Our Lady of Funerals.
O Father of the Dawn, or Janus if you would rather have that name,   20
you watch over the beginning of man's working day,
for such is the will of heaven. So let me begin my song
with you. In Rome you dispatch me to act as a guarantor.
'Hurry, or someone else will answer the call before you!'
The north wind may be rasping the earth, or winter may be drawing
the snowy day into a smaller circle, but go I must.

Then, after swearing loud and clear to my own disadvantage,
I have to barge through the crowd, bruising the slow movers.
   'What do you want, you idiot, and why are you pushing so
                                              [rudely
30   with your angry curses? Do you think you can kick things out of
                                           [your way
because you're dashing back to Maecenas to keep an appointment?'
I like that, I admit, and it's sweet music in my ears.
But as soon as I reach the mournful Esquiline, hundreds of items
of other folks' business buzz in my head and jump round my legs.
   'Roscius would like you to meet him at the Wall by eight
                                        [tomorrow.'
   'The Department said be sure to come in today, Quintus;
an important matter of common concern has just cropped up.'
   'Get Maecenas' signature on these papers.'
                                   'I'll try,'
you say.
         'You can if you want to,' he replies, and won't be put off.

40   Time flies. It's now six, in fact almost seven,
years since Maecenas came to regard me as one of his friends –
or at least he was willing to go so far as to take me with him
when making a journey in his carriage and to risk casual remarks:
'What time do you make it?' 'Is the Thracian Chick a match for the
                                       [Arab?'
'These frosty mornings are quite nippy; you've got to be careful,'
and other comments which might be entrusted to a leaky ear.
All this time, every day and hour, yours truly has become
a more frequent target for jealous comment. Suppose he has sat
in the grandstand with me or played in the Park, there's an instant
                                       [chorus
50   of 'Lucky dog!' If a chilling rumour runs through the streets
from the city centre, everyone I meet asks me for details.
'Excuse me, sir, but you must know, for you are so close
to the supreme power – you haven't by any chance heard some
                                       [news
about the Dacians?'
                   'No, none at all.'
                          'Teasing as usual!'
'I swear it; I don't know a thing.'
                        'No? Well what about the land
Caesar has promised to give his veterans? Will it be in Italy

or Triangleland?'
                    When I protest my ignorance, they regard me with
                                                    [wonder
as a deep man, if you please, of quite unusual reticence!
That's how the day is wasted. In exasperation I murmur:
'When shall I see that place in the country, when shall I be free   60
to browse among the writers of old, to sleep or idle,
drinking in a blissful oblivion of life's troubles?
When shall I sit down to a plate of beans, Pythagoras' kinsmen,
along with greens which are amply flavoured by fat bacon?'

Ah, those evenings and dinners. What heaven! My friends and I
have our meal at my own fireside. Then, after making an offering,
I hand the rest to the cheeky servants. Every guest
drinks from whatever glass he likes, big or small.
We have no silly regulations. One goes for the strong stuff
like a hero, another mellows more happily on a milder blend.   70
And so the conversation begins – not about other folks'
town and country houses, nor the merits of Grace's dancing;
we discuss things which affect us more nearly and one ought to
                                                    [know about:
what is the key to happiness, money or moral character?
In making friends are our motives idealistic or selfish?
What is the nature of goodness, and what is its highest form?

Meanwhile our neighbour Cervius tells us old wives' tales
which are yet to the point. If someone envies Arellius' money
without considering his worries, he begins: Once upon a time
a country mouse is said to have welcomed to his humble hole   80
a mouse from the city – a friend and guest of long standing.
He was a rough fellow, who kept a tight hand on his savings,
though he didn't mind relaxing when it came to a party. Anyhow,
he drew freely on his store of vetch and long oats,
then brought a raisin in his mouth and bits of half-eaten bacon,
hoping, by varying the menu, to please his finicky guest.
The latter would barely touch each item with his dainty teeth,
while the master of the house, reclining on a couch of fresh straw,
ate coarse grain and darnel, avoiding the choicer dishes.
At last the townsman spoke: 'Look old man, why on earth   90
do you want to eke out a living on a cliff edge in the woods?
You ought to give up this wild forest in favour of the city
and its social life. Come on back with me now: I mean it

All earthly creatures have been given mortal souls;
large or small they have no means of escaping death.
So my dear chap, while there's still time, enjoy the good things
of life, and never forget your days are numbered.'

His words
prodded the peasant into action. He hopped nimbly from his house,
and then the pair completed the journey, hurrying on
100 to creep within the city wall under cover of darkness.
Night had reached the middle of her journey across the heavens
when they made their way into a wealthy house. Covers steeped
in scarlet dye shimmered expensively on ivory couches,
and close by, piled in baskets, were several courses
left from a great dinner earlier on that evening.
Inviting the bumpkin to relax on the red material, the host
bustled about, like a waiter in a short jacket, producing
one course after another, not forgetting the house-boy's
duty of testing whatever he brought with a preliminary nibble.
110 The other was lying there, thoroughly enjoying his change of fortune
and playing the happy guest surrounded by good cheer,
when suddenly the doors crashed open and sent them scuttling from
[their places.
They dashed in fright down the long hall, their fear turning
to utter panic when they heard the sound of mastiffs baying
through the great house. Then the countryman said: 'This isn't
[the life
for me. Good-bye: my hole in the woods will keep me safe
from sudden attack, and simple vetch will assuage my hunger.'

SATIRE 7

Like II. 3, *this homily is supposed to be delivered during the Saturnalia.
It is also on a Stoic theme, viz. that only the sage is free. Davus,
Horace's slave, has heard the sermon not from the Stoic Crispinus
himself but from his hall porter who had been listening at the door of
the lecture-room.*

'I've been listening for ages and wanting to say a few words, but as
I'm a slave I haven't the nerve.'

'Is it Davus?'

'Yes, it's Davus –

a servant fond of his master, and reasonably good – though not
so good, I hope, as to die young.'
                                        'Come on, it's December;
enjoy the freedom our fathers decreed, and say what you like.'

'Some people love their faults and follow their aim unswervingly;
most vary, at one time trying to go straight, at another
stooping to something crooked. One day Priscus would be seen
with three rings on his left hand, the next with none.
He had no stability. He would change his stripe from hour to hour;   10
leaving a great house, he would enter a dive from which
the cleaner sort of freedman would blush to be seen emerging;
he rang the changes: lecher in Rome and scholar in Athens.
Vertumnus scowled on his birth, and made him a versatile failure.

The wastrel 'Vólanérius, when the gout he richly deserved
crippled his fingers, hired a servant at a daily wage
to pick up the dice and put them in the box on his behalf.
He stuck steadily to a single vice and accordingly suffered
less distress and was better off than the wretched creature
that is now chafed and now entangled by the rope around it.'   20
'Don't take all day, you crook. Just tell me, what's the point
of all this rot?'
                        'Why *you* are!'
                                        'How do you mean, you scum?'
'You praise the fortune and ways of the men of old, and yet
if a god suddenly urged you to go back you'd refuse point blank,
for you don't believe that what you shout about is really better,
or else you are too weak to defend what's right; so you stick
fast in the mud vainly struggling to pull out your foot.
In Rome you long for the country; there, you praise to the skies
the city you've just left. There's caprice! If no one
has asked you to dinner you talk lovingly of "carefree veg".   30
You hug yourself in delight that you needn't go out drinking,
as if it took handcuffs to get you to a party. About lighting-up time
Maecenas sends round a late invitation to join him at dinner.
"Will someone bring the lamp-oil? Quickly! Is nobody listening?"
Then, with a lot of bluster and bellowing, you dash away.
The hangers-on depart with curses that needn't be repeated.
I can imagine Mulvius saying: "All right, I admit I'm easily
led by my belly, my nostrils twitch at a savoury smell,
I'm weak, spineless – if you like, a glutton into the bargain,

40   but you're exactly the same, if not worse. So why
      should you lecture me in a superior tone, wrapping up your vices
      in polite expressions?" Suppose you were shown to be more of a fool
      than I, who cost you a mere five hundred? You needn't try
      to scare me by making faces; put down your fists and control
      your temper, till you hear the lesson I learned from Crispinus'
                                                          [porter.
      'You fancy someone else's wife, Davus a tart.
      Who commits the graver offence? When I'm prodded on
      by the goad of lust, a girl lying naked in the lamplight submits
      to the strokes of my swollen crop or eagerly urges on
50   with her buttocks the horse on whose stomach she is riding. I wave
                                                          [her good-bye
      without incurring disgrace or feeling any concern
      that someone richer or more handsome may be using the same
                                                          [receptacle.
      Whereas you tear off the badges of your rank – your knight's ring
      and your Roman clothes, changing from a judge to a common slave,
      and hiding your scented hair with a hood. Then aren't you in fact
      the very thing you pretend to be? You walk nervously in,
      and your whole body trembles as fear struggles with lust.
      What matter whether you're handed over to be seared with the birch
      and killed with the sword, or whether you're bundled into a box
60   by a maid abetting her mistress' sin and forced to cower there
      with your head stuffed between your knees? The injured husband
      has a right to take revenge on both the guilty parties,
      but especially on the seducer. (The wife, after all, doesn't change
      her clothes or her rank, nor does she actually inflict the crime.)
      When the woman is apprehensive and doesn't trust your affections,
      will you walk deliberately under the yoke, consigning your goods
      plus body, reputation, and life to that frenzied master within?
      You've escaped. I suppose you'll have learnt to be cautious and
                                                          [careful in future.
      No. You'll look for another chance of terror and ruin.
70   You inveterate slave! Is any animal so degenerate
      that, after breaking free, it crawls back to its chains?

      ' "I'm not an adulterer," you say. No, nor am I a thief
      when I studiously ignore your silver; but remove the danger, and
                                                          [nature
      will bound forward with the reins off and go on the rampage.
      Are you my master, you who submit to other men's orders

and the constant pressure of affairs? However often you are touched
by the rod, it will never free you from the fear which is so degrading.
A further point – and no less cogent: a man who takes orders
from a slave may be called a *sub*-slave, as he is in servants' parlance,
or a *fellow*-slave; at any rate, isn't that what I am to you?   80
For although you dictate to me, you cringe to another master.
You are jerked like a wooden puppet by somebody else's strings.

'Who then is free? The wise man who is master of himself,
who remains undaunted in the face of poverty, chains and death,
who stubbornly defies his passions and despises positions of power,
a man complete in himself, smooth and round, who prevents
extraneous elements clinging to his polished surface, who is such
that when Fortune attacks him she maims only herself. Can you
lay claim to a single one of these qualities? A woman demands
a small fortune, bullies you, slams the door, saturates you   90
with cold water – and invites you back. Tear that degrading
yoke from your neck! Come on, say you are free! You can't.
For a cruel master is riding your soul, jabbing the spurs
in your weary flanks, and hauling round your head when you shy.

'When, like an idiot, you are entranced by a decadent Pausias,
how are you less at fault than I, when with straining hamstrings
I gaze in wonder at the duels of Fulvius or Pácideiánus
or Rútuba, drawn in charcoal or red ochre as if
the men were actually fighting and flashing their weapons to strike
and parry? Davus is a useless layabout, but you, of course,   100
are known as an astute and discerning judge of the old masters.

'I'm trash if I follow the whiff of a cake. Do you
with your lofty mind and character refuse sumptuous dinners?
Why does it do more harm to me to be the slave of my belly?
I suppose because I get walloped. But do you come off more lightly
when you reach for goodies which can't be had at a reasonable
                                                                   [price?

The fact is that an endless series of banquets acidifies,
and the poor overtaxed legs refuse to support the bloated
body. If a slave-boy is guilty when he steals a scraper and swaps it
at dusk for some grapes, what of the man who sells estates   110
at the behest of his gullet? Is there nothing servile about him?
                                                          [Moreover,
you can't stand so much as an hour of your own company

or spend your leisure properly; you avoid yourself like a truant
or fugitive, hoping by drink or sleep to elude Angst.
But it's no good, for that dark companion stays on your heels.'

'Quick, get me a stone.'
                    'What for?'
                                'Where are my arrows?'
'The man's delirious – or composing poetry!'
                                    If you don't get to hell
out of here, you'll end up as drudge number nine on my Sabine farm!'

SATIRE 8

*Fundanius, a comic poet and a friend of Horace (cf. I. 10. 41), describes
a dinner-party given for Maecenas and his friends by the rich parvenu
Nasidienus Rufus. Palmer (pp. 368–9) argues for the theory that the
figure of Nasidienus is based on memories of Salvidienus Rufus, who
after a meteoric career had been executed six or more years earlier
(Velleius II. 76. 4). But there is no evidence that Salvidienus was a gour-
met, and he could hardly have been such a fool as the host described by
Horace. So it is safer to suppose that the occasion is fictitious, though
men of Nasidienus' type would not have been hard to find.*

   *In a Roman dining-room the guests reclined on couches on three sides
of a square. The meal was served from the fourth side. The seating
arrangements described by Horace should be imagined as follows:*

MAECENAS	VIBIDIUS	BALATRO

NOMENTANUS		VARIUS
NASIDIENUS		VISCUS
PORCIUS		FUNDANIUS

How did you enjoy your swell party chez Násidiénus?
Yesterday I was trying to get you to dine with me, but was told
you'd been drinking there since midday.

                                  'I've never had such a time
in all my life.'

            Well tell us then, if you've no objection,
what was the first dish to appease your raging bellies?

'First there was a boar from Lucania, which our gracious host kept
                                       [telling us
was caught in a soft southerly breeze. It was garnished with things
that stimulate a jaded appetite – lettuces, spicey turnips,
radishes, skirret, fish pickle, and the lees of Coan wine.
When this was cleared away, a boy in a brief tunic   10
wiped the maple table with a crimson cloth, while another
swept up scraps and anything else that might annoy
the guests. Then, like an Attic maiden bearing the holy
emblems of Ceres, in came the dark Hydaspes carrying
Caecuban wine, followed by Alcon with unsalted Chian.
Then his lordship said. "If you prefer Falernian or Alban
to what has been served, Maecenas, we do have both varieties."'

It's a terrible thing to have money! But do tell me Fundanius,
who were your fellow guests on this magnificent occasion?

'I was at the top, with Viscus from Thurii next; below,   20
if I remember rightly, was Varius. On the middle couch was Vibídius
with Servilius Bálatro – two 'shadows' who had come with Maecenas.
Our host had Nomentánus above him and Hogg below.
The latter amused us by swallowing whole cakes at a time.
Nomentanus was deputed to point out features that might have
escaped attention. For the uninitiated mob (that is,
the rest of us) were eating fowl, oysters and fish that contained
a flavour totally different from anything we had known before.
This became clear at once when Nomentánus offered me
fillets of plaice and turbot which I hadn't previously tasted.   30
He then informed me that the apples were red because they'd been
                                       [picked
by a waning moon. If you wonder what difference *that* makes, you'd
                                     [better
ask the man himself.
            Vibídius turned to Bálatro:

"If we don't drink him out of house and home we'll die in vain."
And he called for larger tankards. At this a ghastly pallor
appeared on the host's face; he detested strenuous drinkers,
whether because their scurrilous humour gets out of hand
or because a fiery wine dulls the palate's edge.
Vibídius and Bálatro proceeded to tip whole jug-fulls of wine
40   into mugs of the type made in Allífae. The rest followed suit
except for the host's clients, who refrained from hitting the bottle.

'Then a lamprey arrived, stretched on a dish, with prawns swimming
around it, at which his lordship remarked "This one was caught
while she was pregnant; after spawning the flesh is inferior.
The sauce has the following ingredients: Venafran oil (*the first*
pressing of course), liquamen (from the guts of the *Spanish*
                                                            [*mackerel*),
wine that is five years old, but grown in Italy (this
to be added in the course of boiling; after boiling, Chian
is better than anything else), *white* pepper, and one mustn't
50   forget the vinegar, made from fermented Methymnean grape.
I pioneered the practice of boiling sharp elecampane
and green rockets with the sauce. Curtillus uses sea-urchins –
unwashed, for the liquor provided by the shell-fish is better than
                                                            [brine."

'As he spoke, the awning suspended above collapsed on the dish,
wreaking appalling havoc, spreading loftier clouds
of black dust than Boreas raises on Campanian acres.
We feared worse, but on finding there was no danger we emerged.
There was Rufus, his head in his hands, weeping as if
his son had perished young. How would it all have ended
60   if that philosopher Nomentanus hadn't succeeded
in pulling his friend together: "Shame on you Lady Luck!
No other god is so cruel. What pleasure you get from mocking
the plans of men!"
                           Varius struggled to stifle his laughter
with a napkin. Bálatro, who turns up his nose at everything, said
"This is the law which governs life. So it is
that your best efforts will never achieve the fame they deserve.
To think that, just to regale *me*, *you* should be plagued
and tormented with worry, in case the bread should be over-baked
or the sauce be served without proper seasoning, and that all your
                                                            [boys

should be properly dressed and neatly groomed for waiting at table.   70
To say nothing of other hazards – like the canopy falling
as it did just now, or an oaf tripping and smashing a dish.
But as with a general so with a host: adverse fortune
has a way of revealing his genius; good fortune obscures it."

'Násidiénus answered "May heaven send you all
the blessings you pray for! You're a fine man and a courteous
                                                                    [guest!"
And he called for his slippers. Then on every couch heads could be
                                                                    [seen
leaning forward to ears, and a buzz of whispering arose.'

I'd love to have seen it. It all sounds like first-rate slapstick.
Anyhow, go on. What was the next laugh?   80
                                        'Vibídius
wasn't getting the drinks he ordered, so he asked the servants
if the jug was broken as well. We were making jokes to provide
an excuse for our laughter, with Bálatro egging us on, when behold
Násidiénus re-enters wearing the face of a man
resolved to retrieve disaster by inspired improvisation.
Behind come servants carrying a huge dish with a crane
(a male, ready-carved, liberally sprinkled with salt and meal),
the liver of a white female goose fattened on figs,
and hare's wings on their own (allegedly nicer thus
than if you eat them with the back). Then we saw blackbirds served   90
with breasts slightly charred and pigeons minus their rumps –
tasty things if only our host hadn't insisted
on giving a lecture on their causes and properties. We paid him back
by getting away without tasting a thing, as if the banquet
had been blighted by Canidia, whose breath is more deadly than an
                                                    [African snake's.'

HORACE
Epistles

BOOK I

After claiming to give up lyric poetry, Horace turns to questions of moral philosophy.

Named by my earliest Muse and duly named by my last –
Maecenas, I have been tested enough and have now received
my foil. Are you trying to put me back in the old school?
My age and keenness are not what they were. Having hung his
                                     [weapons
on Hercules' door, Veianius is lying low in the country
for fear he might have to plead again and again for discharge
from the edge of the sand. A voice whispers in my well-rinsed ear:
'Have some sense and release the ageing horse in time,
or he'll end by stumbling and straining his flanks to the jeers of
                                     [the crowd.'

So now I am laying aside my verses and other amusements.   10
My sole concern is the question 'What is right and proper?'
I'm carefully storing things for use in the days ahead.
In case you wonder whom I follow and where I'm residing,
I don't feel bound to swear obedience to any master.
Where the storm drives me I put ashore and look for shelter.
Now I'm a man of action and plunge into civic affairs,
doing my highest duty with stern and selfless devotion;
now I slip quietly back to the rules of Aristippus, attempting
to induce things to conform to me, not vice versa.

It's a long night for a man when his girl-friend breaks her promise,   20
a long day for those who must hire their labour; the year
drags for orphan boys in the strict care of their mothers.
For me any time at all is tedious and unrewarding

if it hinders my hopes and plans for following that pursuit
which brings an equal advantage to rich and poor alike,
whereas its neglect will harm young and old alike.
For the present I'll find support and comfort in the rules below.
(You might not be able to rival Lynceus in length of vision,
but that wouldn't make you refuse a salve if your eyes were sore.
30   You'll never enjoy the physique of Glyco the champion athlete,
but you'd still want to keep your body free from the knots of gout.
We can all make *some* progress, in spite of our limitations.)

Suppose your heart is inflamed with greed and wretched craving,
words and sayings exist by which you can soothe the pain
and, to a large extent, get rid of the ailment. Or are you
swollen with ambition? Certain procedures are sure to help you:
read the booklet three times with a pure heart.
Whether he's envious, choleric, indolent, drunken or lustful –
no one is so unruly that he can't become more gentle,
40   if only he listens with care to what his trainer tells him.

Virtue's first rule is 'avoid vice', and wisdom's
'get rid of folly'. Think of the mental effort and physical
risk involved in shunning what *you* regard as the worst
of evils – slender assets and the shame of a lost election.
You never cease – dashing away to India on business,
keeping ahead of poverty through ocean, rock and flame.
Why not trust one wiser than yourself? Listen and learn.
Stop caring for the things you foolishly gaze at and long for.
What wrestler at the village sports and crossroad fairs
50   would refuse the great Olympic prize if given the prospect,
and indeed the offer, of the palm's glory without the dust?
Silver is lower than gold in value, gold than goodness.
'Citizens, citizens, the first thing to acquire is money.
Cash before conscience!' This is propounded from end to end
of Janus' arcade, a lesson recited by young and old
(swinging satchel and writing box from the left arm).
Suppose you've gifts of mind and character, fluent and loyal,
but are six or seven thousand short of the great four hundred:
you'll be one of the throng. But the children chant 'You will be king
60   if you do the right thing.' So let this be your wall of brass:
to have nothing on your conscience, nothing to give you a guilty
                                                              [pallor.

Tell me, is Roscius' law above the children's jingle
which offers the title of king to those who 'do the right thing' –
a jingle repeated by the men of old, like Curius and Camillus?
Who gives the better advice, the man who says 'make money –
if you can, honestly; if not, make it by hook or by crook',
to get a closer view of Pupius' doleful dramas,
or the one who, giving you practical help and advice, equips you
to stand up straight and free and defy the frown of Fortune?

So if the people of Rome should happen to ask me why   70
I share the same colonnades but not the same opinions,
and why I refuse to follow them in all their likes and aversions,
I shall give the same answer as the wary fox in the fable
returned to the sick lion: 'because those footprints scare me;
all of them lead in your direction, none of them back'.
You are like a many-headed beast. What should I follow, or whom?
Some men are eager to secure public contracts, while others
woo wealthy widows with fruit and dainty morsels,
or catch childless dotards in a net to stock their fish-ponds.
Many fortunes are fattened by the quiet growth of interest.   80
But grant that men are engrossed in different aims and activities,
can any bear to enjoy the same thing for an hour?
If the millionaire exclaims 'No bay in the world
outshines glorious Baiae,' lake and sea are subjected
to the master's hurried passion; but if his morbid fancy
gives the sacred signal, he says to his workmen 'Tomorrow
you'll take your tools to Teánum.' If his hall has a marriage bed,
'nothing,' he says, 'but nothing, can beat the bachelor's life'.
If it hasn't, he's perfectly sure that only husbands are happy.
What knot will it take to hold this changeable Proteus?   90
And the poor man? Equally silly. He changes garret and bed,
baths and barber; he hires a boat and is just as sick
as the rich tycoon sailing along in his private yacht.

If I've had a haircut from a rather uneven barber, you laugh
when you meet me; if a grubby vest is visible under my smart
tunic, or say my toga is askew and sloppily folded,
you laugh. Yet what if my mind is all at odds with itself,
rejects what it asked for, returns to what it has just put down,
ebbs and flows, and disrupts my life's entire pattern,
demolishing then rebuilding, changing square to round?   100
You accept my madness as normal. You don't laugh at all,

nor do you think I need a doctor or a guardian assigned
by the court. And yet *you* are in charge of all my affairs;
you even become annoyed with the friend who looks to you
for support and protection, if his nails have not been properly
                                                              [trimmed.

In brief, the sensible man is second only to Jove.
He's free, well thought of, handsome, the very king of kings;
above all, he's *sound* – when he hasn't a blasted cold!

EPISTLE 2

*The first section derives some moral lessons from Homer; this leads
into a homily on ethics.*

While you, Lollius Maximus, are declaiming in Rome, at Praeneste
I have been reading again the tale of the Trojan war.
The poet shows what is fine and foul, what is advisable
and what is not, more clearly and better than Chrysippus and
                                                              [Crantor.
I'm happy to give you my reasons, if you are free to hear them.

The story, which tells how Greece on account of Paris' love
became embroiled in a weary war with a foreign country,
is full of the feverish passions of foolish kings and peoples.
Antenor proposes at a stroke to remove the cause of the war.
10 And what is Paris' answer? He declares that nothing will induce him
to reign in safety and live in happiness! Nestor is anxious
to settle the quarrel of Peleus' son with the son of Atreus,
as the first is ravaged by love and both alike by anger.
For every act of royal folly the Achaeans are scourged.
Sedition, deceit, crime, lust and anger make up
a tale of sin on both sides of the Trojan wall.

Again, Homer has set before us a helpful example
of what goodness and wisdom can do in the shape of Ulysses,
the tamer of Troy, the man of vision, who studied the cities
20 and manners of many peoples, and who, as he struggled home
leading his men across the tracts of the sea, endured
many a horror, yet never sank in the waves of adversity.

You have often heard of the Sirens' song and Circe's cups;
if *he* had been foolish and greedy enough to drink, like his comrades,
he'd have fallen under the brutish degrading spell of a whore,
living the life of a filthy dog or a wallowing pig.
We are the mass, whose role is merely consuming produce –
Penelope's drone-like suitors, or the youths at Alcinous' court,
who spent excessive time in looking after their bodies;
they thought it a fine thing to slumber half the day,   30
and then to woo reluctant sleep with the sound of the lute.

Thugs get up in the middle of the night to cut a throat.
Won't *you* wake up for the sake of your own salvation? But listen –
if you won't run when healthy, you will when you suffer from
                                                                       [dropsy.

Send for a book and a lamp before daylight, and focus
your mind on noble aims and pursuits, or else when you wake
you'll be racked by desire or envy. Why so quick to remove
a speck of dirt from your eye? And yet, if anything eats at
your soul, you say: 'Time enough to attend to it next year'.
Well begun is half done. Dare to be wise.   40
Start now. The man who postpones the hour of reform
is the yokel who waits for the river to pass; but it continues
and will continue gliding and rolling for ever and ever.
I know, you need money and a wealthy wife who will bear you
children; the wild scrub is being subdued by the plough.
But when one's blest with enough, one shouldn't long for more.
Possessing a house or farm or a pile of bronze and gold
has never been known to expel a fever from an invalid's body
or a worry from his mind. Unless the owner has sound health
he cannot hope to enjoy the goods he has brought together.   50
A man with fear or desire has as much pleasure from his house
and possessions as sore eyes from a picture, gouty feet
from muffs, or ears from a lyre when aching with lumps of dirt.
When a jar is unclean, whatever you fill it with soon goes sour.

Despise pleasure: when the price is pain, pleasure is harmful.
The greedy are never content; fix an end to your longings.
Envious people waste away when their neighbours thrive.
Envy is just as painful as any torture invented
by the tyrants of Sicily. The man who fails to control his rage
is sure to regret what his wounded feelings caused him to do   60
when he took hasty and violent revenge to ease his resentment.

Rage is a burst of madness. Restrain your temper: unless it
obeys it will rule you. Keep it in check with bridle and chain.
A colt with his tender neck is pliable; hence the trainer
shapes him to go where the rider wants. The hound begins
to hunt in the woods when once it has barked at a stag's hide
in the yard. So now, when you're still a boy and your heart's
                                                            [untainted,
attach yourself to your betters and absorb their words of wisdom.
A jar retains for years the smell with which it was tinged
70 when new. But mind, don't dawdle or press keenly ahead.
I never wait for the slow-coach or try to catch the leaders!

EPISTLE 3

*Horace inquires about the literary activities of some young friends
who are staff officers in the army of Tiberius.*

Julius Florus, I'm longing to hear what part of the world
Augustus' stepson, Claudius, has reached with his expedition.
Where are you stationed? In Thrace, where snowy fetters confine
the Hebrus, or by the straits which run between the towers
on either side, or in Asia with its fertile plains and hills?

Also, what literary work is his staff engaged in, I wonder.
Who's shouldering the task of recording Augustus' exploits,
spreading the tale of war and peace to distant ages?
What of Titius, who will soon become the talk of Rome?
10 He has had the spirit to despise the tanks and open channels,
and has not blenched at drinking from Pindar, the fountain-head.
How is he? Does he ever think of me? Do the Muses smile
on his efforts to fit the rhythms of Thebes to the Latin lyre,
or does he rave and boom at large in the tragic manner?
What is Celsus up to? He needs constant reminding
to look for resources within himself, and to keep his hands off
the writings received by Apollo within the Palatine temple;
or else, when the flock of birds return to claim their plumage,
the poor little crow will be stripped of all the colours he stole,
20 and exposed to laughter. And what exciting plans have *you* got?
What beds of thyme are you buzzing about? Not that your talent
is in any way small; nor is it coarse or unpleasantly shaggy.

Whether you sharpen your tongue for the courts, or prepare to give
an opinion on civil law, or build your lovely songs,
you will win first prize – the victor's ivy. But if you were able
to get rid of your worries – those cold showers that damp you
                                                        [down –
you would soar above to the place where heavenly wisdom leads.
That is the task, that's the pursuit we should all engage in
(great or small), if we prize our country's esteem and our own.
When you write back, you must also tell me whether you care   30
for Munatius as much as you should; or does the gash in your
                                                        [friendship
reopen and fail to knit, because it's been badly stitched?
You're a wild pair, with tossing heads! But whatever's inciting you
(hot blood or lack of experience), and wherever you are,
it's wrong that such fellows should break the ties of brotherly
                                                        [feeling.
A heifer is being fattened to celebrate your return.

EPISTLE 4

A greeting and exhortation to the poet Albius.

Albius, you were a fair judge of my 'conversations'.
What are you doing, I wonder, in your native haunts at Pedum?
Writing something to outshine Cassius of Parma's pieces,
or taking a quiet stroll through the fresh woodland air,
pondering on all that befits a man who is wise and good?
You always were a soul as well as a body. The gods
have given you good looks, wealth and the sense to enjoy it.
If a man can judge what's right, express what he feels, and also
claim a generous share of charm, prestige and health,
with a decent style of living and a wallet that's never empty,   10
what further gift could a nurse desire for her darling baby?

In a world torn by hope and worry, dread and anger,
imagine every day that dawns is the last you'll see;
the hour you never hoped for will prove a happy surprise.
Come and see me when you want a laugh. I'm fat and sleek,
in prime condition, a porker from Epicurus' herd.

EPISTLE 5

A cheerful invitation to dinner.

If you can bear to recline on one of Archias' couches,
and can face smallish helpings of vegetarian food,
I shall look forward, Torquatus, to seeing you here at sunset.
The wine you will drink was bottled in Taurus' second consulate
between Minturnae in the marsh and Petrinum near Sinuessa.
If *you*'ve something better, have it brought, or obey orders.
The hearth is already polished, and you'll find the furniture tidy.
Forget for a while your chancy prospects and the race for profits
and the Moschus case. Tomorrow is Caesar's birthday, and so
10 we have an excuse for sleeping in. No retribution
if we stretch our pleasant talk into the summer night.

What's the point of money if you haven't the chance to enjoy it?
Someone who scrimps and saves more than he needs, in concern
for his heir, is next door to an idiot; I'll begin
drinking and scattering flowers. Who cares if I'm called
                                          [irresponsible?
Think of the wonders uncorked by wine! It opens secrets,
gives heart to our hopes, pushes the cowardly into battle,
lifts the load from anxious minds, and evokes talents.
Thanks to the bottle's prompting no one is lost for words,
20 no one who's cramped by poverty fails to find release.

I'm under orders, willing and able, to ensure the following:
there'll be no dirty napkins to make you grimace in disgust,
nor any grubby covers; no tankard or plate
that you can't see your face in; no one to noise abroad what is said
to friends in confidence. Getting the right blend of guests
is so important. I shall have Septicius and Butra along
to meet you, and Sabinus if he's not prevented by a previous
                                          [engagement
and prettier company. There's also room for several shadows.
(But at *over*crowded parties one must beware of the goat.)
30 Let me know how many you'd like; then drop what you're doing
and trick the client in the hall by slipping out the back.

EPISTLE 6

*Various approaches to the good life, most of them treated with good-
humoured irony.*

'Never be dazzled' is about the one and only thing,
my dear Numicius, that can make and keep a person happy.
The sun up there, and the stars, and the seasons passing in steady
procession – some can watch them without the least apprehension.
So what do you think of the earth's gifts and those of the sea
that provides such wealth for the distant Arabs and Indians? Also,
what of the shows? And the gifts and cheers of the Roman crowd?
How should *they* be regarded? With what looks and emotions?
As for their opposites, one who fears them is dazzled in rather
the same way as the eager man; the trouble is caused   10
by excitement: both are unsettled by the sight of the unforeseen.
Whether a man feels joy or pain, fear or desire –
what matter, if after seeing something better or worse
than expected he stands and stares, benumbed in mind and body?
The sensible man would be called a fool, the moral immoral,
if he followed Goodness herself beyond the proper limit!

Go on then, gaze at antique silver and bronzes and marbles
and works of art; be dazzled by gems and Tyrian colours;
revel in the fact that a thousand eyes are watching you speak.
Early to the Forum, home late – never let up,   20
or Mute may reap a richer crop from the fields he acquired
with his wife, and (horrid thought, for his people are lower class)
he may prove more dazzling to *you* than vice versa.
Whatever is under ground time will bring to the sunshine;
it will bury and hide what's now in the limelight. After you've been
a familiar sight in Agrippa's Porch and the Appian Way,
you must still go down the road travelled by Numa and Ancus.

If your lungs or kidneys are attacked by an acute disease, you look
for a cure. You also desire *moral* health. (Who doesn't?)
Well if that's produced by goodness alone, forget your fun   30
and set to work.
                   Do you think goodness is just a name,
and a grove just timber? Then see that *you* make harbour first.
(You mustn't lose the trade from Cíbyra or from Bithynia.)

Clear a thousand talents, and as many again; to these
add a third thousand, and then square the pile with a fourth.
As we all know, a wife and dowry, credit and friends,
birth and looks are conferred by her royal highness Money;
and the well-heeled man is blessed with charm and sex appeal.

Cappadocia's king has lots of slaves, but he's short of cash.
40 Don't you be like him. Lucullus, they say, was asked
whether he could lend a hundred cloaks for a stage production.
'A hundred?' he said. 'I doubt it, but I'll have a look and send you
what's there.' A letter followed: 'I find I have five thousand
available; take your pick – or the whole lot if you like.'
A house is sadly inadequate unless there's a large surplus
which the owner can't keep track of and thieves grow fat on. Well
                                                                     [then,
if wealth is the only thing that can make and keep you happy,
every day be the first at work, and the last to leave.

But if success is attained by display and popular favour
50 let's buy a slave to remind us of names, to dig us in the ribs
and make us offer a handshake across the stepping stones.
'*He*'s important in the Fabian tribe; *he* in the Veline;
he can confer the rods at will or remove the chair
of ivory without compunction.' Add 'Brother' or 'Father'
according to age, genially admitting them all to your family.

If good food is the secret of the good life – it's daylight;
let's obey the call of our gullet, going in quest
of fish and game, in Gargilius' style. He would send
his servants, with nets and spears, through the crowded Forum; later
60 one of his mules would carry home, as the people watched,
a boar he had bought. Distended with half-digested food
let's go to the baths, and ignore all questions of decency, acting
like Caere's third-rate townsmen, or Ulysses the Ithacan's crew –
a rotten lot, who preferred forbidden delights to their homeland.
If, as Mimnermus holds, without sexual pleasure
no joy exists, devote your life to sexual pleasure.

Good-bye and good luck. If *you* know anything better, be sure to
pass it on; if not, you can share the above with me.

EPISTLE 7

A crucial point in the relationship of poet to patron.

A week – that is how long I promised to stay in the country.
And I'm gone the whole of August. Most reprehensible. Yet
I know you want me to remain healthy and fit, Maecenas.
You show patience when I'm ill; so please do the same when I'm
                                                                    [trying
to avoid being ill, when the heat that ripens the early figs
brings the undertaker out, complete with his black attendants,
when fathers and doting mothers are pale with fear for their
                                                                    [children,
when conscientious deference and the footling concerns of the
                                                                    [Forum
bring on bouts of malaria and break the seals of wills.
But as soon as the winter covers the Alban fields with snow,   10
your lyric poet will go down to the seaside and take it easy,
curled up with a book. If you, my friend, will let him,
he will come and see you along with the zephyr and the first
                                                                    [swallow.

You've made me a precious gift – not like the man from Calabria
who offered pears to his guest: 'Go on, help yourself.'
'I've had plenty.'
                    'Well take away as many as you like.'
'Thanks all the same.'
                        'They'll make lovely gifts for the children.'
'Really, I'm as grateful as if I'd taken all I could carry.'
'Suit yourself. If you leave them, the pigs will have them for dinner!'
It's silly to fling around what you don't like or value.   20
Such sowing has never produced any thanks, and never will.
The good, sensible man is always ready to help
deserving cases, but he still can tell a coin from a counter.
I for my part will show I deserve such a splendid patron.
But if you want me never to leave, you'll have to restore
the strong lungs and the black hair thick on my forehead,
the charm of words, the well-mannered laughter, and the sad
                                                                    [laments
uttered, with glass in hand, when naughty Cinara left me.

Once a slim little fox crept through a narrow opening
30   into a bin of corn; after filling its belly
with food, it tried again and again to escape, but couldn't.
A weasel close at hand remarked: 'If you want to get out of there,
try that chink again when you're thin; you were thin when you
                                          [entered.'
If the fable is levelled at me, I hand everything back.
I don't sigh for 'penniless slumbers' when full of chicken,
nor would I change my leisure and freedom for the wealth of Arabia.
You have often praised my modesty; I've called you 'Father' and 'Sir'
in your hearing; nor do I use less generous terms in your absence.
If you try me, you'll find I can cheerfully hand your presents back.
40   Remember the words of Telemachus, child of enduring Ulysses:
'Ithaca's not very good for horses; it doesn't possess
broad, level tracks, or pastures of lush grass.
So I'll leave your gifts, son of Atreus; they're better suited to you.'
Small things for the small. It isn't royal Rome
that attracts me now, but quiet Tibur or peaceful Tarentum.

The distinguished lawyer Philippus, a dynamic, hard-working man,
was returning home from his business at two in the afternoon.
Being no longer young, he was grumbling that the Carínae
were now too far from the Forum, when they say he noticed a man,
50   freshly shaven, sitting in a barber's empty booth,
penknife in hand, quietly cleaning his own nails.
'Demetrius,' (this was Philippus' lively messenger boy)
'go and find out who that man is, where he lives,
how well off he is, and who's his father or patron.'
He goes, and returns with the answer: 'His name's Volteius Mena;
he's an auctioneer in a small way – quite respectable;
they say he knows when to work and rest, make and spend;
his home is his own; none of his friends are big people;
he enjoys the games, and he goes to the Park when work is finished.'
60   'I'd like to hear all this from his own lips. So tell him
to come to dinner.' Mena really couldn't believe it,
and scratched his head in silence. In the end he answered 'No
                                          [thanks.'
'Refuse me, will he?'
                     'Yes. The cheeky devil! He's either
insulting you or has something to hide.' Next morning Philippus
went up to Volteius who was selling some cheap bits and pieces
to folk in their working clothes. 'Good morning,' he opened. At once

Volteius began to apologize for not having called sooner;
he had been tied up by his work and business; he was also sorry
for not seeing Philippus first. 'Let's say I'll forget it,
provided you join me for dinner today.'   70
                                          'All right.'
                                                     'Very well then,
come about four. In the meantime, carry on coining money!'
At dinner he spoke about all and sundry, regardless of tact,
till at last he was allowed to go home to bed. Thereafter he often
hurried like a fish to the hidden hook. When he'd become
a morning client and a regular guest, Philippus asked him,
when the Latin holidays came, to go out to his place in the country.
As he rode in the carriage, Volteius praised the Sabine soil
and air again and again; Philippus watched and smiled.
Looking for light relief and amusement from any quarter,
he offered him seven thousand and guaranteed a loan   80
of as much again, urging him to buy a small farm.
He bought it. (I mustn't keep you too long with a rambling story.)
He changed from a dapper type to a peasant; talked about nothing
but furrows and vineyards; prepared his elms; nearly collapsed
from his strenuous efforts; and wore himself out in his passion for
                                                             [gain.
But after his sheep were stolen, and his goats died of disease,
and his crops let him down, and his ox was worked to death at the
                                                             [plough,
he was driven to despair by his losses. And so, in the middle of the
                                                             [night,
he grabbed a horse and rode to Philippus' house in a rage.
As soon as Philippus saw his rough and shaggy appearance,   90
'Volteius!' he cried, 'you look like a man that's overworked
and over-anxious!'
                    'God help me, sir,' Volteius answered,
'you'd call me a wretch if you wanted to use the proper word.
I beg and implore you by your guardian spirit and your own right
                                                             [hand
and the gods of your hearth, let me return to my old life!'

When a person sees how his former condition surpasses the one
he is in, he should hurry back, and resume the things he abandoned.
Every man should measure himself by his own foot-rule.

EPISTLE 8

Horace's self-criticisms prepare the way for a gentle warning.

Please convey, O Muse, to Celsus Albinovánus,
member of Nero's court and staff, my warmest greetings.
If he asks how I am, tell him that in spite of good resolutions
my life is neither right nor pleasant; not because hail
has beaten down my vines, or heat has blighted my olives,
nor because herds of mine are sick on a distant pasture,
but because, although I'm physically fit, I'm spiritually ill.
And yet I don't want to hear or know about possible treatment.
I'm rude to the doctors who wish me well, and can't think why
10 my friends are fussing to rid me of this accursed depression.
I go for things that are bad for me, and avoid what I think would
                                                                [help.
In Rome, I long for Tibur; at Tibur I veer to Rome.

Then ask how *he* is, how he's handling his job and himself,
how he's getting along with the young prince and his staff.
If he answers 'Well', say 'Congratulations!' and then by and by
be sure to drop this advice in his ear: 'Your response
to success, dear Celsus, will govern our response to you.'

EPISTLE 9

*The poet of modest origins is diffident about recommending a young
man to Augustus' step-son.*

It seems, dear Claudius, that only Septimius knows how much
you think of me. For, when he asks and insists, if you please,
that I should try to commend and present him to you as one
who deserves the approval and society of a prince known for
                                                                [discernment
(believing that I'm on closer terms than I really am),
he sees and knows my own capabilities better than I do!

I gave him many reasons why I should be excused;
but I feared I might be thought to have understated my credit,

concealing my influence, keeping favours just for myself.
And so, to avoid being found guilty of a worse offence,   10
I decided to see what might be obtained by suave effrontery.
So if you'll forgive the liberty I've taken at a friend's request,
do admit him to your group – you'll find him staunch and good.

EPISTLE 10

A simple country life is closer to nature than urban sophistication.

All good wishes to Fuscus, a man fond of the city,
from one who is fond of the country. In this respect, to be sure,
we are very different, but in all else we are almost twins
with hearts like brothers'. When one says 'no', so does the other;
we nod together in agreement like old familiar doves.
You stay in the nest; I prefer the streams
and mossy rocks and the woods of the lovely country around us.
In fact I begin to live and enter my kingdom on leaving
the scene which you folk praise to the skies in glowing terms.
I'm like the priest's runaway slave: I abominate cakes.   10
Bread's what I need now rather than muffins and honey.

If we are all supposed to live in accordance with nature,
and we have to start by choosing a site to build a house on,
can you think of any place to beat the glorious country?
Where are the winters milder? Where will you find a more welcome
breeze to soothe the Dog-star's frenzy and the leaps of the Lion,
when the sharp rays of the sun have struck him and driven him mad?
Where is one's sleep less apt to be broken by nagging worries?
Is grass duller in scent or sheen than Libyan chippings?
Is the water which strains to burst the pipes in city streets   20
purer than that which babbles down its hurrying course?
Why trees are coaxed to grow between your coloured pillars,
and a house with a view of distant fields is always envied!
Expel nature with a fork; she'll keep on trotting back.
Relax – and she'll break triumphantly through your silly
                                                        [refinements.

The man who lacks the skill to distinguish Sidonian purple
from wool steeped in the dye of Aquinum will not incur

a surer loss or one that slices nearer the bone
than the fellow who proves unable to tell false from true.
30 Those who are overjoyed when the breeze of luck is behind them
are wrecked when it changes. If you once become attached to a
                                                        [thing,
you'll hate to part with it. Avoid what's big. In a humble house
you can beat kings and the friends of kings in the race of life.

The stag, being stronger than the horse, drove him away from the
                                                        [pasture
they shared, until, having had the worse of the age-old struggle,
the horse turned for help to man, and accepted the bit.
But after routing his enemy and leaving the field in triumph
he never dislodged the rider from his back or the bit from his mouth.
So the man who, in fear of poverty, forgoes his independence
40 (a thing more precious than metals) has the shame of carrying a
                                                        [master;
he's a slave for life, as he *will* not make the best of a little.
A man's means, when they don't fit him, are rather like shoes –
he's tripped by a size too large, pinched by a size too small.

If you are happy with the deal you've received, you'll live wisely,
Aristius; and I trust you won't let me off unpunished
when I seem to be making more than I need and never relaxing.
The money a person amasses can give, or take, orders.
Its proper place is the end of the tow-rope, not the front.

I'm writing this letter behind Vacuna's crumbling temple,
50 perfectly happy – except for the fact that you aren't with me.

EPISTLE 11

A balanced mind has no need of foreign travel.

Bullatius, what did you think of the famous Chios and Lesbos,
elegant Samos, and Sardis, Croesus' royal seat?
What of Smyrna and Cólophon? Are they greater or less than
                                                        [reported?
Did they all seem dull beside the Park and Tiber's stream?
Perhaps you have set your heart on one of Attalus' cities?

Or is it Lébedus you fancy, sick of the sea and roadways?
(You know what Lébedus is – even more of a ghost-town
than Gabii or Fidénae! I'd still be happy to live there –
to forget about all my friends, and be forgotten by them,
sitting on the shore and looking out at the fury of Neptune.)   10

But a traveller from Capua to Rome, who's been soaked with rain
                                                               [and mud,
wouldn't be keen to live the rest of his days at an inn;
the man who is frozen stiff doesn't pretend that a furnace
and bath supply in full the needs of a happy life.
Neither would you, having weathered a gale on the high seas,
promptly sell your ship on the far side of the Aegean.

To a healthy man Mytiléne and Rhodes, for all their charm,
are as welcome as a heavy coat in summer, shorts in a blizzard,
a winter plunge in the Tiber, or a stove in the middle of August.
At Rome, while you have the chance, and Lady Luck is smiling   20
benignly, admire Samos, Chios, and Rhodes – from a distance.
Whatever lucky hour heaven has offered you, take it
gratefully; don't postpone your blessings to another year.
Then, wherever you've been, you can claim to have lived a happy
life. If it's true that worry is banished by reason and wisdom,
not by a place which commands a wide expanse of sea,
emigrants only change their scenery, not their outlook.
We are worn out by the strain of doing nothing; we search for
the good life with yachts and cars. The thing you're searching for
is here – or at Úlubrae, if you preserve a balanced mind.   30

EPISTLE 12

More reflections on money.

The produce you are collecting from Agrippa's Sicilian estates
constitutes, dear Iccius, provided you use it properly,
the greatest wealth that heaven can give you. No more complaining!
The man who enjoys the use of commodities isn't poor.
If stomach, chest and feet are in good condition, then kings
with all their wealth can add nothing of greater value.
Suppose you're the sort that rejects things that are easy to get,

living on greens and nettles, you'd continue to live like that
even if Fortune's stream suddenly drenched you with gold,
either because one's character cannot be changed by money,
or because you hold that goodness is all that matters.

We recall with surprise how Democritus' herds were allowed to eat
his fields and crops while his mind sped abroad, released from his
                                                                    [body.
But you, while the furious itch for profit spreads around you,
have no mean thoughts, but keep your mind on higher things:
why does the sea not rise? What controls the year?
Do the stars wander and roam at will or according to law?
What obscures the circle of the moon, and what reveals it?
What is the meaning and effect of nature's jarring concord?
Is it Empedocles or shrewd Stertinius that's talking nonsense?

But whether you're murdering fish, or only leeks and onions,
welcome Pompeius Grosphus, and be sure to give him whatever
he wants; he'll ask for nothing unless it's right and fair.
When decent men need help, their friendship costs very little.

In case you're wondering about the state of Rome's affairs,
Cantabria has fallen to the gallant spirit of Agrippa; Armenia
to that of Claudius Nero; Phraates on bended knee
has accepted Caesar's imperial rule; golden Plenty
has poured on Italy the fruits of the earth from her brimming horn.

EPISTLE 13

Horace uses the 'asinine' Vinnius to convey his Odes *to Augustus.*

As I told you, Vinnius, at length and often, when you were leaving,
be sure to deliver the rolls to Augustus with seal intact,
if he's well and in good form, and *if* he requests them.
Don't blunder out of zeal for me, and by doing your duty
with excessive ardour make my little volumes unwelcome.
If you find the pages heavy and abrasive, throw them away;
but don't, on reaching the right address, go crashing in
with your load like a wild thing, turning the fine old family name
of Ass into a joke, and becoming a subject of gossip.

Use your strength to get over mountain, stream and bog.   10
Then, when you've struggled through and arrived at your
                                        [destination,
this is how you should hold the parcel – you mustn't carry
the bundle of books under your arm, like a hick with a lamb,
or tipsy Pirria with her stolen ball of wool, or a workman
with cap and slippers at the dinner of a prominent fellow tribesman.
Don't tell all and sundry how much you sweated to carry
poems which I hope Caesar will enjoy reading and hearing.

Those, then, are my many instructions. Press ahead.
Good-bye; and please don't trip and fall down on all you're
                                        [charged with!

EPISTLE 14

Horace's longings are contrasted (somewhat sophistically) with his steward's.

Steward of the woods and the farm which makes me myself again
(and which you despise, although it provides for five households,
and sends to Varia's market their five trusty fathers):
let's see if I am better at pulling thorns from my mind
than you from the ground; is Horace or his land in sounder
                                        [condition?
Although my tender concern for Lamia keeps me in town
(he's mourning his brother, weeping with inconsolable grief
for the brother he has lost), my thoughts keep stealing away to
                                        [where *you* are,
and my mind is eager to break the bar that closes the track.
I envy the countryman, *you* the city-dweller.   10
Whoever admires another's surroundings dislikes his own;
yet each is a fool to blame the place, which doesn't deserve it.
The mind is the real culprit – it never escapes from itself.

When you were an ordinary servant, you secretly pined for the
                                        [country;
now you're a steward, you long for the games and baths of the city.
But I, as you know, am consistent – I depart in gloomy spirits
whenever some tedious business-concerns drag me to Rome.

Our tastes are not the same: that's the root of the difference
between you and me. What you regard as a wilderness, lonely
20   and forbidding, is a beautiful spot to one who feels as I do,
and who doesn't like what fascinates you. I know – it's the brothel
and greasy café that make you long for the town; and the fact
that your plot will produce pepper and spice sooner than grapes,
and that no tavern is round the corner to serve you drink,
and no floosie at hand to provide tunes on her pipe
while you clump up and down on the floor. At the same time
you work in fields which haven't been touched by a hoe for ages,
unyoke the ox and look after him, stripping leaves for his belly.
The river makes further unwelcome work, when after a cloudburst
30   it has to be trained by dykes to avoid the sunny meadows.

Well now, I'll tell you what really prevents us from singing in
                                                                [unison:
the man who went in for fine togas and sleek hair,
who charmed, as you know, the greedy Cinara without a present,
and would drink the clear Falernian wine from midday on,
is content with a simple meal and a doze on the grass by the river.
Fun's fine; but there comes a time when it ought to stop.
Out in the country no one jabs at my happy position
with sidelong glances, or hurts me with venomous back-biting. No,
the neighbours laugh when they see me shifting sods and boulders.
40   You keep thinking of the lads in town chewing their rations,
and would give anything to join them; my wheedling houseboy in
                                                                [Rome
envies you the use of firewood, flock and garden.
From sloth the ox longs for the harness, the horse for the plough.
In my view each should be willing to ply the trade he knows.

EPISTLE 15

The poet looks forward to the pleasures of a health resort.

How is the climate in winter, Vala, at Velia and Salernum?
What sort of people are there? And what is the road like? Baiae,
you see, is ruled out by Antonius Musa; which none the less
makes me unpopular there. As I take cold showers in winter,

the town grumbles that I am deserting its myrtle groves
and slighting the sulphur baths which are said to rid the muscles
of the most tenacious ailments. It is rather indignant at patients
who dare to plunge their head and stomach under the showers
at Clusium's spring, or make for Gabii and the chilly uplands.
I must find a new resort and prevail on my horse to pass   10
the familiar inns. 'Where are you going? We're not on the way
to Cumae or Baiae!' the driver will shout, pulling in anger
on the left rein; but the horse's ear's in its bridled mouth.
Which of the two towns has the better supply of food?
Do they drink from tanks that collect the rain or from wells of
                                                          [water
that never fail? I don't think much of the local wine.
On my own estate I'm willing to tolerate almost anything;
at the seaside, however, I look for something high-class and mellow
to banish my worries, to carry a generous flood of hope
into my veins and heart, to supply me with plenty of words,   20
and make me as attractive as a lad to some Lucanian girl.
Which district is richer in hares, and which in boars?
Whose coastal waters conceal more fish and urchins?
I can then go home from there as fat as a true Phaeacian.
Do write and tell me; I'll abide by your judgement.

After strenuously working his way through all that his father
and mother had left him, Maenius acquired the name of a wit –
a drifting sponger, an eater without a fixed abode,
who accosted friend and foe alike in his quest for lunch,
and cruelly spread malicious lies about all and sundry.   30
Like a tornado or vortex, he spelt disaster for the market;
and whatever he managed to get, he fed to his greedy belly.
When he had extracted little or nothing from those who applauded
or dreaded his spite, he used to devour platefuls of tripe
or cheap lamb – enough to fill a trio of bears.
He would even assert, like Bruty when he had changed his ways,
that wastrels should have their bellies burnt with red-hot plates.
And yet, when he got his hands on a larger piece of plunder,
he'd reduce it to a pile of debris. 'By god, I'm not surprised,'
he would say, 'that some folks swallow their fortunes. There's   40
                                                          [nothing better
than a fat thrush, or nicer than the paunch of a good sow!'

That's me to the life. I admire the safe and humble,
when funds are low; I'm quite a Stoic with plain fare.
But when something finer and more delectable comes, I say
that truth and the good life are only attained by those,
like you, whose solid wealth is reflected in splendid villas!

EPISTLE 16

*After describing his Sabine estate, Horace reflects on the nature of
goodness.*

My dear Quinctius, to save you asking about my farm –
whether it feeds its master from the furrow, or makes him rich
with the fruit of the olive, with apples, or meadows, or vine-clad
                                                              [elms –
I'm writing a chatty letter on the nature and site of the place.

If I told you the chain of mountains was broken by a shady valley,
so that the sun in its morning approach looks on the right side
and warms the left as it speeds away in its flying car,
you'd praise its mildness. What if I added that the bushes grow
lots of cornels and plums, that the oak and ilex delight
10   the herd with plenty of acorns and the owner with plenty of shade?
Why you'd say Tarentum's greenery had been brought nearer to
                                                              [home!
There is also a spring, which deserves to give its name to the river.
(The Hebrus is no more cool or clear as it winds across Thrace.)
The stream is good for an invalid's head – and for his stomach.
This retreat, which I love and which is, I assure you, delightful,
keeps me fit, you'll be glad to hear, in the heat of September.

Your life is in order if you manage to be what you seem.
We in Rome have long been accustomed to call you happy;
but you mustn't put anyone's view of yourself above your own,
20   or count anyone happy apart from the wise and good,
or, if people constantly say you're sound and healthy,
conceal and disguise your fever as dinner approaches, until
with knife and fork in hand you suddenly start to shiver.
Fools, from a wrong-headed shyness, hide their open wounds.

If someone spoke of the wars you had fought on land and sea,
and stroked your eagerly listening ear with words like these:
'May Jove, who cares for both you and the country, keep it a secret
whether the people are more concerned for *your* welfare
or you for the people's', you'd know the praise belonged to
                                                        [Augustus.

When you allow yourself to be called 'wise and faultless',   30
do tell me, is the name you acknowledge really yours?
'Well, I enjoy being called "good" and "wise", as you do.'
What the public gave today it can take, if it likes, tomorrow;
it tears the badge of office from one who has proved a failure.
'Drop it, it's mine.' I drop it, and walk sadly away.
If the same public came after me, shouting 'Thief!' and 'Lecher!',
and alleged I had strangled my own father with a knotted cord,
should I be hurt by such false charges, and change colour?
False honour delights, and lying slander dismays,
no one, unless he's flawed and infirm. So who is the *good* man?   40
'He who abides by the senate's decrees and the laws and statutes;
who as an arbiter settles many important cases,
as a sponsor ensures payment, as a witness victory in court.'
But his own household and his neighbours, one and all, can see
he's rotten inside, and owes his appeal to a handsome skin.
'I haven't stolen or run away' – if one of my slaves
said that, I'd answer: 'As a reward you're not being flogged.'
'I haven't committed murder.' 'You won't feed crows on a cross.'
'I'm sound and honest.' The Sabine shakes his head in dissent.
The wary wolf is afraid of the pit, the hawk of the snare,   50
which it rightly treats with suspicion, and the pike of the hidden
                                                        [hook.

The truly good eschew sin from a love of virtue.
You refrain from crime, because you're afraid of punishment.
If you thought no one would notice, you'd rob the gods themselves.
When, from a thousand bushels, you steal a single bean,
the loss is slighter on that account, but not the crime.
Your good man, who commands the respect of the bench and board,
when he offers a pig or an ox to appease the wrath of the gods,
utters aloud 'Father Janus' or 'Apollo', and then
mutters in a furtive, inaudible whisper 'Lovely Laverna   60
grant I may cheat, and be thought a fine and holy man;
cover my sins in darkness and in clouds my acts of deception.'
I fail to see in what respect a miser is better
or freer than a slave, when he stoops at a cross for the sake of a coin

stuck in the ground. For desire entails fear, and to me
the man who is subject to fear will never attain freedom.
When a person rushes about, engrossed in making money,
he throws away his weapons and deserts the post of Virtue.
If you take him prisoner, don't kill him – you'll get something
                                                         [for him.
70   He'll make a useful slave, toiling in furrow or pasture;
give him a ship and let him winter on the high seas;
or let him serve the market, carrying corn and victuals.

The wise and good man will have the courage to say
'Pentheus, lord of Thebes, what shame, what degradation
will you make me suffer?'
                              'I will take your goods.'
                                             'You mean my
                                                      [cattle,
cash, couches and plate? You're welcome.'
                                    'I'll have you kept
in handcuffs and fetters under the eye of a cruel jailer.'
'God himself will set me free whenever I wish.'
He means, I take it, 'I'll die'. Death is the end of the race.

EPISTLE 17

How to behave to one's patron.

Dear Gauche, although you're alive to your own interests,
and know how one really ought to behave to superior people,
here are the views of your humble friend, who has much to learn.
It's like a blind man wanting to act as a guide; but perhaps
you may find something in my words that you would care to adopt.

If you enjoy the quiet life and sleeping till daybreak,
if you're unable to stand dust and the noise of wheels
and staying at inns, Ferentinum's the place for you.
For the rich are not the only happy people. The man
10   who passes unnoticed from birth to death hasn't lived badly.
If you want to help your friends and coddle yourself a little,
take your bones to one who lives off the fat of the land.

'If Aristippus could put up with a dinner of greens, he wouldn't
mix with princes.'
               'If my critic could learn how to mix with princes,
he'd turn up his nose at greens!' Now tell me, which man's precept
and example do you prefer? Or rather, let me explain,
as I am older, why the outlook of Aristippus
is better. They say he parried the snapping Cynic as follows:
'I perform for myself, you for the people. My way
is far more honest and splendid. I serve in order to drive   20
a carriage and eat with a prince; you only beg for scraps,
but you're still inferior to the giver though you boast of your
                                      [independence.'
Aristippus could adjust to any style and condition.
Though he aimed higher, he was normally happy with what he had.
But I'd be surprised if the man dressed in the double rag
prescribed by austerity could adjust to a change in his style of life.
One won't wait until he is given a purple garment;
he'll walk through the crowded streets wearing anything at all;
and he'll give a perfectly tailored performance in either role.
The other fellow will avoid in horror, as worse than the plague,   30
a cloak made in Miletus; he'll freeze to death if you don't
return his rags. Return them, and save the ass's life!

To do deeds and parade prisoners before the people –
that is to touch the throne of Jove and mount to heaven.
To have won the esteem of Rome's leaders is *some* distinction.
'Not every man has the good fortune to get to Corinth.'
The fellow who dreaded failure stayed in his seat. 'Very well then,
what of the one who made it? Did he act like a man?'
Here, if anywhere, is what we are after. One man shrinks
from the load as too great for his small body and spirit;   40
the other lifts it and carries it home. If manliness isn't
an empty name, the trier deserves the prize and the glory.

Those who never mention their need to a patron obtain
more than those who ask; and polite acceptance is different
from grabbing. And that is the point and purpose of the whole
                                      [business.
'My sister needs a dowry; my mother is badly off;
the farm is unable to support us, and I cannot find a buyer.'
Whoever says that cries 'Give us some food!' Another chimes in
'Me, too!' The loaf is divided and the gift halved.

50 If the crow could feed in silence he'd obtain more to eat,
    and he'd have to cope with a great deal less strife and resentment.
    When a travelling companion on the way to Brindisi or lovely
                                                        [Sorrento
    complains of the jolting, the bitter cold and the torrents of rain,
    or moans that his trunk has been broken open and his money stolen,
    he's like the girl with her well-known tricks, who is always
                                                        [lamenting
    the theft of a necklace or anklet, until in the end, when she's suffered
    a real loss and is really upset, no one believes her.
    A person who has once been laughed at doesn't bother to help
    the prankster who has broken his leg at the cross, though in floods
                                                        [of tears
60 he swears by holy Osiris and cries 'O please believe me!
    I'm not fooling. Be kind, and help an injured man!'
    'Ask a stranger!' the locals shout in a raucous chorus.

                          EPISTLE 18

Further thoughts on the client-patron relationship.

    Dear Lollius, frankest of men: unless I'm mistaken,
    you'd hate to seem like a sponger, having claimed the role of a
                                                        [friend.
    As a lady differs from a whore in appearance as well as in character,
    so one can always tell a friend from a bogus sponger.
    There is also an opposite vice to this, and almost worse:
    namely a boorish rudeness, out of place and abrasive,
    which affects a close-cropped style of hair and discoloured teeth
    in the hope of passing for absolute candour and genuine virtue.
    Virtue is a mean between vices, distant from both extremes.
10 The first is a clown, over-inclined to servility; sitting
    beside the host, he anxiously watches the rich man's nod,
    echoes his words, and prevents the pearls from falling unheeded.
    He's like a schoolboy repeating his lesson, phrase by phrase,
    to a brutal teacher, or a mime acting the second part.
    The other often wrangles on how to define a tomato.
    He dons his armour to fight about non-issues: 'Imagine!
    Not to receive instant credence! Not to yell out
    what I really think! A second life would be poor compensation.'

And what is the question? 'Is Castor or Smart the cleverer fighter?'
'Is the Appian or the Minucian the better road to Brindisi?'   20

The man who is stripped by ruinous sex or the tumbling dice,
who is dressed and perfumed beyond his means to satisfy vanity,
who is gripped by a morbid hunger and thirst for money, and the
                                                              [shame
and dread of poverty – he is shunned by his wealthy friend,
who has often a larger share of vices. The latter dislikes him –
or, if he doesn't dislike him, he bosses him, and like a loving
mother wants him wiser and better than himself. He says,
with a measure of truth, 'Because of my money, I'm allowed
to be a fool; don't try to keep up; you can't afford it.
A narrow toga suits a sensible client. It's pointless   30
trying to rival me.' When he wanted to injure a person
Witt would give him expensive clothes. 'The lucky fellow
will put on, along with his fine tunics, new aspirations
and projects; he'll sleep late, postpone respectable business
for the sake of a tart, and fatten his debts, ending up
as a Thracian, or earning his wages by driving a grocer's nag.'

Never poke your nose into his private affairs.
Keep a secret, even when tortured by wine or anger.
Don't praise your own interests or criticize others'.
And don't become inspired when he wants to go hunting;   40
that's how the brotherly love of the twins Amphíon and Zethus
was wrenched apart, till the lyre which the sterner so distrusted
ceased to play. Amphion, the story goes, gave in
to his brother's feelings. So you accede to the gentle commands
of your powerful friend. Whenever he makes for the country, riding
in front of his hounds and his mules, which carry Aetolian nets,
dismiss the withdrawn, unsociable Muse, jump to your feet,
and work, as *he* does, to earn the relish you eat at supper.
It's the age-old pastime of Roman heroes, improving one's life
and standing and physique. You, moreover, are splendidly fit –   50
well able to outrun the hounds or take on a boar
in a trial of strength. No one can handle a man's weapons
with a finer style. You know how loudly the onlookers cheer
when you compete in the Park contests. As a boy you fought
in the savage campaigns of the Spanish war under a general
who is now removing Roman standards from Parthian temples
and assigning whatever else is lacking to Italy's empire.

Don't opt out, or avoid being present without good reason.
Although you're careful to avoid anything tasteless or foolish,
60 you do occasionally have some fun on your father's estate.
The boats are divided between the armies. You and your brother
command opposite sides (the lake is the Adriatic),
and the lads, with authentic fury, stage the Actian battle,
till Victory swoops to crown with laurel one or the other.
When your patron believes you take an interest in his amusements,
he will gladly turn up his thumbs in favour of yours.

Another word of advice – if in fact you need an adviser:
watch what you say, and of which man, and to whom you say it.
Have nothing to do with inquisitive people – they're also gossips.
70 You cannot rely on ready ears to contain a secret,
and once a word escapes, it flies beyond recall.
Don't let any maid or lad arouse your desires
within the marble hall of the friend you hope to impress.
The owner may give you the pretty boy or the darling girl
(and add nothing of substance), or cause you pain by refusing.
Be very careful whom you present, for fear that later
the other's conduct may cause embarrassment. Sometimes, in error,
we sponsor a second-rater. So, when you've been let down,
don't protect a man who has brought trouble on himself.
80 Then, when someone you're sure of is under attack and relying
on your support, you can clear his name and defend him. You know,
don't you, that when *he* is surrounded and bitten by rats like Theon,
it won't be long before the danger will spread to you.
It's very much *your* affair when the house next door is ablaze.
Ignore a fire, and soon you're faced with a conflagration.

Serving a powerful friend appeals to the uninformed;
others dread it. You, whose ship is well on its way,
stay alert, or the wind may shift and carry you back.
Jovial people dislike the gloomy, and vice versa;
90 lively jars on quiet, slack on keen and dynamic.
To decline a glass when it's offered usually gives offence,
despite your plea that wine at bedtime doesn't agree with you.
Lift the cloud from your brow. The shy man frequently gives
the appearance of being inscrutable; the silent of being morose.

As well as all this, you must read and sift the books of the experts
to find what system may help you to pass your days in peace;

will greed, which is never free from want, plague and torment you,
or fears and hopes about things of no essential importance?
Is moral goodness achieved by learning, or granted by nature?
What reduces worry, makes you at peace with yourself,   100
and gives you perfect calm – prestige, or a nice little nest-egg,
or the hidden path and the course of life that passes unnoticed?

Every time I regain my health in the icy Digentia –
the stream drunk by Mandela, that village wrinkled with cold –
what, my friend, do you think is my state of mind and my prayer?
May I have what I have now, or less, and live for myself
what's left of my life (if heaven decides that *any* is left);
may I have a decent supply of books and enough food
for the year; may my spirits not depend on the hour's caprice.
And yet it's enough to ask Jove, the giver and taker,   110
to grant me life and subsistence; I'll find my own stability.

EPISTLE 19

The rewards and disadvantages of originality.

If, my cultured Maecenas, old Cratínus was right,
poems written by water-drinkers will never enjoy
long life or acclaim. Since Bacchus enlisted frenzied
poets among his Satyrs and Fauns, the dulcet Muses
have usually smelt of drink first thing in the morning.
His praises of wine prove that Homer was fond of the grape;
father Ennius himself never sprang to his tale
of arms, unless he was drunk. 'The Stock Exchange and the City
shall be reserved for the sober; the stern are forbidden to sing' –
since I issued this edict, poets have never ceased   10
drinking in competition by night, and stinking by day.

But wait. If someone were to imitate Cato, going barefoot,
wearing a fierce, grim expression and a skimpy style
of toga, would he reproduce Cato's moral character?
Iarbítas burst in his efforts to rival Timágenes' tongue.
(He was straining so hard to achieve a name for wit and eloquence.)
Models deceive: their faults are easy to copy. And so,
if *I* were sallow, *they*'d drink cumin to make them pale.

Imitators! Bah! A slavish herd. How often their antics
20 have made me wild with rage! How often they've made me laugh!

Beholden to no one I blazed a trail over virgin country;
nobody had trodden that ground. The one who trusts himself
will rule and lead the swarm. I was the first to show
the iambics of Paros to Latium, keeping Archilochus' rhythms
and fire, but not his themes or the words which hunted Lycambes.
In case, however, you think I deserve a smaller garland
because I declined to change his metres and verse technique,
manly Sappho largely retains Archilochus' metres;
Alcaeus does the same, though different in themes and arrangement;
30 he doesn't look for a father-in-law to smear with invective,
or make a noose for his bride out of his scarifying verses.
I, the lyrist of Latium, have made him familiar – a poet
never sung before. I am glad to be held and read
by the better sort, and to offer things that no one has uttered.

Perhaps you would like to know why readers enjoy and praise
my pieces at home, and ungratefully run them down in public?
I'm not the kind to hunt for the votes of the fickle rabble
by standing dinners and giving presents of worn-out clothes.
I listen to distinguished writers and pay them back; but I don't
40 approach academic critics on their platforms to beg their support.
Hence the grief. If I say 'I'm ashamed to recite my writings
(they aren't fit for a crowded hall) and to treat trifles
as important,'
                              'You're teasing,' they say; 'they're reserved for
                                                              [Jupiter's ear.
You're so conceited, you firmly believe that you alone
distil poetry's honey.' I'm afraid to show my contempt;
and so, to avoid getting scratched by a sharp nail in the struggle,
'That position's unfair!' I shout, and call for a break.
For sport tends to give rise to heated strife and anger;
anger in turn brings savage feuds and war to the death.

EPISTLE 20

Horace sends his book of Epistles *into the world.*

Eyeing Vertumnus and Janus, my young book? I suppose
you want to be smoothed by the Sosii's pumice and stand on sale.
You've no patience with the keys and seals which modesty
                                                              [welcomes.
Private viewings are a bore; you want public exposure.
You didn't learn that from me. Well – you're keen to be off.
Good-bye. When you've gone, there's no way back. 'What have I
                                                              [done?
What came over me?' you'll cry, when you're roughly handled, or
                                                              [find
that you're being kept very tight by a weary and sated admirer.

Unless the prophet is misled by pique at your misbehaviour,
you'll be well loved in Rome until your youth deserts you.   10
When, having been through numerous dirty hands, you lose
your attractions, you'll be left unnoticed, gathering boorish maggots;
or be banished to Utica; or tied up and sent to Ilerda.
The friend whose advice you ignored will laugh, like the man who
                                                              [pushed
his stubborn donkey over a cliff in exasperation.
(For who would bother to save a creature against his will?)

This, too, lies ahead: when mumbling age overtakes you,
you'll be teaching children how to read at the end of a street.
When the warmer sun brings you a larger group of listeners,
you will talk about me: 'He was born in a home of slender means,   20
a freedman's son; but his wingspan proved too large for the nest.'
(In this way what you take from my birth you will add to my
                                                              [merits.)
'In war and peace he won the esteem of the country's leaders.
Of small build, prematurely grey, and fond of the sun,
he was quick to lose his temper, but not hard to appease.'
If anyone happens to ask my age, you can let him know
that I arrived at the end of my forty-fourth December
in the year when Lollius declared Lepidus his fellow consul.

BOOK II

To Augustus: a defence of modern poetry.

Since you carry so many weighty affairs on your shoulders,
strengthening Rome's defences, promoting decent behaviour,
reforming our laws, it would damage the public interest, Caesar,
if I were to waste your time with a lengthy conversation.

Romulus, father Liber, and also Castor and Pollux
entered the holy temples *after* their huge achievements.
But while they tended the world of men – putting an end to
savage wars, assigning lands, establishing cities –
they complained of not receiving the gratitude they expected
10 in return for their services. He who crushed the terrible Hydra
and smashed those fabled monsters in inescapable labours
found resentment could only be quelled by ending his life.
A great man oppresses inferior talents; he sears
the eyes with his brilliance. When he's gone out, everyone loves him.
But *you* are honoured in good time while still among us.
We build altars on which to swear by your divinity,
declaring your like has never been and never will be.

But this people of yours, though wise and right in exalting
you alone above other rulers, Greek or Roman,
20 judges everything else by quite a different system
and standard: unless a thing has patently had its day
and passed from the scene, they treat it with disgust and aversion.
They are so biased in favour of the old, they like to insist
that the criminal code which the Ten enacted, the regal treaties
fairly struck with Gabii's men or the tough old Sabines,
the pontiffs' ancient tomes and the musty scrolls of the prophets

were all proclaimed on the Alban Mount by the Muses in person!
True – with the Greeks the oldest writing in every genre
is quite the best. But if, in consequence, Roman writers
are judged by the same procedure, we needn't go any further –   30
a nut hasn't a shell; there's no stone in an olive!
Rome as a country is top dog; so of course it follows
that in painting, music and wrestling we surpass the oily Achaeans!

If poems like wine improve with age, would somebody tell me
how old a page has to be before it acquires value?
Take a writer who sank to his grave a century back –
where should he be assigned? To the unapproachable classics
or the worthless moderns? To prevent argument let's have a limit:
'Anyone over a hundred is old and respectable.' Well then,
what of the man who died a month or a year too late?   40
How shall we classify *him*? Is he a fine old poet
or one who deserves to be spat on by this and the next generation?
    'Naturally one who is just too young by a month or even
a full year may fairly be counted among the classics.'
Exploiting this concession I gradually pluck away
one year after another, like hairs in a horse's tail,
until by 'the dwindling pile' I effect the collapse of the critic
who relies on the calendar, using age as a measure of quality
and spurning whatever has not been hallowed by our Lady of
                                                          [Funerals.

Ennius, whom the pundits call 'the wise' and 'the valiant'   50
and 'a second Homer', need (it is clear) no longer trouble
to vindicate his boast and his Pythagorean visions.
Is not Naevius read and remembered as if he'd been published
almost yesterday? Age ensures canonization.
When the question of placing comes up, Pacuvius is always awarded
the title of 'learned' and Accius that of 'the lofty old man'.
Menander's comic mantle fell, they say, on Afranius;
Epicharmus of Sicily's pace served as a model for Plautus;
Caecilius wins the prize for dignity, Terence for art.
These are the men whom mighty Rome commits to memory   60
and watches, packed in a poky theatre; these are the poets
who comprise her tradition from Livius' time to our own day.
Sometimes the public gets things right; sometimes it blunders.
If, in its worship and adulation of early poets,
it denies that anything's better or even as good, it's wrong.

If it maintains that some of their phrases are too archaic
and quite a number crude, and admits that many are lifeless,
it's right, I'm with it, and Jove himself approves of the verdict.
I'm not attacking Livius' poems, nor do I think
they should be destroyed (I remember learning them off as a
                                                         [schoolboy
70   for 'whacker' Orbilius); still, that they should be thought of as
                                                         [finished
and beautiful works, little short of perfection, astounds me.
We may on occasion catch the glitter of a lovely word,
or a couple of lines may strike us as better made than the rest,
but *they* ought not to carry and sell the entire creation.
It makes me annoyed that a thing should be faulted, not for being
crudely or clumsily made but simply for being recent,
and that praise and prizes should be asked for the old, instead of
                                                         [forbearance.
If I questioned whether a play of Atta's still stood up
80   as it rambled on through the flowers and saffron, all our elders
would cry that shame was dead – because I'd ventured to fault
what the grave Aesopus and accomplished Roscius once appeared in.
They seem to object to whatever hasn't appealed to *them*,
or they're ashamed to heed their juniors and will not admit
that things they learnt in their youth should now be treated as
                                                         [rubbish.
In fact the man who praises Numa's Salian Hymn
and likes to pose as the expert on a work which he understands
as little as I do is not the champion of the mighty dead
but our opponent; he's jealous, and hates us and our works.

90   Suppose the Greeks had resented newness as much as we do,
what would now be old? And what would the people have
to read and thumb with enjoyment, each man to his taste?
As soon as Greece abandoned war and turned to amusements,
lapsing into frivolity as fortune smiled upon her,
she developed a feverish craze for either athletes or horses,
or fell in love with craftsmen in ivory, bronze, or marble;
she acquired a hang-up gazing at surfaces covered with paint,
and became enraptured with pipers or else with tragic actors.
Just like a baby playing under her nurse's eye,
100   she'd clamour for something, and then grow bored and leave it alone.
Such were the blessings brought by the prosperous winds of peace.

At Rome for years they had the agreeable habit of rising
early, opening the door, and telling the client his rights.
They would lend cash to reliable people with good collateral,
hear from their elders and tell the youngsters various ways
of increasing assets and cutting down on ruinous pleasures.
But what likes and dislikes are not subject to change?
Now the fickle public has changed; the only hobby
that turns it on is writing; boys and their stern progenitors
bind their hair with leaves and dictate verse over dinner.   110
I myself, after swearing that I'm writing no more poetry,
prove a worse than Parthian liar; for there I am,
awake before dawn and asking for pen, paper and files.
If he knows nothing of sailing, a man avoids the helm;
no one risks giving wormwood to a patient, unless he's trained;
doctors doctor; carpenters handle carpenters' tools;
but qualified or not we all go in for scribbling verses!

Yet this aberration (or if you like, this mild insanity)
has certain merits; for just think: the soul of a poet
can hardly be greedy; verse is his only love and concern.   120
Fires, losses, runaway slaves – he smiles at the lot.
He never works out plans to cheat his partner in business
or the boy in his charge. He lives on pulse and second-rate bread.
He's too idle to be much of a soldier; yet he serves his country –
if you grant that minor activities further major ends.
The poet shapes the tender faltering speech of a child,
already turning the ear away from coarse expressions.
Later he moulds the disposition by kindly maxims,
using his voice to correct cruelty, envy and temper.
He recounts noble actions, equips the new generation   130
with old examples, and brings relief to the poor and sick.
Where would innocent boys and girls who are still unmarried
have learnt their prayers if the Muse had not vouchsafed them a
                                                          [poet?
The choir asks for aid and feels the deities' presence;
by the poet's prayers it coaxes heaven to send us showers;
it averts disease and drives away appalling dangers;
it gains the gift of peace and a year of bumper harvests.
Song is what soothes the gods above and the spirits below.

Farmers of old – sturdy men, well off with a little –
when the crops were in, at holiday time relaxed the body   140

and the mind as well (which bears a lot when it has an end
in sight) with the sons and loyal wives who had shared the work.
They used to placate Silvanus with milk and Earth with a pig,
and the Genius who knows the shortness of life with wine and
                                                                    [flowers.
These occasions saw the beginning of wild Fescennines –
verses in which they exchanged volleys of rustic abuse.
Freedom was gladly given a place in the year's cycle,
and people enjoyed the fun, until the joking began
to get vicious and turned into sheer madness, becoming a menace
150   and running unchecked through decent houses; its tooth drew blood,
and the victims smarted; even those who escaped were worried
about the state of society. At last a law was enacted
involving penalties; no one, it said, should be traduced
in scurrilous verse. They changed their tune, and in fear of the
                                                                    [cudgel
returned to decent language and the business of giving pleasure.

When Greece was taken she took control of her rough invader,
and brought the arts to rustic Latium. Then the primitive
metre of Saturn dried up; and the fetid smell gave way
to cleaner air; nevertheless for many a year
160   there remained, and still remain today, signs of the farmyard.
It was late when the Roman applied his brains to Greek writing.
In the peace which followed the Punic wars he began to wonder
if Aeschylus, Thespis and Sophocles had anything useful to offer,
and if he himself could produce an adequate version. He tried,
and liked the result, having grand ideas and natural keenness.
(His spirit was tragic enough, and his daring strokes succeeded,
but he had the novice's guilty dread of using a rubber.)
As Comedy draws its themes from daily life, they say
it doesn't require much sweat. In fact it's heavier work
170   because it is judged more strictly. Look at the feeble way
Plautus presents his characters – the teenage boy in love,
the parsimonious father and the shifty devious pimp.
What a buffoon he is in handling his famished spongers!
And think of the slipshod style in which he blunders along.
He's keen to pocket the cash; after that, who worries
whether the play is a steady success or a hopeless flop?
The man who is brought to the stage by Glory's windy car
collapses when given a cool reception, expands at a warm one.
Such is the tiny and trivial thing that breaks or repairs

the heart set on applause. To hell with the stage if a palm-leaf,   180
withheld or given, sends me away haggard or healthy!
Often even the resolute poet is daunted and routed
when those superior in numbers but not in worth or status –
stupid illiterate men who are ready to start a fight
if the knights oppose their wishes – call for a bear or boxers
in the middle of a play. That's the stuff that appeals to the masses.
Nowadays even the knights have stopped listening, and all their
interest is taken up with inane and ephemeral pageants.
The curtain is up for four-hour periods, if not longer,
as squadrons of cavalry and hordes of infantry hurtle past;   190
fallen kings are dragged across with their hands pinioned;
chariots, carriages, wagons and ships rumble along,
carrying works of bronze and ivory taken from Corinth.

If he were still alive, wouldn't Democritus laugh
to see the people turning to gape at a white elephant
or a giraffe, that beast made up of camel and leopard?
He'd watch the crowd more closely than the actual show,
for they would offer him far more astonishing things to look at.
As for the writers, he'd think they were telling their stories
to a deaf ass. For who was ever born with a voice   200
that could rise above the din you get in a Roman theatre?
You'd think it came from the Gargan forest or the Tuscan Sea.
That's the noise through which they watch the production, including
the expensive foreign jewellery with which the actor is smothered.
He walks on stage and at once is greeted with frenzied applause.
'Has he said something already?'
                                    'No.'
                                                'Then why are they clapping?'
'It's his woollen coat, dyed in Tarentum to rival a violet.'
You mustn't think I'm too mean to admit admiration
for things which I would never try and others excel at.
Take the playwright who fills my heart with imaginary grief,   210
illusory rage or fear, and then with peace; to me
that's as hard as walking a tightrope; like a magician,
he whisks me away – one day to Thebes, another to Athens.

I would ask you now to spare a moment's thought for the men
who trust themselves to a reader rather than face the contempt
and snubs of an audience – if, that is, you intend to fill
the shelves of that gift so worthy of Phoebus and to spur our poets

to stretch with greater zeal for the green slopes of Helicon.
We writers, it's true, frequently harm our cause
220 (says he, hacking his own vines) when, though you are worried
or weary, we thrust a book at you; when we are cut to the quick
if a friend dares to see any fault in a single line;
when, unasked, we repeat sections we've read before;
when we complain that the pieces we've shaped with exquisite art
and infinite pains have failed to win the least recognition;
when we hope that eventually things will reach the point
where as soon as you've heard we're writing you'll kindly invite us
                                                                    [to court,
relieve our financial worries and urge us to carry on.
Nevertheless, it's worth considering what type of custodian
230 ought to guard that valour proven in peace and war –
a task not to be given to a poet who doesn't deserve it.
King Alexander the Great, who much admired the wretched
Choerilus, paid him golden sovereigns from the royal mint
by way of reward for all those crude misbegotten effusions.
People who dabble in ink leave blots and stains on the paper;
so your average writer defiles illustrious deeds
with his horrid scrawls. And yet that very monarch who purchased
such a fatuous poem at such a reckless price,
laid it down that no one except Apelles should paint
240 his portrait, and no one except Lysippus should cast in bronze
Alexander's martial features. If, however, you had asked
that judgement which handled visual arts with such acumen
to pronounce on books and poetic creations of the kind described,
you'd have sworn the man was reared in the thick Boeotian climate.

Your own judgement of poets, however, is fully upheld
by your favourite writers Virgil and Varius; also the presents
they have received reflect the greatest credit on you.
The truth is that the mind and character of famous men
come through as clearly in a poet's work as the features do
250 in a bronze statue. For my part, rather than writing talks
that creep on the ground I'd sooner celebrate mighty deeds,
describing the lie of the land, the course of rivers, the setting
of forts on mountain tops, barbarous kingdoms, and then
the ending of strife throughout the world by your command,
Janus guardian of peace locked behind his bars,
and the Parthian foe overawed by your imperial Rome –
if only my powers matched my yearning; but a minor poem

is not in keeping with your pre-eminence, and I should be rash
to venture upon a task so far beyond my abilities.
The centre of stupid and fawning attention finds it vexatious,   260
most of all when it seeks his favour through the art of poetry;
for a thing that causes merriment is always sooner learnt
and longer remembered than what commands respect and approval.
I've no time for the service that irks me, nor do I want to
be shown in wax with a face that has taken a turn for the worse,
nor to have my virtues extolled in hideous lines.
I'd probably flush on receiving so coarse a tribute; in no time
I'd be laid in a closed box beside my poetic admirer,
then carried down to the street that deals in perfume and incense
and pepper, and anything else that's wrapped in useless pages.   270

EPISTLE 2

An apology for not writing lyric poetry.

To Florus: loyal friend of the good and gallant Nero.
Suppose somebody wanted to sell you a slave who was born
at Tibur or Gabii, and said to you: 'Here's an attractive lad
with a fair skin, beautifully built from head to toe.
Eight thousand and he's yours, signed, sealed and delivered.
He's home bred, quick to obey his master's orders;
he has had a touch of basic Greek, and will turn his hand to
any skill that's required; wet clay can be moulded;
he'll even sing you a simple song to go with your wine.
Too many claims reduce credibility. Only a salesman   10
who wants to get rid of his goods will praise them above their
[worth.
I'm not obliged to sell; I'm poor, but not in the red.
None of the dealers would make you this offer. I'll do it for you,
[sir –
but no one else. Once he dodged his work and, as usual,
hid under the stairs in fear of the strap on the wall.
So let's shake – if you're not put off by the lapse I mentioned.'
The man, I fancy, would be in the clear. The goods were faulty,
but you bought them with your eyes open; the terms were stated.
Will you still sue him and waste his time with false allegations?
I told you when you were leaving that I was lazy; I told you   20

I was almost physically incapable of such a commitment (I dreaded
your angry recriminations if your letters went unanswered).
I might have saved my breath; for although the law's on my side
you still contest the case. On top of that you complain
I have let you down by failing to send the lyrics I promised.

One of Lucullus' soldiers had, with enormous efforts,
saved some money. One night, as he snored in exhaustion,
he lost the lot. In a rage at himself as much as at the enemy,
like a savage wolf with teeth sharpened by hunger, he then
30   dislodged the king's troops from a well-defended position,
which also, they say, contained a large amount of treasure.
The exploit won him much acclaim and high decorations.
He also received a cash sum of twenty thousand.
Shortly after, as it happened, the general was anxious to capture
some fort or other; so he addressed the man again
in words which might have inspired even a coward with courage:
'Go, my lad, where your brave heart leads you. Go, and good luck!
Your deeds will win you a handsome reward. Well – what's keeping
                                                          [you?'
      'If you want someone to go, go, wherever you tell him,'
40   said the crafty yokel, 'find a man who has lost his wallet!'

I had the luck to be raised in Rome, where I learned from my teacher
how much harm was done to the Greeks by the wrath of Achilles.
Then a little more training was added by Athens the good,
so that at least I was keen to distinguish straight from crooked
and to go in search of truth among the Academy's trees.
But harsh times tore me away from that pleasant spot,
and the billows swept the raw recruit into a force
which would prove no match for the brawny arms of Caesar
                                                          [Augustus.
Discharged by Philippi, there I was with my wings clipped,
50   no longer a flyer and without my family hearth and home.
At once our Lady Poverty, daring as ever, impelled me
to turn out verses; but now that I have enough to live on
my brain would surely be addled beyond the power of hemlock
if I scribbled verses instead of enjoying a night's sleep!

As the years go by they rob us of one thing after another.
Already they've taken fun, sex, parties and sport;
now they're pulling away my poems. What shall I do then?

Moreover, not everyone likes and admires the same thing.
You put lyric poetry first – he's for iambics –
he prefers the tangy wit of Bion's homilies.   60
You're rather like a trio who can't agree on a menu
asking for different dishes to suit their different tastes.
What should I serve or avoid? You spurn what he has requested,
while your own choice is horrid and foul to the other two.
Apart from that, how can you ask me to turn out poetry
in Rome, with so many worries and so many onerous duties?
One man wants me to act as a sponsor, another to cancel
all my engagements and hear his work; this one is poorly
on the Quirinal, that one across the Aventine; both expect
a visit. (Note how conveniently close they are!) 'The streets,'   70
you say, 'are clear; there's nothing to block your inspiration.'
A feverish builder charges past with his mules and workmen;
a huge contraption heaves a beam and then a boulder;
wailing funerals smash their way through lumbering wagons.
There goes a mad dog; here is a muddy pig.
Try composing tuneful lines in the middle of that!
The poet's company loves the woods and abhors the city
in fealty to Bacchus their lord, who enjoys the drowsy shade.
Am I expected to sing with a din going on around me
night and day, and to follow the minstrels' narrow path?   80
The soul who chooses to live in the peace of Athens, devoting
seven years to his work, turning haggard from study
and the problems of writing, often emerges as dumb as a statue
and becomes a public joke. Here, tossed as I am
in the storms of city life, why should I make the effort
to weave words which will summon forth the sound of the lyre?

A lawyer in Rome and his fan (a teacher of rhetoric) never
conversed except in terms of mutual glorification.
They even addressed one another as 'Gracchus' and 'Mucius'. Well
                                                             [now –
doesn't the same delusion affect our warbling poets?   90
I write lyrics, my friend elegiacs. 'A dazzling achievement;
a work of the purest inspiration!' Note in the first place
the lordly mien and portentous expression we wear as we gaze a–
round the temple with its spaces ready for the bards of Rome.
Then, if you've time, follow, and hear from a tactful distance
what each provides, and how he contrives to win his laurels.
Like Samnites in the arena, giving and taking blows,

we exhaust the foe in a weary duel that lasts till nightfall.
I emerge as 'Alcaeus' on his verdict, and he as
100 'Callimachus', of course, on mine. If he seems unhappy with that,
he at once becomes 'Mimnermus' and swells at the coveted title.
When writing and humbly bidding for popular favour, I suffered
a lot to placate the poets – that hypersensitive species.
Now that my work is over and my mind restored to sanity
I can safely block my spreading ears to our friends' recitations.

People who write incompetent verse are a joke; however,
they *enjoy* composing and treat themselves with sincere respect,
and if *you* say nothing they'll actually praise their own productions.
But the man who wants to achieve a poem of genuine quality
110 will take, along with his notebook, the mind of a rigorous Censor.
Any words deficient in lustre or lacking solidity,
or those which he deems unworthy of honour, he will have the
                                                            [courage
to expel from their place, although they may be reluctant to leave
and still hang back, seeking refuge in Vesta's temple.
He will do well to unearth words which have long been hidden
from the people's view, bringing to light some splendid terms
employed in earlier days by Cato, Cethegus and others,
which now lie buried by grimy dust and the years' neglect.
He will also admit some new ones, proposed by their father Need.
120 Flowing strong and clear like an unpolluted river
he will spread prosperity, enriching the land with the wealth of his
                                                            [language.
He will show his skill and care by pruning the over dense,
stripping untidy pieces, and taking out the feeble.
In spite of the strain he will make it seem like fun, as a dancer
who switches with ease from nimble satyr to blundering Cyclops.

I'd sooner be thought a cracked and incompetent writer
(provided my faults gave *me* pleasure or escaped my notice)
than know the truth, and grimace. A well-known figure in Argos
used to think he was watching a splendid tragic performance
130 as he sat alone excitedly clapping in the empty theatre.
Apart from that he coped with the daily business of life
perfectly well – a good neighbour, a charming host,
kind to his wife, the sort who managed to forgive his servants
and not go mad with rage if the seal of a jar were broken,
who had no trouble avoiding a cliff or an open well.

He was finally cured thanks to his relatives' care and expense.
But when the potent drug had done its work, expelling
the harmful bile, and the man recovered, he cried: 'Ah god!
You've killed me, my friends, not cured me; for now you've ruined
                                                         [my pleasure
by driving away the illusion which gave me such delight.'   140

And yet it's best to be sensible – to throw away one's toys
and leave to children the sort of games that suit their age,
and instead of hunting for words to set to the lyre's music
to practise setting one's life to the tunes and rhythms of truth.
And so in silence I recall and repeat to myself what follows:
If no amount of water could put an end to your thirst,
you'd see a doctor. What of the fact that the more you've got
the more you want? Shouldn't you ask advice about that?
Suppose you've a wound which fails to heal with the cream or
                                                         [powder
that has been recommended, you cease to employ that cream or   150
                                                         [powder,
because it has proved no good. No doubt you've heard the assertion
that when a person is blessed with wealth he is cured of the curse
of folly. But a thicker wallet hasn't succeeded in making
you any wiser; so why do you still believe those voices?
If, however, money brought a sensible outlook,
reducing your lust and fear, why then you would blush with shame
if the whole world contained a greedier man than yourself!

Though personal property is that which is bought with bronze and
                                                         [balance,
sometimes, the lawyers tell us, things are conveyed by use.
Orbius' land, which provides your food, is yours, and his steward   160
thinks of you as the owner, as he harrows the field that will shortly
supply *you* with grain. In return for cash you are given
grapes, poultry, eggs and a jar of wine; so in that way
you are gradually buying a farm which once was purchased
for a price of three hundred thousand, or possibly higher.
What does it matter *when* you paid for the food you live on?
The buyer (long ago) of a farm at Aricia or Veii
eats, though he doesn't know it, bought greens for his dinner,
and he boils his kettle in the chilly evening on bought logs.
But he calls it all his own, up to the line of poplars   170
which marks the boundary, thus avoiding neighbourly wrangles –

as if *any*thing were 'ours', which at a point in the movement
of time changes owners by gift or purchase or force
or at last by death, and passes into another's control.
Therefore, as no one is granted use in perpetuity
and one heir follows another as wave on wave, what advantage
are barns and tenants' houses or those Lucanian pastures
stretching into Calabria, if large and small alike
fall to the scythe of Orcus who cannot be coaxed by gold?

180   Jewels, ivory, marble, paintings, Etruscan bronzes,
silver plate, material dyed in African purple –
some never have such things; some, I know, never want them.
Of two brothers one prefers an oil massage
and a life of ease and pleasure to the palms of Herod; the other,
rich and persistent, tames his woodland property, burning
and digging from dawn to dusk. The cause of the contrast is known
to none but the Genius – the friend who controls the star of our
                                                                    [birth,
the mortal god of human nature who looks with a different
expression, bright or gloomy, on each individual person.
190   I shall enjoy what I have and draw on my modest supplies
as needed, without any fears about what my heir may think of me
when he finds the estate has not increased; and yet I shall also
try to observe the line which divides generous giving
from waste and marks the point where thrift turns into meanness.
For it makes a difference whether you splash your money around,
or without striving to acquire more are not reluctant
to spend, but are eager, in fact, to make the most of the short
and beautiful time, as schoolboys do in the Easter vacation;
(let's not think of a poor and squalid household). For my part,
200   whether sailing in cruiser or dinghy, I'll remain one and the same.
My sails are not puffed out with the north wind in my favour,
nor am I beating into the southern gales of affliction.
In strength, talent, appearance, valour, status and riches
my place is behind the leaders; but I stay ahead of the last.

You aren't a miser, you say; very well, have you banished the other
vices along with that? Is your heart no longer obsessed
with futile ambition, with fear and rage at the prospect of death?
Dreams and the terrors of magic, miracles, ghosts at night-time,
witches, Thessalian portents – do you treat them all as a joke?
210   Are you glad to count your birthdays, quick to forgive your friends?

Are you improving and growing more mellow as the years go by?
Why take out a single thorn and ignore the others?
If you can't live as you ought, give way to those who can.
You've eaten and drunk; you've had your fun; it's time to be going.
Or else, when you've drunk too much, you may be pushed aside
and mocked by youngsters, whose wild behaviour is less out of
                                                                   [place.

THE *ARS POETICA*

*Horace's young friends are offered advice on the craft of writing
poetry. Innate ability is taken for granted (409–10), but does not lend
itself to analysis.*

Suppose a painter decided to set a human head
on a horse's neck, and to cover the body with coloured feathers,
combining limbs so that the top of a lovely woman
came to a horrid end in the tail of an inky fish –
when invited to view the piece, my friends, could you stifle your
                                                              [laughter?
Well, dear Pisos, I hope you'll agree that a book containing
fantastic ideas, like those conceived by delirious patients,
where top and bottom never combine to form a whole,
is exactly like that picture.
                            'Painters and poets alike
have always enjoyed the right to take what risks they please.'   10
I know; I grant that freedom and claim the same in return,
but not to the point of allowing wild to couple with tame,
or showing a snake and a bird, or a lamb and tiger, as partners.

Often you'll find a serious work of large pretensions
with here and there a purple patch that is sewn on
to give a vivid and striking effect – lines describing
Diana's grove and altar, or a stream which winds and hurries
along its beauteous vale, or the river Rhine, or a rainbow.
But here they are out of place. Perhaps you can draw a cypress;
what good is that, if the subject you've been engaged to paint   20
is a shipwrecked sailor swimming for his life? The job began
as a wine-jar; why as the wheel revolves does it end as a jug?
So make what you like, provided the thing is a unified whole.

Poets in the main (I'm speaking to a father and his excellent sons)
are baffled by the outer form of what's right. I strive to be brief,
and become obscure; I try for smoothness, and instantly lose
muscle and spirit; to aim at grandeur invites inflation;
excessive caution or fear of the wind induces grovelling.
The man who brings in marvels to vary a simple theme
30   is painting a dolphin among the trees, a boar in the billows.
Avoiding a fault will lead to error if art is missing.

Any smith in the area round Aemilius' school
will render nails in bronze and imitate wavy hair;
the final effect eludes him because he doesn't know how
to shape a whole. If I wanted to do a piece of sculpture,
I'd no more copy him than I'd welcome a broken nose,
when my jet black eyes and jet black hair had won admiration.

You writers must pick a subject that suits your powers,
giving lengthy thought to what your shoulders are built for
40   and what they aren't. If your choice of theme is within your scope,
you won't have to seek for fluent speech or lucid arrangement.
Arrangement's virtue and value reside, if I'm not mistaken,
in this: to say right now what has to be said right now,
postponing and leaving out a great deal for the present.

The writer pledged to produce a poem must also be subtle
and careful in linking words, preferring this to that.
When a skilful collocation renews a familiar word,
that is distinguished writing. If novel terms are demanded
to introduce obscure material, then you will have the
50   chance to invent words which the apron-wearing Cethegi
never heard; such a right will be given, if it's not abused.
New and freshly created words are also acceptable
when channelled from Greek, provided the trickle is small. For why
should Romans refuse to Virgil and Varius what they've allowed
to Caecilius and Plautus? And why should they grumble if I succeed
in bringing a little in, when the diction of Ennius and Cato
showered wealth on our fathers' language and gave us unheard of
names for things? We have always enjoyed and always will
the right to produce terms which are marked with the current stamp.
60   Just as the woods change their leaves as year follows year
60a   (the earliest fall, *and others spring up to take their place*)
so the old generation of words passes away,

and the newly arrived bloom and flourish like human children.
We and our works are owed to death, whether our navy
is screened from the northern gales by Neptune welcomed ashore –
a royal feat – or a barren swamp which knew the oar
feeds neighbouring cities and feels the weight of the plough,
or a river which used to damage the crops has altered its course
and learned a better way. Man's structures will crumble;
so how can the glory and charm of speech remain for ever?
Many a word long dead will be born again, and others   70
which now enjoy prestige will fade, if Usage requires it.
She controls the laws and rules and standards of language.

The feats of kings and captains and the grim battles they fought –
the proper metre for such achievements was shown by Homer.
The couplet of longer and shorter lines provided a framework,
first for lament, then for acknowledging a prayer's fulfilment.
Scholars, however, dispute the name of the first poet
to compose small elegiacs; the case is still undecided.
Fury gave Archilochus her own missile – the iambus.
The foot was found to fit the sock and the stately buskin,   80
because it conveyed the give and take of dialogue; also
it drowned the noise of the pit and was naturally suited to action.
The lyre received from the Muse the right to celebrate gods
and their sons, victorious boxers, horses first in the race,
the ache of a lover's heart, and uninhibited drinking.
If, through lack of knowledge or talent, I fail to observe
the established genres and styles, then why am I hailed as a poet?
And why, from misplaced shyness, do I shrink from learning the
                                                                     [trade?
A comic subject will not be presented in tragic metres.
Likewise Thyestes' banquet is far too grand a tale   90
for verse of an everyday kind which is more akin to the sock.
Everything has its appropriate place, and it ought to stay there.
Sometimes, however, even Comedy raises her voice,
as angry Chremes storms along in orotund phrases;
and sometimes a tragic actor grieves in ordinary language –
Peleus and Telephus (one an exile, the other a beggar)
both abandon their bombast and words of a foot and a half
when they hope to touch the listener's heart with their sad appeals.

Correctness is not enough in a poem; it must be attractive,
leading the listener's emotions in whatever way it wishes.   100

When a person smiles, people's faces smile in return;
when he weeps, they show concern. Before you can move me to
[tears,
you must grieve yourself. Only then will your woes distress me,
Peleus or Telephus. If what you say is out of character,
I'll either doze or laugh. Sad words are required
by a sorrowful face; threats come from one that is angry,
jokes from one that is jolly, serious words from the solemn.
Nature adjusts our inner feelings to every variety
of fortune, giving us joy, goading us on to anger,
110 making us sink to the ground under a load of suffering.
Then, with the tongue as her medium, she utters the heart's
[emotions.
If what a speaker says is out of tune with his state,
the Roman audience, box and pit, will bellow with laughter.
A lot depends on whether the speaker is a god or a hero,
a ripe old man, or one who is still in the flush and flower
of youth, a lady of high degree, or a bustling nurse,
a roaming merchant, or one who tills a flourishing plot,
a Colchian or an Assyrian, a native of Thebes or Argos.

Writers, follow tradition, or at least avoid anomalies
120 when you're inventing. If you portray the dishonoured Achilles,
see that he's tireless, quick to anger, implacable, fierce;
have him repudiate laws, and decide all issues by fighting.
Make Medea wild and intractable, Ino tearful,
Ixion treacherous, Io a roamer, Orestes gloomy.
If you are staging something untried and taking the risk
of forming a new character, let it remain to the end
as it was when introduced, and keep it true to itself.

It's hard to express general things in specific ways.
You'd be well advised to spin your plays from the song of Troy
130 rather than introduce what no one has said or thought of.
If you want to acquire some private ground in the public domain,
don't continue to circle the broad and common track,
or try to render word for word like a loyal translator;
don't follow your model into a pen from which
diffidence or the laws of the genre prevent escape;
and don't begin in the style of the ancient cyclic poet:
'Of Priam's fate I sing and a war that's famed in story.'
What can emerge in keeping with such a cavernous promise?

The mountains will labour and bring to birth a comical mouse.
How much better the one who makes no foolish effort: 140
'Tell, O Muse, of the man who after Troy had fallen
saw the cities of many people and their ways of life.'
His aim is not to have smoke after a flash, but light
emerging from smoke, and thus revealing his splendid marvels:
the cannibal king Antíphates, the Cyclops, Scylla, Charybdis.
He doesn't start Diomédes' return from when Meleager
died, nor the Trojan war from the egg containing Helen.
He always presses on to the outcome and hurries the reader
into the middle of things as though they were quite familiar.
He ignores whatever he thinks cannot be burnished bright;   150
he invents at will, he mingles fact and fiction, but always
so that the middle squares with the start, and the end with the
                                                          [middle.

Consider now what I, and the public too, require,
if you want people to stay in their seats till the curtain falls
and then respond with warmth when the soloist calls for applause:
you must observe the behaviour that goes with every age-group,
taking account of how dispositions change with the years.
The child who has learnt to repeat words and to plant his steps
firmly is keen to play with his friends; he loses his temper
easily, then recovers it, changing from hour to hour.   160
The lad who has left his tutor but has not acquired a beard
enjoys horses and hounds and the grass of the sunny park.
Easily shaped for the worse, he is rude to would-be advisers,
reluctant to make any practical plans, free with his money;
quixotic and passionate, he soon discards what he set his heart on.
Manhood brings its own mentality, interests change;
now he looks for wealth and connections, strives for position,
and is wary of doing anything which may be hard to alter.
An old man is surrounded by a host of troubles: he amasses
money but leaves it untouched, for he's too nervous to use it;   170
poor devil, his whole approach to life is cold and timid;
he puts things off, is faint in hope, and shrinks from the future.
Morose and a grumbler, he is always praising the years gone by
when he was a boy, scolding and blaming 'the youth of today'.
The years bring many blessings as they come to meet us; receding,
they take many away. To avoid the mistake of assigning
an old man's lines to a lad, or a boy's to a man, you should always
stick to the traits that naturally go with a given age.

An action is shown occurring on stage or else is reported.
180 Things received through the ear stir the emotions more faintly
than those which are seen by the eye (a reliable witness) and hence
conveyed direct to the watcher. But don't present on the stage
events which ought to take place within. Much of what happens
should be kept from view and then retailed by vivid description.
The audience must not see Medea slaying her children,
or the diabolical Atreus cooking human flesh,
or Procne sprouting wings or Cadmus becoming a snake.
I disbelieve such exhibitions and find them abhorrent.

No play should be longer or shorter than five acts,
190 if it hopes to stage a revival 'in response to public demand'.
Don't let a god intervene unless the dénouement requires
such a solution; nor should a fourth character speak.
The chorus should take the role of an actor, discharging its duty
with all its energy; and don't let it sing between the acts
anything not germane and tightly joined to the plot.
It ought to side with the good and give them friendly advice,
control the furious, encourage those who are filled with fear.
It ought to praise the simple meal which is not protracted,
healthy justice and laws, and peace with her open gates.
200 It ought to preserve secrets, and pray and beseech the gods
that good fortune may leave the proud and return to the wretched.

The pipe (which was not, as now, ringed with brass and a rival
of the trumpet, but rather slender and simple with not many
                                                                    [openings)
was once enough to guide and assist the chorus and fill
with its breath the rows of seats which weren't too densely packed.
The crowd was, naturally, easy to count because it was small,
and the folk brought with them honest hearts, decent and modest.
When, thanks to their victories, the people widened their country,
extending the walls around their city and flouting the ban
210 which used to restrain daytime drinking on public occasions,
a greater degree of licence appeared in tunes and tempo.
(What taste was likely from an ignorant crowd on holiday,
a mixture of country and town, riff-raff and well-to-do?)
Vulgar finery and movements augmented the ancient art,
as the piper trailed his robe and minced across the stage.
The musical range of the sober lyre was also enlarged,
while a cascading style brought in a novel delivery,

and the thought, which shrewdly purveyed moral advice and also
predicted the future, came to resemble the Delphic oracles.

The man who competed in tragic verse for a worthless he-goat   220
later presented as well the naked rustic satyrs.
Rough, though without any loss of dignity, he turned to joking;
for the crowd which, after observing the rites, was drunk and
                                                                    [unruly,
had to be kept in their seats by something new and attractive.
However, to make a success of your clownish cheeky satyrs
and achieve a proper transition from heavy to light, make sure
that no god or hero who is brought on to the stage
shall, after just being seen in regal purple and gold,
take his language down to the plane of a dingy cottage,
or in trying to keep aloft grasp at cloudy nothings.   230
Tragedy thinks it beneath her to spout frivolous verse;
and so, like a lady obliged to dance on a public holiday,
she'll be a little reluctant to join the boisterous satyrs.
If *I* ever write a satyr drama, my Pisos, I shan't
confine my choice to plain and familiar nouns and verbs;
nor shall I strive so hard to avoid the tone of tragedy
that it might as well be the voice of Davus or brazen Pythias,
who has just obtained a talent by wiping Simo's eye,
as of Silenus – guardian and servant of the god in his care.
I'll aim at a new blend of familiar ingredients; and people   240
will think it's easy – but will waste a lot of sweat and effort
if they try to copy it. Such is the power of linkage and joinery,
such the lustre that is given forth by commonplace words.
Fauns from the forest, in my opinion, ought to be careful
not to go in for the dandy's over-emotional verses,
or to fire off volleys of filthy, disgraceful jokes,
as if they came from the street corner or the city square.
Knights – free-born and men of property – take offence
and don't greet with approval all that's enjoyed by the buyer
of roasted nuts and chick-peas, or give it a winner's garland.   250

A long syllable after a short is named Iambus.
Being a quick foot, he ordered iambic verses
to be called 'trímeters', in spite of the fact that six beats
occurred in a pure iambic line. At a time in the past,
so as to reach the ear with a bit more weight and slowness,
he was kind and obliging enough to adopt the stately spondees

and share the family inheritance – though never going so far
in friendship as to relinquish the second or fourth position.
Iambus rarely appears in Accius' 'noble' trímeters,
260 and his all too frequent absence from the lines that Ennius trundles
onto the stage leaves them open to the damaging charge
of hasty and slapdash work or a disregard of art.

It isn't every critic who detects unmusical pieces;
so Roman poets have enjoyed quite excessive indulgence.
Shall *I* therefore break out, and ignore the laws of writing?
Or assume my faults will be seen by all, and huddle securely
within the permitted range? Then I've avoided blame;
I haven't earned any praise. My Roman friends, I urge you:
get hold of your Greek models, and study them day and night.
270 To be sure, your forefathers praised the rhythm and wit of Plautus.
On both counts their admiration was far too generous,
in fact it was stupid – assuming that you and I know how
to tell the difference between clumsy and clever jokes,
and discern correctness of sound with the aid of ear and fingers.

We are told Thespis discovered the genre of the tragic Muse
which was never known before; he carried his plays on a wagon
to be sung and acted by men who had smeared lees on their faces.
After him came Aeschylus, introducing the mask
and lordly robe; he laid a stage on lowish supports
280 and called for a sonorous diction and the wearing of high-soled boots.
Old Comedy followed, winning a lot of acclaim;
but its freedom exceeded the proper limit and turned to violence
which needed a law to control it. The law was obeyed, and the
                                                              [chorus
fell silent in disgrace, having lost its right of insult.

Our own native poets have left nothing untried.
They have often been at their best when they have had the courage
to leave the paths of the Greeks and celebrate home affairs
with plays in Roman dress, whether serious or comic.
Latium now would be just as strong in her tongue as she is
290 in her valour and glorious arms if the patient work of the file
didn't deter our poets each and every one.
Children of Numa, condemn the piece which many a day
and many a rub of the stilus have not smoothed and corrected
ten times over, to meet the test of the well-pared nail.

Because Democritus holds talent a greater blessing
than poor despised technique and debars a poet from Helicon
unless he's mad, many no longer cut their nails
or beard; they make for secluded spots and avoid the baths.
For a man will surely acquire the name and esteem of a poet
if he never allows the scissors of Lícinus near his head –   300
a head which three Antícyras couldn't cure. And me?
Like a fool I banish madness by taking springtime sedatives.
No one could put together better poems; but really
it isn't worth it. And so I'll play the part of a grindstone
which sharpens steel but itself has no part in the cutting.
Without writing, I'll teach the poet his office and function,
where he can find his resources, what nurtures and shapes him,
what is correct, what not; what is right and wrong.
Moral sense is the fountain and source of proper writing.
The pages of Socrates' school will indicate your material;   310
once that is provided, words will readily follow.
First be clear on what is due to your country and friends;
what is involved in loving a parent, brother, or guest;
what is the conduct required of a judge or member of senate;
what are the duties imposed on a general sent to the front.
Then you will give the proper features to every character.
The trained playwright, I say, should turn to life and behaviour
for dramatic models – and as a source of living speech.
A play with attractive moral comments and credible characters,
but wholly lacking in charm and poetic force and finish,   320
sometimes pleases the public and holds its interest better
than lines devoid of content – mere melodious wind.
The Muse bestowed on the Greeks talent and also the favour
of eloquent speech; they craved for nothing but admiration.
Roman children learn by doing long calculations
how to divide the *as* a hundred times. 'Very well then,
young Albanus: five twelfths – we subtract one of them,
what's the remainder? Come on, hurry up!'
                                        'A third, sir.'
                                                  'Splendid!
You'll look after your money! Now *add* a twelfth to make it –'
'A half.' But when this craze for coppers, this verdigris,   330
has formed on our hearts, how can we hope to fashion poems
fit to be oiled with cedar and stored in polished cypress?

The aim of a poet is either to benefit or to please
or to say what is both enjoyable and of service.
When you are giving advice, be brief, to allow the learner
quickly to seize the point and then retain it firmly.
If the mind is full, every superfluous word is spilt.
Make sure that fictions designed to amuse are close to reality.
A play should not expect us to take whatever it offers –
340   like 'child devoured by ogress is brought alive from her belly'.
The senior bloc refuses plays which haven't a message;
the haughty young bloods curl their nostrils at anything dry;
everyone votes for the man who mixes wholesome and sweet,
giving his reader an equal blend of help and delight.
That book earns the Sosii money; it crosses the ocean,
winning fame for the author and ensuring a long survival.

There are, of course, certain mistakes which should be forgiven.
A string doesn't always sound as mind and finger intended
[when you want a bass it very often emits a treble],
350   nor does a bow invariably hit whatever it aims at.
In a poem with many brilliant features I shan't be offended
by a few little blots which a careless pen has allowed to fall
or human nature has failed to prevent. Where do we stand, then?
If a copying clerk persistently makes the same mistake
in spite of numerous warnings, he is not excused; if a harpist
always misses the same note he causes laughter.
So for me the inveterate bungler becomes a Choerilus,
whose rare touches of goodness amaze and amuse me; I even
feel aggrieved when Homer, the pattern of goodness, nods.
360   Sleep, however, is bound to creep in on a lengthy work.

A poem is like a picture. One will seem more attractive
from close at hand, another is better viewed from a distance.
This one likes the gloom; this longs for the daylight,
and knows it has nothing to fear from the critic's searching eye.
That pleased once; this will please again and again.

My dear Piso major, although your father's voice
and your own good sense are keeping you straight, hear and
                                                            [remember
this pronouncement: in only a limited number of fields
is 'fairly good' sufficient. An average jurist and lawyer
370   comes nowhere near the rhetorical power of brilliant Messalla,

nor does he know as much as Aulus Cascellius; still,
he has a certain value; that *poets* should be only average
is a privilege never conceded by men, gods, or bookshops.
When, at a smart dinner, the orchestra's out of tune,
or the scent is heavy, or poppyseeds come in Sardinian honey,
we take it amiss; for the meal could have been served without them.
It's the same with a poem, whose *raison d'être* is to please the
[mind;
as soon as it misses the top level, it sinks to the bottom.
A man who is hopeless at field events avoids the equipment,
keeping his ignorant hands off shot, discus and javelin,   380
for fear of giving the crowds of spectators a free laugh.
The fellow who is useless at writing poetry still attempts it.
Why not? He's free, and so was his father; his fortune is rated
at the sum required of a knight; and his heart's in the right place!

You will compose and complete nothing against the grain
(you have too much sense and taste). If you do write something
[later,
be sure to read it aloud to the critic Tarpa, and also
to your father and me. Then hold it back 'till the ninth year',
keeping your jotter inside the house. You can always delete
what hasn't been published; a word let loose is gone for ever.   390

Before men left the jungle, a holy prophet of heaven,
Orpheus, made them abhor bloodshed and horrible food.
Hence he is said to have tamed rabid lions and tigers.
It is also said that Amphíon, who built the city of Thebes,
moved rocks by the sound of his lyre and led them at will
by his soft appeals. This was the wisdom of olden days:
to draw a line between sacred and secular, public and private;
to bar indiscriminate sex, and establish laws of marriage;
to build towns and inscribe legal codes on wood.
That is how heavenly bards and their poems came to acquire   400
honour and glory; after them Tyrtaeus and Homer
won renown, for their verses sharpened the courage of men
to enter battle. Song was the medium of oracles, song
showed the way through life. By means of Pierian tunes
a king's favour was sought, and an entertainment devised
to close a season of long work. So don't be ashamed
if you love the Muse's skill on the lyre and Apollo's singing.

Is it a gift or a craft that makes outstanding poetry?
I fail, myself, to see the good either of study
410   without a spark of genius or of untutored talent.
Each requires the other's help in a common cause.
The Olympic athlete who strains to breast the finishing tape
worked and suffered a lot as a boy, sweating and freezing,
leaving wine and women alone. The piper competing
at Delphi was once a learner and stood in awe of his teacher.
Is it enough to proclaim 'I'm a marvellous poet!
The last one home is a cissy; I hate to lag behind
or admit I'm utterly ignorant of something I never learnt'?

As an auctioneer attracts a crowd to bid for his goods,
420   a poet with large estates and large sums invested
encourages toadies to come and obtain something for nothing.
If he's also the sort who knows how to serve delicious dinners,
who will sponsor a shifty and penniless client or come to his rescue
when he's up to his neck in a lawsuit, then I'll be very surprised
if the lucky fellow can tell a true friend from a sham.
When you have given someone a present, or plan to do so,
and he's pleased and excited, never invite him to hear any verses
you have written. He'll shout 'Fine! Lovely! Oh yes!'
He will turn pale at this, at that he will squeeze a tear
430   from his loyal eyes; he will jump to his feet and stamp the ground.
Just as those who are hired to come and wail at a funeral
say and do, if anything, more than the truly bereaved,
so the fake is more visibly moved than the real admirer.
When kings are keen to examine a man and see if he merits
their trust, we are told, they make him submit to the test of wine,
plying him with a succession of glasses. So if *you* compose,
make sure you are not deceived by the fox's hidden malice.

When you read a piece to Quintilius he'd say 'Now shouldn't you
                                                              [alter
that and that?' If you swore you had tried again and again
440   but couldn't do any better, he'd tell you to rub it out
and to put the lines which were badly finished back on the anvil.
If, instead of removing the fault, you chose to defend it,
he wouldn't waste another word or lift a finger
to stop you loving yourself and your work without a rival.
An honest and sensible man will fault lines that are feeble,
condemn the clumsy, proscribe with a black stroke of the pen

those which haven't been trimmed, prune pretentious adornment,
where a place is rather dark insist that light be admitted,
detect ambiguous expressions, and mark what ought to be changed.
He'll be a new Aristarchus; nor will he say 'Why should I   450
annoy a friend over trifles?' For such 'trifles' will lead
to serious trouble once he is greeted with laughter and hisses.

As with the man who suffers from a skin disease or jaundice
or religious frenzy caused by the lunar goddess's anger,
sensible people are wary of touching the crazy poet
and keep their distance; children unwisely follow and tease him.
Away he goes, head in the air, spouting his verses;
and if, like a fowler watching a bird, he happens to tumble
into a pit or a well, however long he may holler
'Somebody! Help!' no one will bother to pull him out.   460
If anyone does bring help and drops him down a rope,
'How do you know,' I'll say, 'he didn't throw himself in
on purpose, and doesn't want to be *left* there?' I'll add the tale
of the poet of Sicily's death – how Empedocles, eager to join
the immortals, leaped into Etna's inferno (thus catching fire
for the first time). Dying is a poet's right and privilege.
To save him against his will is tantamount to murder.
He's done it before; and it's not as if, when you hauled him up,
he'd become human and cease to yearn for a notable death.
One wonders why he persists in writing poetry. Is it   470
a judgement for pissing on his father's ashes, or has he profaned
a gruesome place where lightning has struck? He's certainly mad,
and like a bear that has managed to smash the bars of its cage
he scatters everyone, cultured or not, by the threat of reciting.
For he firmly grips the person he catches, and reads him to death.
The leech never lets go the skin till he's full of blood.

PERSIUS

PROLOGUE

'I have not undergone any of the usual rituals of consecration. I only
half belong to the fraternity of bards. But, as we know, the prospect
of cash makes all kinds of untalented people poetic.'

I never drenched my lips in cart-horse spring,
nor dreamed upon Parnassus' two-pronged height
(I think) to explain my bursting on the scene
as poet. Pale Pirene and Helicon's Maids
I leave to those whose portraits are entwined
with clinging ivy. I present my song,
a semi-clansman, at the bardic rites.
Who coached the parrot to pronounce 'Bonjour!'?
Who helped the magpie mimic human speech?
Teacher of art, giver of genius' gift –   10
the belly, adept at bending nature's laws.
If cash sends out a tempting ray of hope,
then raven poets and magpie poetesses
you'd swear were singing Pegasus' nectar-flow.

SATIRE I

In the course of this dialogue between the satirist and an anonymous
interlocutor Persius says that he expects to have few readers because
the Romans do not want poetry to have any bearing on real life.
Fashionable verse is false and affected, written without a proper
apprenticeship to the craft and designed solely to win applause. This
decadence in literary taste is directly related to the general decadence
in morals. Romans have lost their traditional virility. The satire ends

with a list of certain types whom Persius does not hope to have as
readers.

Ah, the obsessions of men! Ah, what an empty world!
  'Who will read this?'
                              Are you asking me? Why, no one.
                                                        'No one?'
Well, perhaps one or two.
                          'Disgraceful! Pathetic!'
                                          But why?
Are you worried in case 'Polýdamas and the Trojan ladies' prefer
Labeo to me? What the hell? If woolly old Rome attaches
no weight to a piece of work, don't you step in to correct
the faulty tongue on her balance. Ask no one's view but your own.
Is there any Roman who hasn't – if only I could say it – but I can,
when I look at our venerable hair and that austere demeanour
and all we've been at since we gave up marbles and assumed the
                                                            [wisdom
of disapproving uncles, then – sorry, it's not that I want to –
but what can I do? It's my wicked humour – I must guffaw!

  Behind our study doors we write in regular metre,
or else foot-loose, a prodigious work which will leave the strongest
lungs out of breath. No doubt you'll finally read the product
from a public platform, carefully combed, in a new white toga,
with a birthday gem on your finger, rinsing your supple throat
with a clear preparatory warble, your eyes swooning in rapture.
Then, what a sight! The mighty sons of Rome in a dither,
losing control of voice and movement as the quivering strains
steal under the spine and scratch the secret passage.
You old fraud – collecting titbits for other men's ears –
ears which will puff your skin out of shape until you cry 'Whoa
                                                              [there!'

  'What's the point of study if that frothy yeast, that fig-tree
which has once struck root inside never bursts out of the heart?'

  So that's why you're pale and peevish! My god, what have we
                                                          [come to?
Is it so futile to know things unless you are *known* to know them?

'But it's nice to be pointed out, and for people to say "that's him!"
Isn't it something to be set as a text for a mob of long-haired
schoolboys?'   30
                    Look, the Roman elite with well filled stomach
are inquiring over the port 'What has deathless verse to say?'
Then a creature with a hyacinth mantle draped around his
                                                              [shoulders
mumbles some putrid stuff through his nose, filtering out
a Phyllis or Hypsípyle or some other tear-jerking bardic rot,
letting the words trip prettily against his tender palate.
The great men murmur approval. Now surely the poet's ashes
are happy; surely the gravestone presses more lightly on his bones!
The humbler guests applaud. Now surely violets will spring
from those remains, from his tomb, and from his blessed dust!

'You're making fun,' he says, 'and curling your nostrils unfairly.   40
Who would deny that he hoped to earn a place on the lips
of the nation, to utter words that called for cedar oil,
and to leave behind pages that feared neither mackerel nor incense?'

You, whoever you are, my fictitious debating opponent,
if in the course of my writing something special emerges
(a rare bird, I admit), but if something special emerges,
I'm not the man to shrink from applause; my skin's not that tough.
But I do say your 'Bravo' and 'Lovely' are not the final
and ultimate test of what's good. For just shake out that 'Lovely'.
What does it not contain? Why Attius' Iliad's there,   50
dotty with hellebore. Yes, and all the dear little elegies
thought up by dyspeptic grandees, all the stuff in fact
that is scribbled on citrus couches. You cleverly serve at dinner
hot sow's udders, give a threadbare coat to a shivering client,
then say 'I'm a lover of truth; tell me the truth about me.'
How can he? Shall I oblige? You're an airy doodler, baldy,
though your fat pot protrudes at least a foot and a half!
Janus, you have no stork pecking you from behind,
no wagging hands that mimic long white ears, no tongue
stuck out like a thirsty dog's when his star is parching Apulia.   60
My noble lords, who must live with a blind rear wall in your skull,
run and confront the jeering grimace at your back door!

'Well what does the public say?'
                              What you'd expect – that poems

at last have a smooth-flowing rhythm; where the joint occurs, it
                                                                    [sends
the critical nail skidding across the polished surface.
He *rules* each line, as if stretching a cord with one eye shut.
Our poet's Muse always provides him with great themes –
the royal way of life, perhaps, or its splendours, or its dinners!

Just look, we are teaching them to voice heroic sentiments –
                                                                    [amateurs
70 who used to doodle in Greek! They haven't the skill to depict
a clump of trees or the well-fed land with its baskets and hearths
and pigs, and the hay smoking on Pales' holiday – that's where
Remus came from and Quintius, who was polishing his share in the
                                                                    [furrow
when his flustered wife, with a quorum of oxen, invested him
                                                                    [Dictator,
and the sergeant took home the plough. Bravo my noble bard!

Nowadays one man pores over the shrivelled tome
of Accius the old Bacchanal, others over Pacuvius
and his warty Antiopa – 'a dolorous heart weighed down by woe'.
When you see myopic fathers dinning these daft ideas
80 into their sons, why ask who's to blame for putting this sizzling
mish-mash into their mouths, and for that degrading rubbish
which makes our pumiced knights of the realm jitter on their seats?
You should be ashamed! Why you can't defend that venerable head
in court without eagerly listening for a murmur of 'Very nice!'
'You, Pedius, are a thief!' In answer Pedius weighs
the charges in trim antitheses and is praised for his clever figures.
'How lovely!' Well *is* it lovely? Or is Romulus wagging his tail?
Would that move me? If a shipwrecked mariner sang would I give
                                                                    [him
a penny? Do you sing as you tote on your shoulders a picture of
                                                                    [you
in the flotsam? Whoever would bowl me over will have to produce
90 some genuine tears, not rehearsed the night before.

'But the crude old verses have been given a new smoothness and
                                                                    [grace.
A metrical role has now been assigned to "Berecyntian Attis"
and to "The dolphin slicing his way through dark blue Nereus",

and to "We stole a rib from the long spine of the Apennines."
"Arms and the man" – what desiccated, antiquated stuff that is,
like the branch of an old cork tree enveloped in cakey bark!'

Well what is fresh, and good for reciting with limp-held wrist?
'They filled their frightening horns with Bacchanalian brays.
The Bassarid carrying the head torn from a frisky calf   100
and the Maenad ready to guide the lynx with reins of ivy
cry Euhoe! Euhoe! The shout's taken up by restorative Echo.'
Could such things happen if we cherished a spark of our fathers'
                                                    [spunk?
This emasculated stuff, this Maenad and Attis, floats on the spit,
always on the tip of the tongue, ready to come drooling out.
It doesn't pummel the back-rest or taste of bitten nails.

  'But why do you feel obliged to rub the rasp of truth
on sensitive ears? Better watch it. You may get a chilly reception
from those baronial porches. Don't you hear the rolling r
of an angry dog?'   110
                    From now let's say everything's white.
I don't care. Bravo! Superb! You're all just marvellous.
How's that? You erect a notice which says 'Refrain from shitting.'
Paint two holy snakes: 'This is sacred ground, my lads;
find somewhere else to piss.' I'm going. Lucilius crunched
the city – Lupus and Mucius and all – and smashed his molar.
While his friend is laughing, that rascal Horace lays his finger
on all his faults; gaining admission, he plays on the conscience –
so clever at holding the public up on that well-blown nose.
Am I forbidden to whisper – to myself – to a ditch – to anything?
Never mind; I'll bury it here in my book. I've seen it myself: 120
EVERY MAN JACK HAS AN ASS'S EARS! That's my secret;
that's my joke. Slight as it is, I still wouldn't sell it
for all your *Iliads*.
                    If you've caught the spirit of brave Cratínus
or are pale from devotion to angry Eúpolis and the Grand Old
                                                    [Man,
if you've an ear for a concentrated brew, then look at this.
I want a reader with his ears well steamed by that comic vinegar,
not the lout who is eager to jeer at Greek-style sandals,
and is willing to shout 'Hey one-eye!' at a man with that affliction,
who thinks he's somebody just because as Aedile at Arezzo

130   he has smashed a few short measures with full municipal pomp,
nor the witty fellow who sniggers on seeing cones and numbers
traced in the sand of the abacus, and is vastly amused if a Nones-girl
cheekily pulls a philosopher's beard. For them I suggest
the law reports in the morning, and *Calliroë* after lunch.

SATIRE 2

Men's secret prayers are discreditable and foolish, revealing an ignor-
ant and debased conception of divinity.

Count this a red-letter day, Macrinus! Another year
rolls in to your credit. Pour a drink for your guardian angel.
You never offer covetous prayers, asking the gods
for things that you wouldn't dare to mention except in private.
But most of the wealthy offer incense from a silent casket.
Not everyone is ready to rid our temples of all that low
whispering and mumbling and to bring his prayers into the open.
'Good sense, good name, good character' – these words ring out for
                                          [strangers
to hear; under his breath he privately mutters 'If only
10   uncle would pop off, what a splendid funeral we'd have!' 'If only
Hercules would let my spade thump on a crock of silver!'
'Although I'm his guardian, I'd like to rub that youngster out.
I'm next in line, and he's mangy and swollen
with jaundice.' 'That's his third wife that Nerius is burying.'
To ensure these prayers are holy you duck your head each morning
three times or more in the Tiber and wash away the night.

    Well now, tell me – it's only a tiny point to clear up –
what's your opinion of God? Would you rate him higher than –
                                          ['Whom?'
Whom? Shall we say Staius? Or perhaps you balk at that?
20   Is there a finer judge, a more suitable guardian for orphans?
Well take this supplication, with which you are doing your best
to bend God's ear, and make it to Staius. 'Oh God!' he would cry,
'Good God!' So why shouldn't God himself cry 'Good God!'
Do you think you're forgiven when an oak is split in a tempest
by a sulphurous bolt from heaven while you and your house escape?
You don't lie buried in a clump of trees where lightning has struck,

obeying the ritual of a Tuscan crone and her sheep's liver,
an object of dread and abhorrence. Does that mean Jove will let you
tweak his stupid beard? And what, may I ask, have you used
to bribe the ears of the gods? Offal and greasy guts?   30

Here we have a granny or superstitious aunt who has taken a baby
from his cot and now protects his forehead and dribbling lips
by smearing prophylactic spit with her horrible middle finger –
she's skilled at checking the searing blast of the evil eye.
Dandling the scrap of hope in her arms, in fervent prayer
she projects him into Licinian domains or the hall of a Crassus.
'May a king and queen choose him as a husband for their daughter;
                                                          [may girls
scramble to get him; may roses appear wherever he treads!'
I'd never allow a nurse to pray for me. Refuse,
O God, to grant her requests, though she ask in her Sunday best.   40

You pray for strong muscles, a physique that won't let you down
when you're old. Fine, but huge platefuls of thick goulash
prevent the gods from granting your prayer and impede Jove.
You hope to build up your assets by killing a bullock; you summon
Mercury with its liver. 'Grant that my house may prosper;
grant growth to my flocks and herds!' And how is that possible,
fat-head, when the tripe of so many heifers melts in the fire?
Yet the fellow strives to prevail on heaven with piles of innards
and cakes: 'Now for more land, now for more sheep, yes now
my prayer will be answered, now!' till the coin left at the bottom   50
of the money-box, cheated and hopeless, heaves a sigh of despair.

If I brought you a present of silver bowls heavily embossed
with gold, you'd break into a sweat; in the left side of your chest
your heart would beat with impetuous joy, expelling the drops.
That's how you got the idea of smearing the faces of the gods
with gold proudly looted from the foe. 'Within that bronze
fraternity, those who send us dreams most clear of catarrh
should stand out from the rest. Let them have beards of gold.'
Gold has pushed out Numa's crockery and Saturn's copperware;
Vestal urns of Tuscan clay are becoming outmoded.   60
Souls bent on earth, devoid of the things of heaven!
What profit is there in carrying our ways into the churches,
using this sinful flesh to decide what's good for the gods?
The flesh has spoilt olive oil by mixing it into a perfume,

and soaked Calabrian fleece in unnatural crimson dye.
It's the flesh that drives us to gouge pearl from shell and rip
the veins of glowing ore out of the raw slag.
The flesh is guilty, yes guilty; but at least it *profits* from sin.
But tell me, you men of god, what use is gold in a church?
70 As much as the dolls which a young bride offers to Venus.
Let's give to the gods what mighty Messalla's bloodshot offspring
can't give from his mighty dish; a soul in which human
and divine commands are blended, a mind which is pure within,
a heart steeped in fine old honour. Let me bring *these*
to the temple, and I'll win the favour of heaven with a handful of
                                                                [grain.

SATIRE 3

In the first half of the poem a lazy student, who represents Persius
himself, is lectured by an older and wiser companion on the evils of
sloth. In the second half (from v. 63 on) the address becomes more
general. Sin is a form of disease; better nip it in the bud. Find out the
true nature of human existence; forgo sensual pleasures; and live by
the rules of Stoic philosophy.

'So this is your diligent study!'
                                        The bright morning sunshine
is streaming through the shutters, widening the narrow chinks
with its light. My snores continue, allowing the fierce Falernian
to simmer down as the shadow nudges the fifth line
on the dial.
                        'Well, what's this?' says a friend. 'It's late. The mad
dog-star is baking the corn dry; the cattle are huddled
under the spreading elm.'
                                        'Really? Are you sure? Hurry up, then!
Someone! Is nobody there?' My glistening bile swells up
and I burst. You'd think Arcadia's asses were braying in concert.
10 I reach for a book and the two-tone parchment with its hair
                                                                [removed,
also for sheets of paper and a pen of knotty reed.
First I complain that a thick blob is hanging from the nib.
I make the black stuff thinner by adding water, and then

complain that the pen deposits a series of runny drops.
'God help us! Things get worse every day. Has it come to this?'

'Ah, why not do like a pampered dove or a rich man's baby –
demand to have your din-din pre-chewed, and then throw a fit
of temper refusing to let your mammy sing you a lullaby?'
    'How can I work with such a pen?'
                                    'Who are you kidding? No
                                                  [more
snivelling excuses; the joke's on you; You're oozing away   20
mindlessly; you'll be rejected. When a half-baked jar is tapped,
the greenish clay gives a dull answer betraying its quality.
You are soft, damp, earth; away and have yourself moulded
on the whirling wheel till you're properly finished. Oh yes, your
                                                  [family
estate gives a fair yield; you've a pure and spotless salt-cellar
(no need to worry) and a comfortable dish for the rites of the
                                                  [hearth.
Is that enough? Or again, should you puff up your lungs till they
                                                  [burst
because you, descendant one thousand, trace your family tree
to Tuscan stock and parade for your Censor in full regalia?
Let the mob have your trappings; I know what you're like   30
                                                  [underneath,
in the flesh. Aren't you ashamed to live like sloppy Natta?
But vice has made *him* insensible; thick fat has surrounded
his conscience; he has no feelings of guilt, no notion of loss.
Lying on the bottom, he has ceased to send any bubbles to the
                                                  [surface.
    O mighty father of the gods, when sadistic lust with its dagger
dipped in fiery poison incites dictators to crime,
may it please thee to punish their cruelty in this and this way only:
let them see Goodness, and waste with remorse at having betrayed
                                                  [her.
Were the roars more frightful which came from Sicily's brazen bull,
and did the blade dangling from the gilded ceiling cause more   40
                                                  [terror
to the purple neck below than for a man to say to himself
"I'm falling, falling headlong!" and blanch in his heart, poor devil,
as he thinks of a crime which his own dear wife must never hear of?

'I remember as a youngster I often smeared olive oil on my eyes
to avoid learning the dying Cato's magnificent speech.
(I knew my moronic teacher would praise it highly, and my father
would listen in a sweat of excitement with the friends he had
[dragged along.)
Why not? My highest aim was to learn what I stood to win
from a treble six, what I'd lose on three ruinous ones,
50 never to let the narrow-necked jar avoid my marble,
never to yield first place at whipping a wooden top.
But *you're* no novice at spotting crooked behaviour and grasping
the doctrines of the learned Porch with its mural of trousered
[Persians –
doctrines swotted to the small hours by sleepless, crew-cut
students sustained by lentil soup and bowls of porridge.
Pythagoras' Ч betokens a young man's moral choice.
Your eyes are set on the path which climbs steeply to the right.
Still snoring! Your head's lolling, neck-joints undone
and jaws unfastened at both sides, yawning off yesterday.
60 Have you any goal to strive for? Any target to hit?
Or do you chase wild geese with stones and broken bottles,
not caring where your legs carry you, living at random?

'It's no use clamouring for hellebore when your flesh is already
[sick
and bloated. Nip the disease in the bud. Just what's the point
of promising the earth in fees to Doctor Cráterus? Listen,
you poor unfortunates, and learn the purpose of human existence –
what we are, what kind of life we are born to live;
which is our lane, where the turn, and when to begin it;
how much money's enough, what prayers are right, what advantage
70 are crisp notes, how much should be set aside for the state
and for your nearest and dearest; what role the lord has asked you
to play, what post you have been assigned in the human service.
Learn *this*; never mind those jars piled in a barrister's larder
as rewards for defending some greasy Umbrians, rotting beside
the pepper and hams ("tokens of gratitude" from a Marsian client)
while the first tin of sardines still contains a survivor.

'Here a sergeant-major – one of that smelly fraternity –
may say "I know all I need to know. The last thing I want
is to be like Arcésilas or a woebegone Solon – people who wander
80 about with head hanging down, their eyes fixed on the ground,

champing their silent mutterings in rabid self-absorption,
protruding their lips to serve as a balance for weighing their words,
repeating over and over the dreams of a sick old fool:
'Nothing comes from nothing, nothing reverts to nothing.'
Is this why you're pale? Would this detain a man from his dinner?"
That gets a laugh from the crowd, and the lads with the big muscles
send brays of merriment ringing through their contemptuous
                                                              [nostrils.

  ' "Have a look," says the patient to his doctor. "I'm getting
                                              [odd palpitations
here in my chest; I've a sore throat, and I'm short of breath.
Please have a look." He is ordered to bed. By the third night   90
his veins are flowing gently. So he sends a thirstyish flagon
to the house of a rich friend, requesting some smooth Surrentine
to drink at bath-time.
                       "I say, old man, you're a bit pale."
"It's nothing."
                "Still, you'd better watch it, whatever it is.
Your skin's rather yellow and it's quietly swelling up."
   "Your own colour's worse. Stop acting like nanny. I buried her
years ago; you're next."
                         "Carry on. Sorry I spoke."
Bloated with food and queasy in the stomach our friend goes off
to his bath, with long sulphurous belches coming from his throat.
As he drinks his wine, a fit of the shakes comes over him, knocking   100
the warm tumbler from his fingers; his bared teeth chatter;
suddenly greasy savouries slither from his slackened lips.
The sequel is funeral march and candles. The late lamented,
plastered with heavy odours, reclines on a lofty bed,
pointing his stiff heels to the door. He is raised on the shoulders
of men whose caps proclaim them citizens – as of yesterday.
   You poor fool – just take your pulse and put your hand
on your heart.
               "No fever here."
                                 Feel your fingers and toes.
"They aren't cold."
                    What if your eye falls on a bundle
of notes, or you get an enticing smile from the pretty girl   110
next door? Is your heart-beat steady? You are served some leathery
                                              [greens
on a cold plate with meal shaken through a common sieve;

let's see your throat: very tender, with a septic ulcer at the back
which certainly mustn't be chafed by rough proletarian beet.
You shiver when ghastly fear raises hairs on your body;
when a match ignites you, your blood boils, your eyes sparkle
with anger, and you do and say things which Orestes himself,
that legendary madman, would swear were signs of utter madness.'

SATIRE 4

'The conceited young Alcibiades aspires to govern his country,
although he manages his private life on the lowest principles.

'No one looks into his own soul. Instead we carp at the faults of
others. As a result we in turn are open to malicious attack. Self-
deception cannot be maintained indefinitely, and popular acclaim is
unreliable. Examine your own soul and see how inadequate it is.'

The first twenty-two verses are supposed to be addressed by Socrates
to the young Alcibiades. The latter, who was active in the last quarter
of the fifth century BC, represents the politician whose brilliance is not
supported by moral integrity.

The setting is based on the pseudo-Platonic dialogue known as
Alcibiades I.

Running the country are you? (The question comes from the bearded
sage who was carried off by that deadly swig of hemlock.)
By what right? Tell me, mighty Pericles' ward.
Of course your native ability and ready grasp of affairs
have developed ahead of your beard. You can sense what has to be
                                                                    [said
and what suppressed. And so, when the proles are seething with
                                                                    [anger,
you feel impelled to reduce the feverish mob to silence
with a lordly gesture. And then what will you say? 'My friends,
this, for instance, isn't right; that's bad; but that is better.'
10   You can weigh justice in the double pans of the swaying balance;
you can see the straight when it runs between two types of crooked,
or when the rule misleads because of a different standard,
and you don't hesitate to condemn faults with a black x.
So why not doff that attractive skin (it does you no good),
and stop wagging your puppy's tail at the flattering rabble?
You'd be better to lower whole Antícyras of neat hellebore!

What's your idea of the highest good? To dine for ever
among the flesh-pots and pamper your skin with regular sunshine?
But wait – this hag will give the very same answer. Go on, then,
puff out your chest: 'I'm Lady Dinómache's son; and I'm   20
                                                          [handsome.'
Fine, but your motives aren't any higher than those of wizened
old Baucis as she hawks her sexy herbs to a slob of a slave.

   No one – no one – tries to delve into his heart;
everyone watches the bag on the back of the man in front.
If you ask 'Do you know Vettidius' place?'
                                          'Which Vettidius?'
'The squire at Cures – the one with acres a kite couldn't cross.'
   'Oh *that* damned creature. Even his own mother couldn't love
                                                          [him.
On a public holiday he hangs up his yoke at the cross-road shrines;
reluctantly scraping the dirty old seal off his little wine-jar,
he groans "Cheers!" and downs the shrivelled dregs of his senile   30
vinegar, munching an onion in its jacket with a pinch of salt.
His slaves cheer excitedly at getting a bowl of porridge.'

   But if, after a rub, you relax and focus the sun
on your skin, a stranger appears beside you, digs you with his elbow,
and spits abuse: 'What a way to behave, weeding your privates
and the recesses of your rump, displaying your shrivelled vulva to
                                                          [the public!
On your jaws you keep a length of rug which you comb and
                                                          [perfume;
so why is your crotch plucked smooth around your dangling worm?
Though half a dozen masseurs in the gym uproot this plantation,
assailing your flabby buttocks with hot pitch and the claws   40
of tweezers, no plough ever made will tame that bracken.'

   We shoot and in turn expose our legs to the barbs of others.
That's how we live; it's the way we know. You've a hidden wound
down in your groin, but it's covered by a broad golden belt.
As you wish; play tricks and deceive your muscles, if you are able.
   'But the neighbours insist I'm a splendid fellow. Am I not to
                                                          [believe them?'
If you're so greedy that you turn pale at the sight of cash,
if you do whatever occurs to your prick, if you carefully whip up
the harsh rate of interest, causing many a weal,

50 there's no point in lending a thirsty ear to the public.
    Spit out what isn't you; let the crowd take back what they
    have conferred; live alone, and learn how sparse your furniture is.

SATIRE 5

*'Poets conventionally ask for a hundred tongues.' 'But surely your
verse is of a less pretentious kind.' 'It is, but I would gladly have a
hundred tongues to express my gratitude to you, Cornutus; for you
taught me the Stoic way of life.*
     *'Only the wise man, who has subjected his impulses to the control
of reason, can claim to be truly free.'*
     The satire has many points in common with Horace II. 7.

This is the poet's age-old cry: 'Give me a hundred
voices, a hundred mouths, and a hundred tongues for my songs!'
whether he's writing a play to be mouthed by a dismal tragedian,
or showing a wounded Parthian pulling a spear from his groin.

     'What's the point of all this? What lumps of nutritious verse
are you cramming in, that you need a hundred throats to ingest
                                                        [them?
Bards committed to the elevated style may gather mists
on Helicon – those who would bring Thyestes' or Procne's saucepan
to the boil to provide a regular supper for tasteless Sweetman.
10 You're different; you don't squeeze air from a bellows which gasps
as the furnace smelts the ore, or go in for hoarse and pent-up
muttering, inanely cawing to yourself some deep observation,
nor do you strain to blow up your cheeks until they go plop.
You keep to the dress of everyday speech, clever at the pointed
juxtaposition; you've a fairly well-rounded diction; you're expert
at scraping unhealthy habits and nailing vice with a stroke
of wit. Draw your material from there. Leave to Mycenae
its menus of heads and feet, and get used to common food.'

     It's certainly not my aim to swell my page with frivolities
20 dressed in mourning in the hope of lending weight to smoke.
What I have to say is private; now, with the Muses' encouragement,
I'm offering my conscience to you, Cornutus, for a thorough
                                                        [inspection.

I want to show you, my dear friend, how much of my soul
belongs to you. Go on – tap it. You're adept at telling
what sounds solid from painted stucco put on by the tongue.
For this I *would* venture to ask for a hundred throats
to enable me to utter in clear tones how firmly I have tucked you
inside my heart's folds, that my words may reveal what lies
obscure and beyond expression within its deepest fibres.

On shyly removing the purple band which had kept me out of   30
                                                              [trouble,
and presenting my locket to the family gods in their old-fashioned
                                                              [clothes
(when a young man's friends are enticing, and his new white toga
                                                              [allows him
to run his eyes along the whole Subura at will,
when the road forks, and minds wandering in ignorance of life
are led in fear and confusion along the branching paths),
I took you as a father. You lifted my tender years
in your Socratic arms, Cornutus. With quiet dexterity,
you laid your ruler down to straighten my twisted behaviour.
My mind struggled to submit as it felt the pressure of reason,
and under your thumb it took on the right form and features.   40
Together, I remember, we enjoyed those long and sunny days;
together we spent the early part of the night at supper.
The two of us planned a single scheme of work and rest,
and relaxed our serious concerns as we ate a simple meal.
Make no mistake about it, our days are held together
by a solid pact; from the first they have followed the same star.
Fate, with truth in its hand, holds our every minute
poised in the even Scales; or the hour which dawned when the loyal
pair was born has assigned to the Twins our harmonious lives,
and with Jove's help we are breaking Saturn's baleful power.   50
There is certainly *some* star which makes me blend with you.

   Thousands of human types: variegated life-styles.
Each with his own aim, all with different prayers.
Under an Eastern sun one man exchanges Italian
goods for shrivelled pepper and seeds of anaemic cumin,
while another lies replete and bloated in well-soaked sleep.
One is a sports fanatic, another gambles his shirt,
another is soft about sex. But then, when stony arthritis
smashes their fingers into the branches of an old beech-tree,

60 they moan too late that their days have passed in a thick miasma,
with the sun choked by smog, and they've turned their backs on life.
But *you* enjoy acquiring a pallor from your books at night.
Tending the young like a farmer, you clear their ears and sow
Cleanthes' seed. Young and old, you should draw from that
a clear aim for your urges, supplies for your dismal greyness.
        'Tomorrow will do for that.'
                        'Well do it tomorrow.'
                                        'What?
A day's grace? That's a big concession!'
                        When the next day dawns
we have finished yesterday's tomorrow, and look – a new tomorrow
is baling away our years; it will always be just ahead.
70 Although you are under the same carriage and close to the rim
of the wheel that revolves in front, it's futile trying to catch it,
for you are running in the rear position on the back axle.

    We need *freedom* – not the sort which Jack acquires
when he appears as John Smith on the voters' list and is issued
with coupons for mouldy bread. So barren of truth, you imagine
Romans are made by a whirl. Tom is a worthless yokel,
bleary with booze; you couldn't trust him with a bucket of mash.
Then his master turns him round; from that quick spin he emerges
Tom Jones. What's this? You won't authorize a loan
80 which Jones has endorsed? You quail at the sight of Jones on the
                                                        [bench?
It's true – Jones has said so! Would you sign this document, Jones?
That's the real freedom; that's what our cone-caps give us!
    'Well who can be called free, if not the man who is able
to spend his life as he chooses? I'm able to live as I choose;
am I not freer than Brutus?'
                        'Your conclusion is false,' replies
the Stoic here, who has rinsed his ears with biting vinegar.
I grant the rest, but you'll have to remove that 'able' and 'choose'.

    'I walked away from the Praetor and his rod as my own boss.
So why am I not able to do what I like – provided
90 it's not forbidden by a section of *Sabinus on Civil Law?*'

    Very well, listen – but drop that angry screwed-up grimace
while I pull those weedy old granny notions out of your skull.
It wasn't in the Praetor's power to confer a delicate conscience

on fat-heads, or grant them a proper use of their hurrying lives –
it would be easier to train a ham-fisted bruiser to play the harp.
Common sense intervenes and gabbles softly in your ear
that no one should be let do anything that he's sure to make a
                                                [mess of.
Human and natural law lay down a general rule
that bungling ignorance should bar a person from performing an
                                                [action.
Do you mix a dose of hellebore if you can't adjust the weights   100
on a steel-yard? No – such an act is banned by the rules of medicine.
If a clod-hopping yokel who couldn't locate the morning star
tried to take over a ship, Melicerta himself would cry
that shame had vanished from the world. Has philosophy taught
                                                [you to live
a good upstanding life? Can you tell the true from the specious,
alert for the false chink of copper beneath the gold?
Have you settled what to aim for and also what to avoid,
marking the former list with chalk and the other with charcoal?
Are your wants modest, your housekeeping thrifty? Are you nice to
                                                [your friends?
Do you know when to shut your barns and when to throw them   110
                                                [open?
Can you walk steadily past a coin stuck in the mud
and not have to gulp down the Lord of Lucre's saliva?

  When you can truly say 'I possess those goods, they're mine',
deem yourself free and wise in the sight of the Praetor and God.
But if, after just being counted as one of our batch, you retain
the skin of your old disguise and wear a glossy exterior
while keeping a cunning fox inside your rotten heart,
I revoke the concession I made above and draw in the rope.
It stands to reason you'll do nothing right. Waggle your finger
and you're wrong. Is anything smaller? But none of your incense   120
                                                [will lead
the gods to place a gram of what's right in a fool's head.
It's against nature to mix them. If you're a clumsy oaf,
you couldn't do three steps of Bathyllus' satyr routine.

'I'm free.'
            On what grounds, when a slave to so many things?
Do you know no master but the one which the rod lifts from your
                                                [back?

'Here boy – run and take Crispinus' scrapers to the baths.'
If he shouts 'You good-for-nothing loafer!' you aren't jabbed into
                                                              [action
by the goad of slavery, nor does any external force
galvanize your muscles; but if inside, in your sickly heart,
masters come into being, how do *you* get off more lightly
than the lad who ran for the scrapers in fear of his owner's strap?

    It's daylight and you're lying snoring. 'Get up,' says Lady Greed,
'Hey, get up!' You won't. She persists, 'Up!'
                                                      'I'm unable.'
'Up!'
   'What for?'
                              'What a question! Go and fetch kippers from
                                                              [Pontus,
plus beaver-musk, oakum, ebony, frankincense, slippery silk.
The pepper's arrived, unload it before the camel's had a drink.
Do a shady deal, then swear you haven't.'
                                                  'But God will hear.'
'Ha! Listen, you numskull, if you want God on your side
you'll spend your days happily scraping the bottom of the barrel.'

    You're dressed for the journey, loading the slaves with bundles
                                                              [and wine-jars.
'Get this aboard right away!' The huge vessel is ready
to hurry you over the Aegean, when Luxury slyly draws you
aside for a word of advice: 'Just where the hell are you off to?
What do you mean? Are you mad? Why a whole jar of sedatives
couldn't quell the frenzy that's raging in that hot head!
You – hopping over the sea, having your supper on a bench
with your back propped against a coil of rope, while a squat mug
reeks of Veientine rosso ruined by stale resin!
All for what? That the cash you reared at the modest rate
of five per cent should strain to sweat out a greedy eleven?
Give yourself a treat; let's make some hay. What you live is ours.
Soon enough you'll turn into dust, ghost, and hearsay.
Live with death in mind; time flies – my words reduce it.'

    Well then, two hooks are pulling in opposite ways.
Which will you follow, this or that? Your loyalty is bound
to vacillate, obeying and deserting each master in turn.

Even if you once succeed in making a stand and defying
their incessant orders, you can't say 'I've broken my bonds!'
For a dog may snap its fastening after a struggle, but still
as it runs away a length of chain trails from its neck.   160

  'Davus, look – I really mean it – I intend to stop
the hell I've been through,' Chaerestratus says as he gnaws his nails
to the quick. 'Why should I bring disgrace to my decent relatives –
earning a bad name, squandering the family fortune
at the entrance to a house of ill repute, drunkenly singing
outside Goldie's dripping door with my torch doused?'
  'Splendid my boy! Now take my advice and slaughter a lamb
for the gods who protect us.'
                            'But Davus, do you think she'll cry
                                          [when I leave her?'
'Nonsense, my boy! You'll get a whack from her red slipper –
that'll teach you to struggle and gnaw at the tight net!   170
Now you're wild and fierce; if she called, at once you'd say:
"What'll I do? Not go near her, not even now
when she asks me – begs me?"
                                  Not even now, if you've made a clean
and genuine break.'
                      There, I tell you, is the freedom we're after,
not in the piece of stick waved by a silly official.

  The man who is led agape by the charms of whitened Ambition –
is he his own master? 'Do without sleep, let the mob
scramble for showers of peas, so that old men in the sunshine
may one day remember our Festival of Flora. A fine aspiration!'
But when Herod's day arrives, and lamps entwined with violets   180
are placed on the greasy window-sills spewing out heavy clouds
of smoke, and when the tunny's tail swims, encircling
the cheap red dish, and the white jar is bloated with wine,
you move your lips in silence and blanch at the circumcised
                                                        [sabbath.
Demons in the dark, perils portended by an exploding egg,
Cybele's towering eunuchs, a one-eyed priestess of Isis
complete with rattle – they fill you with gods who will puff up your
                                                        [body,
unless on rising you take, as prescribed, three heads of garlic.

If you make such remarks in the presence of varicose
                                              [sergeant-majors,
190   at once the mighty Pulfenius gives vent to a bray of laughter,
      and offers a clipped coin of bronze for a hundred Greeks.

                              SATIRE 6

A letter from Persius, who is spending the winter on the Ligurian coast
at Luna (modern Luni now inland off the Bay of Spezia), to the lyric
poet Caesius Bassus.
    After the preliminary greetings Persius takes up the topic of money,
rejecting in the Horatian manner the way of the miser and that of the
spendthrift.
    The main body of the poem, however, recommends that one should
spend and enjoy what one has in a sensible way without worrying
overmuch about the expectations of one's heir.

      Has the winter brought you out to your Sabine fireside, Bassus?
      Are the lyre-strings waking beneath your stern highland quill?
      You excel at turning the oldest words of our tongue into verse
      and setting them to the virile sound of the Latin harp.
      Though old in years, you're an expert in the sport of young love,
      playing with a tasteful touch.
                              The Ligurian coast is mild,
      and I'm wintering here with my stretch of sea, where the cliffs
                                              [present
      a massive wall and the shore falls back in a deep gulf.
      'Good people, get to know the port of Luna – it's worth it!'
10   So said Ennius the wise, on snoring off the dream
      of being Quintus Homer descended from Pythagoras' peacock.
      Here I couldn't care less for the toiling masses or the mischief
      which the south wind is plotting for my cattle; couldn't care less
      that a certain corner of my neighbour's land is richer than mine.
      If all my social inferiors grew rich, I'd never become
      hunched and shrivelled with resentment or forgo a tasty dinner,
      or poke my nose at the seal of a bottle that's gone flat.
      Others may differ. Twins born under the same star
      vary in temperament. One, for a birthday treat, will dip
20   his dry greens in brine which he has cunningly bought in a cup;
      he personally shakes the precious pepper on his plate. The other,

a stylish lad, chews through a huge inheritance. For me
it's 'Enjoy what you have', though I can't feed my dependants on
                                                            [turbot,
nor can I tell the subtle flavour of a hen thrush.
Live up to your harvest; grind your granaries, as you should.
Why worry? Harrow again, and a new crop's in the blade.

   But you say you have obligations. A friend's ship has gone down;
he's clinging to the rocks of Bruttium, destitute – all his possessions
and his futile prayers committed to the deep; he's sprawled on the
                                                            [beach,
with the mighty gods from the stern beside him; the ribs of the   30
                                                            [mangled
vessel are already drawing the gulls. Well, cut a sod
off your landed capital and give it to the poor fellow, to save him
from carting around his picture on a sea-blue board.
                                              But your heir
will blame you for truncating your property; he'll skimp the funeral
                                                            [feast,
put your bones in the urn without scent. Is the cinnamon flat,
or the cassia debauched with cherry bark? He wouldn't know.
'Serve you right,' he'll say, 'for not keeping up the estate.'

Like Bruty, he blames it on Greek intellectuals: 'That's how it goes;
since these fancy ideas arrived from abroad with pepper
and dates, our farmhands have spoilt their porridge with greasy   40
                                                            [sauces.'
Will such things worry you beyond the pyre? But you, my heir,
whoever you are, may I have a word with you – here, in private?
I say – haven't you heard? A dispatch decked with laurels
has come from Caligula; the prime of Germany has crashed to
                                                            [defeat.
They're raking the cold ashes from the altars; the Empress has
                                                            [ordered
arms for the doorways, royal mantles, yellow wigs
for the prisoners, chariots of war, colossal figures of the Rhine.
So for these brilliant successes I'm staging a hundred fights
in honour of the gods and our beloved leader. Who's going to
                                                            [stop me?
Just try it. Turn a blind eye or else! I'm dishing out oil   50
to the mob – and bread and meat. Any objections? Speak up.
'That field nearby,' you say, 'is too full of stones.' Well if none

of my father's sisters or his brother's daughters and none of my
[uncle's
great-great-granddaughters are left, and my maternal aunt has died
without issue, if my granny's line is extinct, I'll go to the beggars'
hill at Bovillae and in no time I'll find some Jack for an heir.

'An offspring of the soil?'
                                       Ask who my grandfather's grandfather
[was.
It'll take a while, but I'll tell you. Go back a stage – and another;
we've now reached a son of the soil. So in point of kinship
60   this Jack turns out to be some kind of great-great-uncle.
       You're next; why shout for the baton before I've finished?
I'm your Mercury, offering a purse like the god in his picture.
Do you refuse it? Or will you take what's left and be thankful?
       'Some of it's missing.'
                                       It went to meet my expenses. But all of it's
yours, whatever is there. Forget what became of the sum
Tadius left me, and don't call me to account: 'Put down
the sum inherited, add the interest, subtract the expenditure,
what's the remainder?'
                                       Remainder? Come on, boy, drown the
[cabbage,
drown it in oil and damn the expense! Shall I on holidays
70   eat boiled nettles and a smoked pig's cheek with a hook-hole in
[the ear,
so that one day your young wastrel may gorge on goose's liver,
and when the fastidious vein throbs in his roving cock,
relieve himself into an upper-class pouch? Am I to be left
with transparent skin, while his priest-belly wobbles with fat?

       Sell your soul for profit, scour each quarter of the globe;
clinch your smart deals; make sure that *you* are pre-eminent
at standing on the hard platform and slapping fat Cappadocians.
Double your capital.
                                       'I have; now it's trebled; and now
it's in four folds, now in ten. Pinpoint where I'm to stop?
80   You're the first ever to have checked Chrysippus' heap!'

Notes

HORACE

Satire 1. 1

1. *Maecenas*: Horace's patron and friend. He was a knight from an old Etruscan family. Although he never became a senator he was Augustus' chief adviser on home affairs for over twenty years. See also the introductions to *Satires* I. 5, I. 6, and II. 6.

13. *Fabius*: A Stoic bore.

25. *presenting the truth with a laugh*: The Latin is *'ridentem dicere verum'*.

49–50. *nature's limits*: I.e. too much food and too little food are both harmful.

58. *Aufidus*: A swift river near Venusia, Horace's birthplace.

68. *Tantalus*: He abused the hospitality of the gods, but as he had eaten divine food he could not be killed. He was therefore condemned to eternal punishment, being always hungry and thirsty but never satisfied.

91. *the Park*: The Campus Martius.

101–2. *Naevius or Nomentanus*: These names typify prodigality. Naevius the wastrel is not mentioned elsewhere. Some scholars read Maenius, a name which, like Nomentanus, occurs in Lucilius.

104–5. *There is ... massive vassal*: The Latin is *'est inter Tanain quiddam socerumque Viselli'* – 'there is a point between Tanais and the father-in-law of Visellius.' The ancient commentator Porphyrion (third century AD) says that Tanais was a eunuch and that Visellius' father-in-law represented the opposite extreme. This is not a particularly reliable or informative comment, but we have nothing else to go on, and so I have used it as the basis of my translation, which refers to the riddle: 'What is the difference between an Eskimo and a eunuch?' Answer: 'One is a frigid midget with a rigid digit; the other is a massive vassal with a passive tassel.'

108. *I return ... greed*: For a defence of this reading see N. Rudd, *SH*, pp. 274–5.

121. *Crispinus*: Another wordy Stoic. Cf. I. 4. 14–16 and II. 7. 45.

Satire 1. 2

3. *Tigellius*: This Tigellius, who is mentioned also in I. 3. 3, is apparently a different man from the Hermogenes Tigellius who is referred to in I. 3. 129. See *SH*, p. 292, n. 15.

12. *Fufidius*: Unknown.

20–21. *Terence's play*: The *Heautontimorumenos* or 'The man who punished himself'. Horace is referring to the description of Menedemus in the opening scene.

25–7. *Maltinus minces ... Gargonius of goat*: Maltinus, Rufillus, and Gargonius are unknown.

29. *flounce*: The *instita* was an ornamental border worn around the lower edge of the *stola*. This was the dress of married ladies.

32. *Cato*: The Censor M. Cato (234–149 BC) who was famous for his strict views on morality. We do not know whether the anecdote is authentic, but in its full form it had a sequel. After meeting the man several times in the same place Cato said 'I commended you, young man, for paying an occasional visit, not for becoming an habitué.'

37–8. *It is worth ... adulterous men*: This is a parody of Ennius: 'It is worth your while to give ear, ye who wish all success to the Roman state' (*Annals* Frag. 471–2 in Warmington, *Remains of Old Latin*, vol. 1, Loeb Classical Library).

46. *Galba*: An unidentified member of the aristocratic family of the Sulpicii Galbae.

47–8. *How much safer ... freedwomen*: Relations with freedwomen do not involve the dangers enumerated in the previous lines. Nor do they necessarily entail disgrace or ruin. But here too infatuation can lead to serious trouble.

48. *Sallust*: Horace seems to be referring either to the historian Sallust or to his adopted son. But there are difficulties in either case. See *SH*, pp. 135–6.

55. *Marsaeus*: Unknown.

   Miss Newcome: The Latin name is Origo. She is also unknown.

63. *wench with a cloak*: It is not certain whether the phrase *ancilla togata* refers to a freedwoman or a slave. The former gives a tighter sequence but the latter corresponds more closely to the actual words. In any case the three-term Aristotelian treatment, where a satisfactory mean (the freedwoman) is distinguished from two opposing extremes (the married lady and the lowest whore), is not continued. Instead, from now on we have a simple contrast between married ladies and prostitutes. The *toga* was worn by *meretrices* (prostitutes), who might be either freedwomen or slaves.

64. *Villius*: Sextus Villius Annalis. His adulterous liaison with Sulla's daughter was so regular that he is here called Sulla's son-in-law.

   Joy: Fausta, Sulla's notorious daughter, was born in 86 BC. She would have been about forty-seven if she was still alive when the satire was written. Her affair with Villius was one of yesterday's scandals.

67. *Longarenus*: Another of Fausta's lovers. Otherwise unknown.

80–82. *She may be decked ... boasts*: The text which I have translated runs as follows: '*nec magis huic, inter niveos viridisque lapillos sit licet, hoc Cerinthe tuo tenerum est femur aut crus rectius, atque etiam melius persaepe togatae.*' See E. Fraenkel, *Horace*, Oxford, 1957, pp. 84–5.

91. *Lynx*: A member of the Argonautic expedition, famous for his keen sight.

　　Hypsaea: Unknown.

92. '*O legs! O arms!*': This recalls the poem of Philodemus beginning 'O feet! O legs!' See the *Greek Anthology* 5. 132.

95. *Catia*: A noble lady with a bad reputation.

101. *Coan silk*: From the island of Cos in the Aegean sea.

105. *The poet*: In these lines Horace cleverly summarizes an epigram by Callimachus (*Greek Anthology* 12. 102). Callimachus, writing in the third century BC, was one of the most important Alexandrian poets.

113. *distinguish solid from void*: Solid (i.e. atoms) and void were the two basic realities of Epicurean physics. Here the terms are transferred to ethics.

121. *the Gauls*: *Galli* was the name given to the eunuch priests of Cybele, the mother goddess of Phrygia. See Persius 5. 186.

　　Philodemus: (*c.* 110–*c.* 37 BC) The *Greek Anthology* contains twenty-five of his epigrams, but not the one referred to here. He had an important influence on Roman Epicureanism in the middle of the first century BC. For an outline of his work see G. M. A. Grube, *The Greek and Roman Critics*, chapter 12.

126. *Lady Ilia*: The mother of Romulus.

　　Countess Egeria: A nymph who, according to legend, was the wife and adviser of King Numa.

130–31. *the maid for her legs ... her dowry*: Guilty slaves sometimes had their legs broken. A wife convicted of adultery would forfeit part of her dowry.

133. *my cash ... has had it*: Cf. v. 44, where the louts in question are the stable-hands of the aggrieved husband. For other relevant forms of punishment see Mayor on Juvenal 10. 315–17, and Ellis on Catullus 15. 19.

134. *Fabius*: The point seems to be that even a Stoic like Fabius would acknowledge that the consequences were painful.

Satire 1. 3

3. *Tigellius*: See note on I. 2. 3.

4–5. *Caesar*: Octavian, the future Emperor Augustus. He was adopted by

Julius Caesar and therefore counted as his son, though in fact he was his great-nephew.

10–11.   *carrying the sacred vessels*: I.e. in a religious procession.

21.   *Maenius*: Probably a real person who had figured in the satires of Lucilius.

   Newman: Unknown. The Latin is '*Novius*'.

21–3.   *'Hey there . . . said Maenius*: The Latin is '*ignoras te, an ut ignotum dare nobis verba putas?' 'egomet mi ignosco' Maenius inquit*. Literally ' "Do you not know yourself, or do you think you are deceiving us as unknown?" "I pardon myself," said Maenius.' It is as if Maenius had said *non ignoro sed ignosco*. The play on words, which cannot be translated, turns on the fact that *ignotum* can mean both 'unknown' and 'pardoned'.

27.   *Epidaurian snake*: Snakes were supposed to have keen sight. They were sacred to Aesculapius the god of medicine, whose main centre of worship was at Epidaurus in Greece. He also had a temple on the island in the Tiber.

40.   *Balbinus . . . Hagna*: Unknown.

45–8.   *'Castor' . . . 'Bowie'*: The euphemistic names recommended by Horace, viz. *paetus, pullus, varus*, and *scaurus* all belonged to well-known Roman families.

82.   *Labeo*: Cannot be identified with any certainty.

92.   *Evander*: A mythical king who emigrated from Arcadia to Italy before the Trojan war. He founded Pallanteum, later the Palatine Hill. In the *Aeneid* Virgil describes how he welcomed Aeneas and sent his son Pallas to fight on the Trojan side.

127.   *Chrysippus*: (*c*. 280–207 BC) Head of the Stoic school.

129.   Hermogenes: Mentioned in I. 4. 72, I. 9. 25, I. 10. 17–18, 80, 90. Although his surname was Tigellius, he was not, it seems, the same man as Tigellius the Sardinian. See *SH*, p. 292.

130.   *Alfenus*: Sometimes identified with the famous jurist Alfenus Varus, but this is uncertain.

139.   *Crispinus*: See note on I. 1. 121.

Satire 1. 4

1.   *Cratinus, Eupolis, and Aristophanes*: Comic writers of fifth-century Athens.

6.   *Lucilius*: See Introduction, pp. xi–xv.

8.   *harsh*: The Latin is '*durus componere versus*', and some scholars take this to mean 'indefatigable in writing verses'. It is a fine point, but in view of I. 10. 56ff., where the word *dura* occurs again, it seems better to suppose that Horace is talking about harshness.

14.   *Crispinus*: Mentioned already in I. 1. 121 and I. 3. 139.

21.   *Fannius*: A complacent poet. The Latin does not make it clear whether

he gives or receives the presents. For arguments in favour of the former see *Hermathena* 87 (1956) 52–5.

28. *Albius*: Apparently the father of the man mentioned in v. 109. Statuettes and vases of Corinthian bronze were collectors' items.

34. *hay*: A wisp of hay was tied to the horns of a dangerous bull.

34–5. *For the sake . . . his friends*: I have translated the Oxford text, which prints '*dummodo risum/excutiat sibi non non cuiquam parcet amico.*' Most editors read '*dummodo risum/excutiat sibi, non hic cuiquam parcet amico*' 'provided he raises a laugh for himself this fellow will not spare any of his friends.' It seems more likely that *non non* would be changed to *non hic* than vice versa; in the context *hic* does not carry much force; and the former reading has a good parallel in Aristotle, *Nicomachean Ethics* IV. 14, where the buffoon 'will not spare himself or anyone else if he can raise a laugh'. But certainty is impossible. Some editors read *tibi* for *sibi*.

42. *a style rather close to prose*: The Latin is '*sermoni propiora*'.

45. *comedy*: From the example given in 48ff. it is clear that Horace is thinking of Roman comedy.

52. *Pomponius*: Usually regarded as a real person, but more likely to be a character in the play referred to.

60–61. *when loathsome Discord . . . war*: A quotation from Ennius. Cf. Virgil, *Aeneid* 7. 622.

66. *Sulcius and Caprius*: Apparently soap-box orators who specialized in denunciation. The names suggest types of fig, recalling the Greek for 'informer'. See Radermacher, *Wiener Studien* 53 (1935) 80–84.

69. *Caelius or Birrius*: Unknown.

87. *one who throws all kinds of dirt*: This line refers to the type of person known as a *scurra* (hence our 'scurrilous'). Such men relied on being invited to dinner-parties, where they were expected to amuse the company.

92. *Rufillus . . . of goat*: A quotation from I. 2. 27.

94–5. *the theft . . . Capitolinus*: This refers to a *cause célèbre* in which a Petillius Capitolinus was tried for embezzlement. To judge from I. 10. 27 the defence counsel had great difficulty in securing an acquittal. Petillius may have been the man whose name appears on a coin dated about 43 BC.

109. *Albius . . . Baius*: Unknown.

112. *Scetanus*: Unknown.

114. *Trebonius*: Unknown.

120. *without a ring*: Literally 'without cork'.

129. *That is the reason*: The Latin is '*ex hoc*'. It is normally translated 'as a result of this training', but it seems preferable to make the *hoc* refer to the immediately preceding lines. The general sense is much the same either way.

143. *the Jews*: The Jewish colony in Rome was well known for its proselytiz-
ing zeal (Matthew 23:15) and for its community spirit (Cicero,
Flacc. 66).

Satire 1. 5

1. *Aricia*: About sixteen miles from Rome; famous for the worship of
Diana Nemorensis (see Frazer, *Golden Bough*, chapter 1).

2. *Heliodorus*: T. Frank plausibly suggests that this may be the scholar
Apollodorus who was a well-known teacher in Rome at the time
and whose name could not be included in a hexameter. See *Classical
Philology* 15 (1920) 393. Apollo was often identified with the sun,
and the Greek for sun is *helios*.

9–23. *Night was preparing . . . we landed*: The journey is continued by
barge through the Pomptine marshes.

24. *Feronia*: An Italian goddess, consort of Jupiter at Anxur.

25. *Anxur*: The old Volscian name of Tarracina; on the west coast of Italy
sixty-five miles south of Rome.

28. *Cocceius*: L. Cocceius Nerva. He had helped to negotiate the earlier
treaty of Brundisium in 40 BC which divided the Mediterranean world
between the triumvirs Antony, Octavian, and Lepidus.

32. *Fonteius Capito*: After this conference he was given another com-
mission, that of escorting Cleopatra from Egypt to Syria, where she
was to spend the winter with Antony. Fonteius Capito became Consul
Suffectus in 33 BC.

34. *the Praetorship of Aufidius Luscus*: A grandiloquent phrase.

36. *the pan of glowing charcoal*: Apparently for burning incense in honour
of the guests' arrival.

37. *the Mamurras' city*: Formiae, birthplace of the notorious Mamurra
who was Caesar's chief engineer in Gaul.

38. *Murena*: Varro Murena, Maecenas' brother-in-law. He was Consul in
23 BC, but was involved in a conspiracy with Fannius Caepio and was
executed in 22.

40. *Plotius*: Plotius Tucca who, with Varius, edited the *Aeneid* after Virgil's
death.
    Varius: He and Virgil introduced Horace to Maecenas – see I. 6. 55.
    Horace speaks of him as an epic poet in I. 10. 43–4. He also attained
    distinction in tragedy.

41. *and Virgil*: Virgil probably came to join the party from Naples, where
he spent most of his time.

49. *inflamed eyes . . . stomachs*: Horace had sore eyes. Virgil had a chronic
stomach ailment.

52–5. *Sarmentus*: A former slave, emancipated by Maecenas and given a
job in the Treasury. His name, which meant 'faggot', apparently suited
his physique.

Messius: His cognomen Cicirrus meant 'cock'. The cock-man was a stock figure in local farces. The Oscans were proverbially oafish.

62–3.   *'Campanian disease'*: Unknown. Guesses vary from warts on the forehead to satyriasis.

65–9.   *Had Sarmentus . . . scrap like him*: The implication is that Sarmentus had once been kept in chains and had obtained his freedom by running away. The normal ration for a slave was about four pounds of meal a day; this may well have been reduced during the blockade of Sextus Pompeius.

98.   *Then Gnatia . . . scowled*: Gnatia was also short of water.

100–101.   *Apella the Jew may believe it*: The Romans regarded the Jews as credulous and superstitious.

101–3.   *the gods live a life . . . the sky*: These lines are a parody of Lucretius, who maintained that the gods lived a life of serenity, undisturbed by human wickedness. See, e.g., *De Rerum Natura* 5. 83.

Satire 1. 6

1.   *all the Lydians . . . Tuscan soil*: According to Herodotus 1. 94 half the people of Lydia in Asia Minor migrated to Etruria as a result of a famine. Maecenas' family came from Arretium, the modern Arezzo.

6.   *men with unknown . . . fathers*: I have translated Palmer's text: *'ignoto aut, ut me, libertino patre natos.'* See his critical note.

8.   *a gentleman*: The Latin is *ingenuus*, which could mean both 'free-born' and 'of noble character'.

9.   *Tullius*: Servius Tullius, sixth king of Rome, was a man of no pedigree. His mother was a slave.

12.   *Laevinus*: A descendant of P. Valerius Publicola the colleague of Brutus in the consulship of 509 BC.

17–18.   *So what is . . . the masses*: The Latin is *'quid oportet/nos facere a vulgo longe longeque remotos?'* This has been interpreted in two ways: (1) 'How much more should we, who stand apart from the mob, assess a man at his true worth?' (2) 'What am I to do who am so far removed from the public gaze?' I have preferred to follow (1), although it does not lead smoothly to what follows. The fact is that no rendering can succeed in producing a tight connection between the second and third paragraphs.

20.   *Decius*: Decius Mus was the first member of his family to become Consul.

24.   *Tillius*: A man of lowly origins who had reached the Senate. He was apparently expelled but later regained his position. In v. 108 he is referred to as a Praetor.

30.   *Barrus*: An effeminate fop. The girls regarded him as a rival and were anxious to discover his faults. It is unfortunate that a man of such a temperament should have had a name which meant 'elephant'.

38. *Syrus, Dionysius, or Dama*: Slave names.

39. *the rock*: Criminals were sometimes executed by being hurled from
     the Tarpeian rock on the Roman Capitol.
        Cadmus: He is supposed to have been the public executioner.

40. *My colleague . . . behind me*: In the theatre senators sat in the space in
     front of the stage; the knights (*equites*) occupied the next fourteen
     rows; behind them sat the general public.

42. *Paulus or Messalla*: Aristocratic names.

48. *as a military tribune*: Horace was a tribune in the army of Brutus.

55. *Varius*: See note on I. 5. 40.

59. *Tarentum*: A wealthy Greek colony in southern Italy. Lucilius may
     have owned property in the area. See C. Cichorius, *Untersuchungen
     zu Lucilius*, reprinted Berlin, 1964, pp. 23–8.

72. *Flavius' school*: The local school at Venusia.

97. rods: The *fasces* were symbols of the Praetors' and Consuls' power.

98. *thrones*: The senior magistrates had ivory chairs.

118. *Campanian ware*: Cheap pottery.

120. *Marsyas*: The statue represented an attendant of Bacchus with a wine-
     skin over his left shoulder and his right arm raised. Horace suggests
     that the arm is raised in a gesture of abhorrence.

124. *Natta*: Unknown.

126. *triangle*: A kind of ball-game played by three people.

Satire 1. 7

2.   *outlaw*: Rupilius Rex had been proscribed by the Triumvirs and had
     fled to Brutus in Asia.

3.   *sore eyes*: People with sore eyes would congregate and gossip in the
     apothecary's shop.

8.   *Sisenna and Barrus*: Unknown. Horace uses the expression *equis prae-
     currere albis* – 'to outstrip with white horses'. White horses were
     thought to be the fastest.

11–12. *the wrath . . . murderous*: The reference is to the famous fight in
     Iliad 22.

16. *Diomedes . . . Glaucus*: In *Iliad* 6. 119–236, Homer describes how
     Glaucus of Lycia met the Greek Diomedes. They eventually exchanged
     armour, and Glaucus got the worst of the deal. But there was no
     question of cowardice or appeasement.

25. *the infamous Dog*: Sirius, the dog-star, whose appearance in late July
     was frequently accompanied by drought and fever. The phrase is mock-
     heroic; cf. *Iliad* 22. 30–31 and Theocritus 25. 168.

28. *Praeneste*: The modern Palestrina, about twenty-three miles east-
     south-east of Rome.

31. *Cuckoo*: It was thought that vines should be pruned before the arrival
     of the cuckoo. Therefore a passer-by who shouted 'Cuckoo!' was
     taunting the workman in the vineyard.

Satire 1. 8

11. *Grab-all*: Pantolabus is a nickname formed from the Greek πᾶν + λαβεῖν – 'to grab everything'.

13–14. THIS MONUMENT . . . HEIRS: This formula was intended to preserve the ground as a grave; it was not to pass, like the rest of the dead man's property, to his heirs.

15. *the wall*: An embankment closing off the valley which separated the Esquiline from the Quirinal Hill. It was supposed to have been made by Servius Tullius and enlarged by Tarquinius Superbus.

23–5. *Canidia*: A witch who plays an important role here and in *Epodes* 5 and 17; she also makes brief appearances in II. 1. 48 and II. 8. 95. She is described in horrifying and ludicrous terms that are appropriate to any witch, but there are also a few specific details which suggest that the caricature may be based on some notorious figure. Canidia is barefoot and her hair undone, because one who binds another must not be bound.

Sagana: The Latin is '*cum Sagana maiore*', which is most naturally interpreted as implying the existence of a younger sister. This in turn indicates that Horace may be alluding to some contemporary figure. The name itself, however, may have been chosen because, in spite of the quantity, it recalled the word *sāga*, a witch.

26–8. *They scraped . . . their teeth*: The lamb is black, being an offering to the powers of darkness. The witches use nails and teeth because iron, being a late invention in the history of magic, is tabu.

28–9. *letting the blood . . . questions*: By drinking the blood the spirits of the dead regain the power of speech – a parody of the great scene in *Odyssey* 11. One assumes that they then assist Canidia in some way to carry out her purposes. Exactly how they do so is not made clear.

30–31. *a woollen doll . . . the smaller*: The larger doll represents Canidia, the smaller her lover, who is being punished for his lack of devotion.

33. *Hecate*: A goddess of the underworld, associated with sorcery. She often represented the infernal aspect of Diana, the moon.

34. *Tisiphone*: One of the Furies.

38–9. *Julius . . . Miss Pediatius . . . Voranus*: Unknown. The name Julius must belong to a freedman of the Julian family.

42. *a wolf's beard . . . fang*: The beard and fang are buried as a precaution against counter-spells.

Satire 1. 9

13. Bolanus: Unknown.

22. Viscus: One of the two sons of Vibius Viscus, a knight. In I. 10. 80 the brothers are mentioned among the men whose approval Horace is eager to obtain.

23. *Varius*: See note on I. 5. 40.

25.   *Hermogenes*: See note on I. 3. 129.

26–7. *Have you a mother . . . home*: The Latin is '*est tibi mater, / cognati, quis te salvo est opus?*' For a discussion of this uncertain passage see *SH*, p. 284, n. 41.

38–9. *I could never . . . in the box*: It is perhaps a mistake to ask *why* Horace couldn't stand in the box. The poet is prevaricating.

59–60. *'Not without . . . prizes won'*: The commentators point out that the adage appears in many forms in Greek literature.

61.   *Aristius Fuscus*: A friend who is addressed in the two light-hearted poems *Odes* 1. 22 (*Integer vitae*) and *Epistles* 1. 10. He obviously had a sense of humour and he is said to have written comedies.

69.   *the thirtieth – the Sabbath*: The exact meaning is uncertain.

70.   *affront*: The Latin is '*oppedere*' (to break wind at). This is a case where an English translator cannot be both accurate and idiomatic.

76.   *touch my ear*: This ritual gesture was supposed to indicate that the ear was the seat of memory.

78.   *Thus did Apollo save me*: A parody of *Iliad* 20. 443 where Apollo rescues Hector. Apollo is the patron of poets.

Satire 1. 10

1–4.   *I did say that Lucilius' . . . caustic wit*: These lines refer back to the second paragraph of I. 4.

6.   *Laberius*: D. Laberius (*c.* 115–43 BC), a Roman knight who wrote popular comedies in verse. He revived archaisms, coined words, and was often obscene. And so he did not meet Horace's classical standards. The loss of his work is regrettable.

18.   *Hermogenes*: the musician and literary man mentioned in I. 3. 129, 4. 72, 9. 25, and again at the end of this satire.

      that ape: He cannot be identified with certainty, but may be the Demetrius mentioned along with Hermogenes Tigellius in v. 90.

19.   *Calvus and Catullus*: Calvus had died twelve years and Catullus about twenty years before this satire was written. It is important to remember that Horace is attacking not them but their admirers. We do not know what he thought of Catullus. It would be reasonable to imagine that he admired certain qualities in the earlier poet, e.g., his easy self-portrayal, and agreed with a number of points in his literary theory, e.g., his avoidance of the major genres and the more refined aspects of his wit. Yet Catullus' indifference to the themes of moral philosophy, his absorption with love, and his passionate temperament make it unlikely that his work had much influence on Horatian satire. As far as lyric is concerned, Horace had at this stage written very little and published none.

20–35. *'It was a great feat . . . forest'*: For Lucilius' use of Greek see *SH*, pp. 111–14. Not infrequently Catullus and the neoterics used Greek expressions to achieve a sweet or sensuous or romantic effect. Horace, however, took the view that Roman satire should be written in Latin. And romantic effects were alien to the genre. In vv. 25–30 he points out that when language is used for a serious practical purpose, as in the law-courts, Greek importations are avoided. The implication is that satire is a serious poetic form.

22. *Pitholeon*: Usually identified with the Pitholaus who, according to Suetonius (*Julius Caesar* 75), wrote abusive epigrams.

27. *Petillius*: See note on 1. 4. 94.

Pedius Publicola: An unidentified aristocrat.

28. *Corvinus*: Messalla Corvinus, soldier, statesman, orator, and man of letters. He shared the Consulship with Octavian in 31 BC.

30. *Canusiun*: A town in Apulia mentioned in I. 5. 91. Its population was part Greek, part Oscan.

33. *Quirinus*: The name given to the deified Romulus, hence the embodiment of the Roman national spirit.

36. *Alpman*: This epic poet is probably identical with the Furius mentioned in II. 5. 41. Memnon, son of Tithonus and Aurora, was king of Ethiopia. He went to Troy to assist Priam but was killed by Achilles. Zeus then made him immortal. His story was a traditional epic theme. The point of 'the head of the Rhine' is not clear. It may refer to a description of the river's source, or to a personification of the Rhine-god. In any case Horace is ridiculing the poet's language, which, he contends, has ruined the subject.

38. *Tarpa*: Spurius Maecius Tarpa, who twenty years earlier had been appointed by Pompey to choose what plays should be performed in the theatre. The scholiasts on this verse say that he adjudicated poetic competitions in the temple of the Muses.

41. *Fundanius*: A friend of Horace's who describes the dinner-party of Nasidienus in II. 8.

42. *Pollio*: Asinius Pollio, another man of amazing versatility. Consul in 40 BC, he fought a successful military campaign in the following year. By the time of this satire he had withdrawn from political life but was still active as a writer. In addition to the tragedies mentioned here he wrote a history of the civil war and also speeches, criticism, and letters.

43. *with triple beat*: I.e. in iambic trimeters in which there were three beats in a line.

Varius: See note on I. 5. 40.

44. *Virgil*: Horace is here referring to the *Eclogues*.

46. *Varro of Atax*: Born in Narbonese Gaul in 82 BC, died shortly before this poem was written. He wrote an epic on Caesar's campaign of 58 BC. He also wrote an *Argonautica* in the manner of Apollonius and a number of elegies.

50. *Flowed muddily on*: Cf. I. 4. 11.

53. *Accius*: L. Accius (170–c. 85 BC) adapted numerous Greek tragedies to the Roman stage. His flamboyant and rhetorical style lent itself to

parody. For his fragments see *Remains of Old Latin*, vol. 2, in the
Loeb Classical Library.

54. *Ennius*: Q. Ennius (239–169 BC), 'father of Roman poetry'. He
composed in many different forms but was best known for his *Annals*
(an epic on Roman history) and tragedies (adapted from Greek
models).

62. *Cassius*: Unknown.

66. *more polished than the author of a crude verse*: Horace grants that
Lucilius may have been more polished than some early Italian poet
working in a verse-form which, unlike the hexameter, had not been
shaped by the Greeks. He may also have been superior to poets like
Ennius, Pacuvius, and Accius, who did take over Greek verse-forms.
Nevertheless, had he been living in Horace's day he would have been
required to observe stricter standards. For a defence of this interpret-
ation see *Phoenix* 14 (1960) 36–44.

Others (most recently W. Barr in *Rheinisches Museum* 113 (1970)
204–11) think that the 'author' is Lucilius himself. This makes good
sense, but it is hard to extract it from the Latin. Others again (most
recently C. A. van Rooy in *Studies in Classical Satire*, p. 45, note 6)
think that the 'author' is Ennius. This is difficult to accept, because
Ennius is not mentioned elsewhere by Horace as a writer of *saturae*
and because Lucilius is called the *inventor* of the genre in I. 10. 48. Cf.
II. 1. 62–3.

76. *Miss Tree*: Arbuscula was a famous actress mentioned by Cicero, *Att.*
IV. 15. 6.

78. *Carper*: The name Pantilius is found in inscriptions but no doubt
Horace chose it because of its apparent derivation from πᾶν + τίλλειν
– 'to bite at everything'.

79. *Demetrius*: The musician mentioned in v. 90 below.

80. *Fannius*: The poet mentioned in I. 4. 21.
Hermogenes Tigellius: The musician mentioned in I. 3. 129.

81. *Plotius and Varius*: See note on I. 5. 40.

82. *Valgius*: C. Valgius Rufus, an elegiac poet. He became Consul in 12 BC.
Octavius: Octavius Musa, a historian.
Fuscus: See note on I. 9. 61.

83. *the Viscus brothers*: One was mentioned in I. 9. 22.

84. *Pollio*: See note on v. 42.

85. *Messalla*: See note on v. 28.

86. *Bibulus*: L. Calpurnius Bibulus, stepson of Brutus. After Philippi he
supported Antony and served him as a naval commander. Later he
was appointed governor of Syria, where he died in 32 BC. Horace
probably knew him as a student in Athens.
Servius: Usually identified as the son of the famous jurist Servius
Sulpicius Rufus. He may also be the writer of light erotic verse men-
tioned by Ovid in *Tristia* 2. 441.

      Furnius: A distinguished orator who became Consul in 17 BC.

92. *Off with you . . . volume*: Instructions to a slave.

Satire II. 1

4. *Trebatius*: C. Trebatius Testa, a distinguished jurist, recommended to Julius Caesar by Cicero as a legal adviser. He also enjoyed the esteem of Augustus. He was considerably older than Horace.

14. *Gauls*: According to the historian Dio Cassius campaigns against the Gauls took place in 36, 35, and 34 BC and victories were celebrated in the triumph of 29. Heinze, however, thinks that Horace is speaking of the future.

15. *Parthian*: Octavian was in the east in 30 BC and it was expected that he would lead a campaign against the Parthians to avenge the defeat of Crassus in 53 BC. In fact the standards of Crassus were recovered by negotiation in 20 BC.

17. *Scipio*: Scipio Aemilianus Africanus (*c.* 184–129 BC), son of L. Aemilius Paulus, adopted by the son of Scipio Africanus the Elder. He was responsible for the final overthrow of Carthage in 146 BC and for the destruction of Numantia in Spain in 133 BC. In the Spanish campaign he was accompanied by Lucilius.

18. *Floppy*: Horace's cognomen was Flaccus.

22. *Grab-all . . . Nomentanus*: An echo of I. 8. 11.

24. *Milonius*: Unknown.

26. *Castor's . . . of the twin*: Castor and Pollux were sons of Leda by Zeus who visited her in the form of a swan.

47–53. *Cervius points . . . by instinct*: Cervius, an informer, Turius, a crooked judge, Hand (*scaeva* = left hand), a poisoner. Nothing is known about them, but it seems likely that they were real people whose reputation still survived, though they were no longer living.

48. *Canidia*: See note on I. 8. 23.

      Albucius: Unknown and apparently unconnected with his namesake in II. 2. 67.

65. *Laelius*: C. Laelius, close friend of Scipio Aemilianus with whom he served in Africa and Spain. He was nicknamed *Sapiens* for his sagacity, and he enjoyed a high reputation as an orator.

67. *Metellus*: Q. Caecilius Metellus Macedonicus, Consul 143 BC, led campaigns in Macedonia, Greece, and Spain. He was a political opponent of Scipio.

      Lupus: L. Cornelius Lentulus Lupus, Consul 156 BC, Censor 147, and leader of the Senate from 130. He also was an opponent of Scipio.

84. *Caesar*: Octavian, the future Augustus.

Satire II. 2

16. *Falernian*: One of the finest Italian wines, grown in Campania.

      Hymettus: A mountain near Athens famous for its honey.

32.   *the bridges*: The main sewer discharged into the Tiber between the
       Aemilian Bridge and the Sublician Bridge.

33.   *the Tuscan river*: The Tiber rises in Etruria.

41.   *'cook'*: I.e. taint.

47.   *Gallonius*: A glutton attacked by Lucilius. He was a rich auctioneer.

50.   *the Praetor*: Probably the C. Sempronius Rufus who is mentioned
       several times in Cicero's letters (Sempronius no. 79 in Pauly-Wissowa).

56.   *Avidienus*: Called 'the Dog' because he existed on dirty scraps.

64.   *Here's the wolf . . . here's the dog*: Gallonius is the glutton, or wolf:
       Avidienus is the miser, or dog. Both modes of life are to be rejected.

66.   *he will not come to grief in either way*: He will not fall into either
       extravagance or meanness.

67.   *Albucius*: Possibly another Lucilian character. See *SH*, p. 141 and
       pp. 293–4.

68.   *Naevius*: A different type from the Naevius of I. 1 101. Also unknown.

77.   *'problem meal'*: The problem is what delicacy to take first. See Terence,
       Phormio 342.

99.   *Trausius*: Unknown.

115.   *re-assigned*: After Philippi (42 BC) Octavian's ex-servicemen were
       allotted farms in various districts of Italy. The former owners were
       evicted.

Satire II. 3

1.   *asking for parchment*: Poems were composed on tablets and then,
       when finished, were transferred onto parchment.

11–12. *Plato*: Several scholars believe that this is Plato the writer of com-
       edies (writing from *c.* 425–390 BC), because the other men mentioned
       are all poets. But Roman authors say nothing about this Plato, and the
       reader of Horace's day would surely have thought immediately of the
       philosopher. In form, tone, and content the *Satires* have quite a lot in
       common with the *Dialogues*.
             Archilochus: (seventh century BC) Archilochus of Paros was a writer
       of abusive iambic verse. His work served as a model for Horace's
       Epodes, which were being composed at this period, though the *Epodes*
       are much less personal and less directly related to the people and events
       of the day.
             Eupolis: A writer of old comedy. Cf. I. 4. 1.
             Menander: (342–*c.* 290 BC) The most famous representative of the
       Greek new comedy. His plays were adapted for the Roman stage and
       he is frequently mentioned by Roman writers.

17.   *a barber*: Damasippus, like all self-respecting Stoics, had a flowing
       beard.

21.   *Sisyphus*: The mythical founder of Corinth, a city famous for its
       bronzes. His footbath, which is mentioned by Aeschylus, represents a
       much sought after antique.

26. '*Lucre's lad*': Favourite of Mercury, the god of gain.

43. *Chrysippus*: Cf. I. 3. 127. The Porch was the home of Stoicism. See note on Persius 3. 53.

60–62. *he'll pay ... 'Mother, I'm calling you!'*: In the *Iliona* of Pacuvius the ghost of the murdered Deiphilus appeared to his mother Iliona as she slept, reproaching her and asking for burial. Iliona was meant to start from her sleep and reply, but in one celebrated performance Fufius, the actor playing Iliona, was so drunk that he could not be wakened by the appeals of the ghost (played by Catienus), even though the whole audience joined in, chanting '*mater, te appello!*'

68. *Lord of Luck*: Mercury.

69–71. *Write ten of Nerius' I.O.U.s ... tied down*: 'No legal formulae are strong enough to bind a dishonest debtor' (Palmer). The details are obscure and controversial. I have understood *tabulas* with *decem* in v. 69; others understand *sestertia*. Nerius apparently draws up and issues the I.O.U., which is signed by the borrower.

75. *Perellius*: The creditor.

82–3. *hellebore:* A plant produced in the Phocian town of Anticyra in Greece. It was supposed to cure madness by reducing the element of black bile in the system. There were two varieties, but even the milder had extremely violent effects including vomiting, diarrhoea, and convulsions.

84. *Staberius*: Unknown.

86. *Arrius*: Q. Arrius had given a lavish feast at his father's funeral. Cf. Cicero, *In Vatin*. 30ff.

94–8. *The fact is that goodness ... upright*: These lines are an ironical inversion of the Stoic belief that the wise man is whatever he wishes to be, including king. Cf. I. 3. 124.

100. *Aristippus*: Founder of the so-called Cyrenaic school of philosophy, which preached a doctrine of hedonism.

132. *Argos*: A town in the east Peloponnese. It shared with Mycenae in the disasters of the house of Atreus.

161. *Craterus*: A famous physician in Cicero's day, twenty-five years before; used by Horace as a type.

168. *Servius Oppidius*: He and his sons are unknown.

175. *Nomentanus*: The spendthrift.
      Hemlock: (*Cicuta*) The acquisitive man.

182. *waste your money ... and lupines*: The magistrate distributed food to acquire popularity.

185. *Agrippa*: M. Vipsanius Agrippa (64/63–12 BC) was the man largely responsible for Octavian's victories over L. Antonius, Sextus Pompeius, and Mark Antony. As Aedile in 33 BC he used his wealth liberally, thus achieving popularity for himself and for Octavian's cause.

187. *son of Atreus*: Agamemnon. Ajax, when defeated by Odysseus in

his claim for the arms of Achilles, resolved to murder Agamemnon, Menelaus, and Odysseus. He was made mad by Athena and slew a flock of sheep instead. On regaining his senses he committed suicide out of shame. Agamemnon and Menelaus gave orders that his body should be left unburied.

199–201. *making your darling daughter . . . with salt meal*: Agamemnon sacrificed his daughter Iphigenia to Artemis so that the Greek fleet might sail against Troy.

212. *a pompous inscription*: Honorific inscriptions were put on the statues of victorious generals and also in the halls of their houses.

223. *Bellona*: An Italian war goddess, sister of Mars. In Horace's time her rites were accompanied by frenzy and self-mutilation.

239. *Aesop's son*: Aesop, a famous actor and a friend of Cicero. He left a large fortune to his worthless son.

240. *Metella*: Usually identified with Caecilia Metella the wife of P. Cornelius Lentulus Spinther. She had an affair with Cicero's son-in-law, Dolabella. She was gay and dissolute like the other members of her set.

243. *Arrius*: See note on v. 86.

253. *Polemon*: A young Athenian who, on his way home from a party, happened to hear a lecture on temperance given by Xenocrates. He was converted to sobriety and eventually became Head of the Academy (314/13 BC). He died in 270 BC.

255. *leg-bands, pillow and muffler*: The paraphernalia of fops.

260ff. This scene is based on Terence, *Eunuchus* I. 1.

276. *passion is playing with fire*: The Latin is '*ignem gladio scrutare*' – 'poke the fire with a sword'. This is a rendering of the Pythagorean saying πῦρ μαχαίρᾳ μὴ σκαλεύειν – 'Don't poke the fire with a sword.' The Greek meant 'Don't provoke a man of savage temper.' But by '*ignem*' Horace means, of course, the fire of *amor*.

277. *Marius . . . Miss Hellas*: Unknown. Miss Hellas was presumably a freedwoman.

287. *Menenius' flourishing family*: Clearly a family of lunatics, but we do not know why.

303. *Agave*: Mother of Pentheus king of Thebes. When he prohibited the worship of Dionysus, the god had him torn to pieces by Agave and the other maenads. In Euripides' *Bacchae* Agave enters, still in a frenzy, carrying her son's head. Eventually she is brought to realize what she has done.

310. *Turbo*: A small but tough gladiator.

314ff.. *When a mother frog . . . never be as big*: This well-known Aesopic fable is found with certain differences in *Phaedrus* 1.24 and *Babrius* 28.

Satire 11. 4

3.   *the condemned Athenian*: Socrates. Horace uses the periphrasis 'the man accused by Anytus'.

12–14. *the long variety . . . a male yolk*: Aristotle believed that round eggs were male and long eggs female. In this he was opposed by Antigonus of Carystus and (after Horace) by Columella and Pliny. For references see *SH*, p. 301, note 23.

16.   *a watered garden*: Apparently the market-gardens near Rome were irrigated.

24.   *Aufidius*: probably M. Aufidius Lurco who, according to Pliny (*Natural History* X. 20. 45), made a fortune by fattening peacocks about 67 BC.

29.   *white Coan*: White wine from the island of Cos in the Aegean.

32.   *Lucrine cockle*: From the Lucrine lake near Cumae on the coast of Campania.
        Baiae: A fashionable resort on the north-west end of the bay of Naples.

33.   *Circeii*: On the coast of Latium about fifty miles south-east of Rome.
        Misenum: A promontory on the north-west end of the bay of Naples.

34.   *Tarentum*: An old Greek colony inside the heel of Italy.

41.   *Umbrian*: From Umbria, a district in central Italy.

42.   *Laurentian*: From Laurentum, a marshy district between Ardea and Ostia.

44.   *the wings*: I.e. the forelegs.

51.   *Massic wine*: From the Mons Massicus in Campania.

55.   *Surrentine*: From Surrentum (Sorrento) in Campania.

66.   *the brine . . . Byzantine jar*: Pickled fish was imported from Byzantium.

68.   *Corycus*: A mountain on the coast of Cilicia in Asia Minor, north of Cyprus.

69.   *Venafran olive*: From Venafrum in Campania.

70.   *Picenum*: East of the Apennines between Ancona and the river Sangro.

71.   *Venuculan grapes*: Not a local variety. Mentioned by Columella III. 2. 2 and Pliny, *Natural History* XIV. 4. 34.

72.   *Alban*: From the Alban Hills about thirteen miles south-east of Rome.

84.   *Tyrian*: From Tyre on the coast of Phoenicia, which produced an expensive crimson dye from the shellfish called the *murex*.

Satire 11. 5

17.   *be sure to keep outside him*: It was a mark of respect to walk on the outside of one's companion.

20.   *what you spoke of*: I.e. giving the privileged position to a social superior. This line and the next echo *Odyssey* 20. 18. Throughout the poem epic reminiscences are used for satirical effect.

39–41. *'The glowing Dog-star . . . with hoary snow'*: These are quotations from a contemporary epic. In the second the poet's name, Furius, is substituted for Jupiter as the subject of 'bespews'. For Furius see the note on I. 10. 36.

55–6. *a raven ... a minor official*: The legacy-hunter is thought of as a raven because ravens fed on corpses – see Petronius 116. After being a minor magistrate Coranus became a secretary (*scriba*) in the civil service. No doubt there is some topical reference here which is now irrecoverable.

57. *Coranus ... Nasica*: Unknown.

59. *What I say ... come to pass*: This is a claim to precognition, but it can also be read as an absurd tautology.

62–4. *In the days when ... and sea*: An honorific reference to Octavian who had recently won the battle of Actium (31 BC) and who was expected to take reprisals against the Parthians for their victory over Crassus in 53 BC. The formula 'In the days when ...' is a parody of the Delphic oracle.

110. *Proserpine*: Wife of Pluto and queen of Hades.

Satire II. 6

5. *son of Maia*: Mercury, god of luck.

19. *enriches Our Lady of Funerals*: The Latin is '*Libitinae quaestus acerbae*'. The death-goddess Libitina (cf. *Odes* III. 30. 7) had a temple in Rome where funeral equipment was stored and hired.

33. *the mournful Esquiline*: Because it used to be a burial ground. Cf. 1. 8.

35. *the Wall*: The site of the Roman exchange. The Latin word is *puteal*, which meant the wall around the top of a well. This particular wall was erected by Libo and bore his name.

36. *The Department*: The Treasury, in which Horace had been a *scriba*. His exact connection with the Department at this time is not clear.

38. *Maecenas*: In charge of affairs during Octavian's absence in 31 BC.

54. *the Dacians*: Before Actium some of the Dacians, who lived on the Danube, had sided with Antony against Octavian.

55–7. *what about the land ... or Triangleland*: Italians hoped that Octavian (Caesar) would reward his soldiers with grants of land in Sicily (Triangleland).

63. *Pythagoras' kinsmen*: Pythagoras forbade the eating of beans. Several explanations were given for this in antiquity. Horace seems to be referring to the suggestion that beans contained souls and therefore, by the doctrine of transmigration, could be related to human beings.

72. *Grace*: The stage name of a male dancer who is supposed to have been admired by Caesar.

77–8. *Old wives' tales which are yet to the point*: This literal translation seems to be reasonably appropriate. See *SH*, pp. 245–53, and West's article in Woodman and West (1974).
    Arellius: Unknown.

Satire II. 7

3–4. *though not ... die young*: It was a commonplace that 'the good die young'.

December: On the Saturnalia (17–19 December), which marked the end of sowing, the distinction between master and slave was temporarily suspended in memory of the golden age of Saturn when all were free and equal.

8.   *Priscus*: Unknown.

10. *Change his stripe*: Senators had a broad stripe on their tunic, knights a narrow one.

14. *Vertumnus*: An old Italian god of the changing year.

15. *Volanerius*: Unknown.

37. *Mulvius*: Mulvius and the others had expected to dine with Horace.

53–4. *your knight's ring ... Roman clothes*: The knights, who possessed fortunes of 400,000 sesterces or over, wore a gold ring. By 'Roman clothes' Horace means the dress of the free Roman citizen.

66. *to walk deliberately under the yoke*: This signified the loss of one's freedom.

67. *that frenzied master within*: Lust.

77. *the rod*: A slave, when being manumitted before the Praetor, was touched with the *vindicta* or rod.

95. *Pausias*: A fourth-century Greek painter distinguished for his subtle technique and his wanton subjects.

97 8. *Fulvius or Pacideianus or Rutuba*: Famous gladiators; whether they were contemporary or not is uncertain.

Satire II. 8

6–7. *Lucania*: A district in the south of Italy. The soft, warmish wind had given the animal a strong flavour.

9.   *skirret*: A kind of water parsnip.

15. *Caecuban wine*: From Caecubum in southern Latium.

unsalted Chian: Wine from the island of Chios which had not been treated with salt water (a common preservative).

22. *shadows*: Guests who had not been invited in their own right. In this case they were Maecenas' hangers-on.

23. *Nomentanus*: the name typifies someone who has run through his patrimony and now relies on other people to provide him with dinner.

Hogg: The Latin name is Porcius, chosen for its associations with gluttony.

40. *Allifae*: A town in Samnium where earthenware mugs were made.

45. *Venafran oil*: The best kind of olive oil from Venafrum in Campania.

46. *liquamen*: Fish sauce.

50. *Methymnean grape*: From Methymna on the island of Lesbos.

54–6. *As he spoke ... Campanian acres:*. The lines have a mock epic tone.

Boreas: North wind.

86–93. *a huge dish with a crane ... properties*: The male crane, the female goose, and the rumpless pigeons are all, in the host's view, refinements on the normal diet.

95. *Canidia*: The witch who figured in 1. 8.

Epistle 1. 1

3. *foil*: The wooden sword presented to gladiators on retirement.
      school: The gladiatorial school.

5. *Hercules' door*: On the door of Hercules' temple, which, according to Porphyrion, was in Fundi in Latium.
      Veianius: A gladiator.

18. *Aristippus*: A fourth-century philosopher from Cyrene in North Africa, founder of the so-called Cyrenaic school, which preached a doctrine of hedonism.

28. *Lynceus*: One of the Argonauts, gifted with exceptional sight.

34. *words and sayings*: Horace uses language equally applicable to magic, quasi-medical formulas and to philosophy.

55. *Janus' arcade*: The centre of the banking business.

56. (*swinging satchel ... left arm*): Probably spurious; cf. *Satires*, I. 6. 74.

58. *the great four hundred*: (Thousand sesterces.) This was the qualification for membership of the equestrian order.

60. *wall of brass*: An image of security, perhaps referring to 'home' or 'den' in the children's game.

62. *Roscius' law*: In 67 BC the tribune L. Roscius Otho carried a law which reserved the first fourteen rows in the theatre for the knights. Senators sat in the *orchestra*, which was not required for the chorus in Roman times.

64. *Curius*: M'. Curius Dentatus, a hero of the Samnite and Pyrrhic wars in the early part of the third century.
      Camillus: M. Furius Camillus captured the Etruscan outpost of Veii about 396 BC and led the Romans to victory after the Gallic invasion in 387–386.

67. *Pupius*: A tragedian. By acquiring a fortune of 400,000 sesterces one would obtain a seat in the first fourteen rows and so get a closer look at his plays.

84. *Baiae*: A fashionable resort on the Bay of Naples.

86. *sacred signal*: *Auspicium* was a sign indicating the gods' approval. For the rich man his own caprice is sufficient sanction.

87. *Teanum*: An inland town over thirty miles north of Baiae.

102. *guardian*: A *curator* was appointed by the Praetor to look after a lunatic. The general point is that care for one's personal appearance (e.g. *curatus* in v. 94) ought not to be thought more important than care for one's mental and spiritual welfare.

Epistle 1. 2

1. *Lollius Maximus*: From *Epistles* 1. 18 we learn that Lollius served
    under Augustus in Spain (26 and 25 BC). He is now a student of
    rhetoric in Rome, so the epistle belongs to the latter half of that decade.
    Praeneste: The modern Palestrina; a hill resort twenty-three miles
    east-south-east of Rome.

4. *Chrysippus*: (*c*. 280–207 BC). Head of the Stoic school.
    Crantor: (*c*. 340–275 BC). A leading philosopher of the Academy.

9. *Antenor proposes*: In *Iliad* 7. 347ff. he proposes that Helen be returned
    to the Greeks. Paris refuses to agree, but offers money instead.
    (Horace's version of Paris' reply is deliberately prejudiced.)

11. *Nestor is anxious*: In *Iliad* 1. 247ff. Nestor tries to persuade Agamem-
    non, son of Atreus, to return the girl Briseis to Achilles, son of Peleus.
    He also urges Achilles to recognize the superior status of Agamemnon.

23. *Sirens*: See *Odyssey* 12. 39ff.
    Circe: See *Odyssey* 10. 135ff.

28. *Alcinous*: King of Phaeacia: see *Odyssey* 7 and 8.

59. *the tyrants of Sicily*: Phalaris of Acragas (sixth century BC) and Diony-
    sius of Syracuse (*c*. 430–367 BC). Cf. Persius 3. 39–40.

Epistle 1. 3

1. *Julius Florus*: Later the recipient of *Epistles* II. 2; a young aristocrat
    who, according to Porphyrion, wrote satires.

2. *Claudius*: Tiberius Claudius Nero, the elder of Livia's sons and the
    future emperor Tiberius. He was sent to the east by Augustus to place
    Tigranes on the throne of Armenia, which he did in 20 BC.

4. *the straits*: The Hellespont. The towers were at Sestus and Abydos; the
    former in particular was associated with Hero and Leander.

9. *Titius*: Possibly the lyric poet Rufus mentioned by Ovid, *Ex Ponto*
    IV. 16. 28.

10. *tanks and open channels*: The public water supply; hence Greek writers
    who have been frequently imitated.

15. *Celsus*: Albinovanus Celsus, secretary on the staff of Tiberius (see
    Epistles 1. 8).

17. *Palatine temple*: Apollo's temple, celebrating the victory at Actium,
    was dedicated by Augustus in 28 BC. It contained a library of Greek
    and Latin works.

21. *buzzing*: The metaphor of the bee is expounded by D. A. West, *Reading
    Horace* (Edinburgh, 1967), p. 30ff.

31. *Munatius*: Perhaps a son of L. Munatius Plancus addressed in *Odes*
    I. 7.

Epistle 1. 4

1. *Albius*: Probably the poet Albius Tibullus; cf. *Odes* I. 33.
   'conversations': Horace's *Sermones*. The term includes both *Satires* and *Epistles*, but here it refers only to the *Satires*.
2. *Pedum*: An old town between Tibur and Praeneste.
3. *Cassius of Parma*: Like the more famous Cassius Longinus, he was one of the conspirators against Julius Caesar. Having fought on Antony's side at Actium, he was executed by order of Octavian. His pieces (*opuscula*) were probably elegies.
16. *herd*: The word *grex* could be used of a philosophical school as well as of animals. Epicurus, though in fact rather ascetic, was later represented as a voluptuary.

Epistle 1. 5

1. *Archias*: Apparently a maker of unpretentious furniture.
3. *Torquatus*: An aristocrat descended from T. Manlius Torquatus who killed a Gaul in single combat, and later, after a battle against the Latins at Trifanum in 340 BC, had his son executed for disobedience on the battlefield. The severity of this order led to the phrase *imperia Manliana*.
4. *Taurus*: T. Statilius Taurus was Consul for the second time in 26 BC.
5. *Minturnae*: In Latium near the Campanian border, three miles from the sea.
   Petrinum: A mountain.
   Sinuessa: Twelve miles south-east of Minturnae. The area is probably chosen because this was the scene of the battle of Trifanum (see note on v. 3 above).
6. *obey orders*: An allusion to the *imperia Manliana* (see note on v. 3 above).
9. *Moschus*: A rhetorician from Pergamum, unsuccessfully defended by Torquatus on a charge of poisoning and exiled to Marseilles.
   Caesar's birthday: Augustus was born on 23 September 63 BC.
21. *under orders*: see note on v. 3 above.
26–7. *Septicius and Butra . . . Sabinus*: All unknown.
28. *shadows*: (*Umbrae*) men who followed an important figure around and who might accompany him to dinner although not guests in their own right.
29. *the goat*: 'Body-odour', particularly that from the armpits.

Epistle 1. 6

1. *'Never be dazzled'*: The Latin *admirari* here denotes an undesirable disturbance, whether of fear or acquisitiveness, brought about by visual contemplation. The maxim in question was attributed to

Pythagoras and Democritus; similar notions of imperturbability were current among the Stoics and Epicureans.

2. *Numicius*: Unknown.

15–16. *The sensible man . . . proper limit*: The types of behaviour described in vv. 1–14 are all unrestrained. A proper limit must be observed – even (paradoxically) in the pursuit of goodness.

21. *Mute*: (Mutus) unknown.

26. *Agrippa's Porch*: Erected by Augustus' general Agrippa in 25 BC.
    Appian Way: The main road leading south from Rome to Capua and Brundisium.

27. *Numa and Ancus*: The second and fourth kings of Rome; examples of greatness and popularity.

33. *Cibyra*: A town in south Phrygia in Asia Minor.
    Bithynia: A territory on the south-west end of the Black Sea.

39. *Cappadocia's king*: Probably Ariobarzanes III (d. 42 BC), whose desperate financial problems (resulting from Roman exploitation) are mentioned more than once in Cicero's letters. A reference to his successor Archelaus would be more topical, but topicality is not a decisive factor here. (See next note.)

40. *Lucullus*: Campaigned against Mithridates in the east with considerable success between 72 and 69 BC. In his private life he was a by-word for luxury.

45–6. *A house is sadly . . . grow fat on*: This is, of course, ironical.

52. *Fabian . . . Veline*: Two of the thirty-five tribes in which Roman citizens were enrolled.

53. *the rods*: The *fasces*, symbol of the higher magistrates' authority.

53–4. *the chair of ivory*: Occupied by the higher magistrates.

58. *Gargilius*: Unknown, perhaps a figure taken from the satires of Lucilius.

63. *Caere's third-rate townsmen*: According to Livy, the inhabitants of Caere, an old town in south Etruria, were deprived of the franchise as a punishment for a revolt against Rome in the third century. But the facts are obscure. The sense of Horace's phrase is: 'behaving in a way unworthy of a Roman citizen'.

65. *Mimnermus*: An elegiac poet of Colophon, writing in the seventh century BC. Horace is paraphrasing lines which say: 'What is life, what is enjoyable without golden Aphrodite? May I die when such things no longer interest me – secret love, gentle gifts and bed.'

Epistle 1. 7

5–9. *the heat . . . bouts of malaria*: refer to late August and September.

10. *Alban fields*: The slopes of the Alban hills south-east of Rome.

14. *gift*: The Sabine farm.
    Calabria: At this period, the area in the heel of Italy.

28. *Cinara*: A girl mentioned more than once in the *Odes*.

41–3. '*Ithaca's not very good for horses . . . to you*': These words are taken from *Odyssey* 4. 601ff. The son of Atreus is Menelaus.

45. *Tarentum*: A wealthy colony (the modern Taranto) inside the heel of Italy.

46. *Philippus*: There were at least three Philippi whom Roman readers might have identified as Horace's figure; speculation is futile.

48. *Carinae*: A fashionable district on the southern spur of the Esquiline, little more than a quarter of a mile from the Forum.

59. *Park*: The Campus Martius.

94. *guardian spirit*: The Latin *genius*, on which see Rose's note in the *Oxford Classical Dictionary*.

98. *foot-rule*: A measure which is thought of here as varying with the size of the man.

Epistle 1. 8

1. *Celsus*: On the staff of Tiberius. See notes on *Epistles* I. 3. 2 and 15.

16. *drop*: A medical metaphor.

Epistle 1. 9

1. *Claudius*: The future emperor Tiberius.
       Septimius: Also addressed in *Odes* II. 6. See Nisbet-Hubbard.

Epistle 1. 10

1. *Fuscus*: M. Aristius Fuscus: a literary friend. One of the scholiasts (the pseudo-Acron) says he was a school teacher, which would fit v. 45. See also *Satires* I. 9. 61ff. and *Odes* I. 22.

10. *cakes*: Used for sacrifice.

12. *live in accordance with nature*: A Stoic principle.

16. *Dog-star . . . Lion*: The dog-star becomes visible on 26 July; the sun enters Leo on 23 July.

19. *Libyan chippings*: Numidian marble, used in mosaics.

26. *Sidonian purple*: From Sidon, the Phoenician port.

27. *Aquinum*: In Latium on the via Latina, about eighty miles south-east of Rome. It was the home town of the satirist Juvenal.

49. *Vacuna*: A Sabine goddess with an old temple near Horace's farm. The poet may be playing with the etymology *vacare*: to be idle.

Epistle 1. 11

1. *Bullatius*: Unknown.
       Chios and Lesbos: Two large islands off the coast of Asia Minor.

2. *Samos*: Another island, about forty miles south-east of Chios.
       Sardis: Capital of Lydia in Asia Minor, ruled over by Croesus from about 560–546 BC.

3. *Smyrna and Colophon*: Famous cities in the west of Asia Minor.

5. *Attalus*: Attalus III bequeathed his kingdom to Rome in 133 BC. The kingdom included cities like Pergamum, Apollonia, and Ephesus.

6. *Lebedus*: A small coastal town fifteen miles west of Colophon.

7–10. (*You know what Lebedus is . . . fury of Nepture*): Some editors give these lines to Bullatius, but it seems better to regard them as a brief reverie of Horace's, which is corrected in what follows.

8. *Gabii*: Fifteen miles east of Rome.
    Fidenae: Six miles north of Rome. Like Gabii, it was an old town now half deserted.

17. *Mytilene*: Chief city of Lesbos.

30. *Ulubrae*: An insignificant village in the Pomptine marshes south-east of Rome.

Epistle 1. 12

1. *Agrippa*: M. Vipsanius Agrippa (born *c.* 64 BC), Augustus' general and admiral, who in 21 BC was married to the emperor's daughter Julia.

2. *Iccius*: Also addressed in *Odes* I. 29.

12. *Democritus*: Democritus of Abdera in Thrace (*c.* 460–*c.* 370 BC). A man of powerful and wide-ranging intellect, he was one of the pioneers of the atomic theory, which was taken over by Epicurus. This is the kind of story that tends to be associated with philosophers.

20. *Empedocles*: A thinker from Acragas in Sicily, who died *c.* 433 BC at the age of about sixty. He wrote an important work in hexameters *On Nature*. See also *Ars Poetica* 464n.
    Stertinius: A Stoic philosopher; in *Satires* II. 3. 33ff. he is represented as a contemporary of Horace, though perhaps somewhat older.

22. *Pompeius Grosphus*: Addressed in *Odes* II. 16.

26. *Cantabria*: The Cantabri, a tribe in northern Spain, were finally defeated by Agrippa in 19 BC, but Horace may be referring to a campaign of the previous year.
    Armenia: In 20 BC Tiberius installed Tigranes on the throne of Armenia without any opposition, but the episode was represented on coins and elsewhere as a military victory.

27. *Phraates*: King of Parthia; in 20 BC he returned to the Romans the standards which had been captured from Crassus at Carrhae in 53 BC. He was induced to do so by the return of his son, who had been kidnapped by his rival Tiridates five years before. Augustan propaganda made much of this diplomatic success.

28–9. *golden Plenty . . . brimming horn*: The cornucopia figured in numerous works of art as a symbol of abundance. I have translated *defudit* (which implies that the harvest is over) rather than *defundit*.

Epistle 1. 13

1. *Vinnius*: A well-known strong-man called Vinnius Valens was a cen-
turion in Augustus' praetorian guard; note the reference to strength in
v. 10. The recipient's father had the *cognomen* of Asina (Ass). In the
view of McGann (*Classical Quarterly* 13 (1963) 258ff.) the phrase
paternum cognomen (8–9) means that the name Asina belonged only
to Vinnius' father and was not borne by Vinnius himself. Whether or not
this is right, Vinnius himself is described in terms suitable to an ass.

10. *Use your strength ... bog*: The most natural assumption would be
that Augustus was somewhere in Italy rather than in Rome or overseas.
But in view of the comic nature of the epistle one cannot be sure.

14. *Pirria*: According to the pseudo-Acron, Horace is referring to a servant-
girl in a comedy by Titinius, who was writing in the middle of the
second century BC. There is doubt, however, about the form of the
name.

17. *poems*: *Carmina* refers to the first collection of *Odes*, published in
23 BC. M. L. Clarke in *Classical Review* 22 (1972) 157–9, thinks it
means the present collection of *Epistles*, but their send-off comes in
Epistles I. 20.

Epistle 1. 14

3. *Varia*: A town on the Anio (now Vicovaro) two or three miles south
of Horace's farm.

6. *Lamia*: One of the Aelii Lamiae, a distinguished family from Formiae
in south Latium. He may be the man who became Consul in AD 3.
The brother was probably Quintus Aelius Lamia, a commissioner of
the mint in 21 or 20 BC. E. J. Kenney suggests that this brother had
not died but had fallen for a girl (*Illinois Classical Studies* II (1977)
235 ff.). But Horace's language seems too heavy for this.

32. *The man*: Horace himself.

Epistle 1. 15

1. *Vala*: a member of the family Numonius Vala. A Q. Numonius Vala
was a prominent figure in Paestum (about half way between Velia and
Salernum). But we cannot be sure that he was the man in question.
Velia: On the coast of Lucania, about seventy miles south-east of
Naples. It was founded as a Greek colony in the middle of the sixth
century BC.
Salernum: The modern Salerno, twenty-five miles north-west of
Paestum.

3. *Antonius Musa*: A freedman physician who in 23 BC cured Augustus
of an illness by a treatment involving cold baths and cold drinks.

9. *Clusium*: The modern Chiusi, in Etruria about eighty-five miles north-
west of Rome.

Gabii: See *Epistles* I. 11. 8.

12.   *Cumae*: A coastal town just north of Baiae.
      Baiae: A fashionable resort on the north-western end of the Bay of
      Naples.

13.   *the horse's ear's in its bridled mouth*: I.e. shouting is no good; the
      horse will only be guided by the rein.

24.   *Phaeacian*: A member of the carefree and indolent community
      described in *Odyssey* 7 and 8: see especially 8. 248–9.

27.   *Maenius*: A figure satirized by Lucilius.

36.   *Bruty*: For Bestius see note on Persius 6. 38.

Epistle 1. 16

1.   *Quinctius*: A successful young man, perhaps identical with Quinctius
      Hirpinus in *Odes* II. 11.

11.   *Tarentum*: See note on *Epistles* I. 7. 45.

27–9. '*May Jove ... the people's*': The lines are said by the scholiasts to
      come from a panegyric on Augustus by L. Varius Rufus, the friend of
      Horace and Virgil.

49.   *The Sabine*: I.e. Horace himself, but the name also implies old-
      fashioned rustic integrity.

60.   *Laverna*: The patron goddess of thieves and impostors.

74–9. '*Pentheus, lord of Thebes ... I'll die*': These lines are ultimately
      based on Euripides, *Bacchae* 492–8, but the direct ancestor may be
      the Roman Pacuvius' *Pentheus*, written in the second century BC.

79.   *Death is the end of the race*: This is Horace's allegorical interpretation.
      In Euripides the speaker (who, unknown to Pentheus, is the god Dion-
      ysus) means that he will be set free from jail.

Epistle 1. 17

1.   *Gauche*: The Latin name is Scaeva (left hand). The appropriateness of
      the name to the subject would seem to justify this translation. The
      individual himself (if indeed he existed) is unknown.

8.   *Ferentinum*: A lonely town on the via Latina, about forty-five miles
      south-east of Rome.

13.   *Aristippus*: Born *c.* 435 BC in Cyrene in North Africa; he preached a
      doctrine of hedonism. It is a matter of debate whether he or his grandson
      should rightly be thought of as the founder of the Cyrenaic school.

25.   *double rag*: Instead of wearing a tunic underneath, the Cynics doubled
      the cloak. The scholiasts recount that one day, when leaving the baths,
      Aristippus put on Diogenes' cloak, leaving his own crimson one for
      Diogenes. The latter refused to put it on and demanded his own back.
      Aristippus then remonstrated with him for being a poseur: 'You'd
      sooner freeze than be seen in a crimson garment.'

31.   *Miletus*: The most southerly of the great Ionian cities of Asia Minor.
      It was famous for its wool.

36. 'Not every man . . . to Corinth': This is a rendering of a Greek proverb, meaning 'The highest prizes are reserved for the lucky few.' The original context had to do with Lais and other expensive Corinthian courtesans. Here the remark comes from an imaginary objector, who implies that finding favour with the great (as Horace did) is wholly a matter of luck.

38. 'Did he act like a man?': This is the fundamental question.

55–62. he's like the girl . . . raucous chorus: These lines recall the boy who cried 'Wolf!'

60. Osiris: Egyptian cults were familiar at Rome.

Epistle 1. 18

1.   Lollius: See Epistles I. 2. He clearly belonged to a well-to-do family (60–64).

15. how to define a tomato: The equivalent question in Latin was whether a goat's hair could be called wool.

18. A second life: I.e. 'I would not choose to have a second life if it meant surrendering the right to say what I think.'

19. Smart: The Latin name is (probably) Docilis.

20. Appian or the Minucian: The question seems to have been whether the longer but smoother Appian was preferable to the shorter but rougher Minucian. If, as seems probable, the Minucian was the road later known as the via Traiana, that was the route travelled by Maecenas and Horace in the journey described in Satires I. 5. It started from Beneventum and ran north of the via Appia through Canusium and Barium. To judge from Satires I. 5. 95–6 stretches of it were certainly in bad repair at this period.

32. Witt: The knight P. Volumnius, an acquaintance of Antony, Atticus, and Cicero, who was well known for his wit and so given the name Eutrapelus (Witty).

36. a Thracian: A type of gladiator, armed with a scimitar and a small round shield.

41. Amphion and Zethus: Twin brothers, sons of Zeus and Antiope. Amphion was a musician, Zethus a herdsman. Together they built the walls of Thebes, but their different tastes led to a quarrel, which was represented in Euripides' Antiope and Pacuvius' Antiopa.

46. Aetolian: Calydon in Aetolia was the scene of the famous boar-hunt in which Meleager took part. Hence 'Aetolian' is a learned, 'literary' epithet.

55–7. the savage campaigns . . . Italy's empire: Augustus led campaigns against the Cantabri in Spain in 26 and 25 BC. For his recovery of the standards from the Parthians see note on Epistles I. 12. 27.

63. Actian battle: Actium is a promontory of Acarnania in western Greece, scene of the naval battle (31 BC) in which Octavian's fleet defeated those of Antony and Cleopatra.

64. *Victory swoops*: Because she is winged.
82. *Theon*: Unknown.
103. *Digentia*: The modern Licenza, a tributary of the Anio.
104. *Mandela*: A village on a hillside across the Digentia, about two miles from Horace's farm.

Epistle 1. 19

1. *Cratinus*: A fifth-century comic poet, mentioned for his candour along with Aristophanes and Eupolis in *Satires* I. 4. 1. His reputation for drunkenness was fostered by himself in a play called *The Flagon*.
12. *Cato*: M. Porcius Cato (95–46 BC), great-grandson of Cato the Censor (*Satires* I. 2. 32). A genuine but rather ostentatious Stoic.
15. *Iarbitas*: According to the scholiasts he was a Moor, but nothing definite is known about him.
    Timagenes: A rhetorician and historian from Alexandria who was brought to Rome in 55 BC. He knew Augustus but later incurred his displeasure by his criticisms of the imperial family.
24. *Archilochus*: From the island of Paros in the middle of the Aegean. His iambics, written in the seventh century BC, served as a model for Horace's *Epodes*. According to tradition, when Lycambes refused to allow his daughter Neobule to marry Archilochus, the latter wrote a venomous poem accusing Lycambes of perfidy and his daughters of immorality. As a result the girls are supposed to have hanged themselves. Cf. vv. 30–31 below.
28. *Sappho*: Born *c.* 612 BC, she lived and wrote on the island of Lesbos. To judge from the fragments, her lyric poetry can hardly have been a major influence on Horace, but he did take over the form of stanza which she used in her first book. Doubtless the adjective 'manly' refers to her poetry, but there is no point in trying to exclude any allusion to her sexual orientation.
29. *Alcaeus*: Born *c.* 620 BC, also from Lesbos. He was a major influence on Horace both in metre (the Alcaic stanza) and in subject-matter (he wrote about politics as well as about love, wine, and death).
43. *Jupiter's ear*: I.e. the ear of Augustus.
47. *That position's unfair*: The Latin is *displicet iste locus*, which I have interpreted as referring (metaphorically) to a wrestling bout. Others prefer to think of a gladiatorial combat.

Epistle 1. 20

1. *Vertumnus*: A god of change (*verto*) and hence associated with the changing seasons, metamorphoses, and (as here) commercial transactions. He was of Etruscan origin, and his statue stood in the *vicus Tuscus* (cf. *Epistles* II. 1. 269).
    Janus: A temple of Janus stood on the opposite side of the Forum

to that occupied by Vertumnus. Nearby was the Argiletum, a street with numerous bookstalls.

2. *the Sosii's pumice*: Two brothers called Sosius ran a publishing firm and a bookshop (cf. *Ars Poetica* v. 345). Pumice was used both for trimming book-rolls and for removing hair. In an extended double entendre the book is represented as a young slave-boy.

8. *kept very tight*: Tight shut (for the book), tight for money (for the slave).

13. *Utica*: On the coast of North Africa, near Carthage.

      Ilerda: A Spanish town on the Ebro. These names stand for 'the provinces' ('what a come-down'), but at another level they can also stand for 'the empire' ('what glory').

18. *the end of a street*: The Latin is *extremis in vicis*, which many interpret as the outlying quarters of the city. For the whole passage see S. F. Bonner, *American Journal of Philology* 93 (1972) 509–28.

19. *warmer sun*: School started very early in the morning; as the day warmed up, passers-by would stop to listen.

28. *Lollius*: In the year 21 BC M. Lollius was for some time sole Consul, the second place being kept for Augustus. The emperor, however, declined to fill it, and later in the year Q. Aemilius Lepidus was declared Lollius' colleague (*dixit*). Horace was born on 8 December 65 BC.

Epistle 11. 1

5. *Liber*: Bacchus.

10. *He who crushed*: Hercules.

24. *the criminal code*: The twelve tables, drawn up by the Decemvirs in 450 BC.

      regal treaties: Made by Tarquinius Superbus with Gabii (late sixth century) and by Tullus Hostilius with the Sabines (mid seventh century).

31. *a nut hasn't a shell … olive*: I.e. faulty comparisons lead to absurd conclusions. The same point is made in vv. 32–3.

47. *'the dwindling pile'*: see note on Persius 6. 80.

49. *our Lady of Funerals*: Libitina; cf. *Satires* II. 6. 19.

51–2. *no longer trouble … Pythagorean visions*: For Ennius' dream see notes on Persius *Prologue* 2 and *Satires* 6.10–11.

53. *Naevius*: See introduction pp. x–xi.

55. *Pacuvius*: (219–129 BC) Nephew of Ennius, wrote tragedies on Greek models.

56. *Accius*: (170–*c.* 85 BC) See note on *Satires* I. 10. 53.

57. *Menander*: (342–*c.* 290 BC) The most famous representative of Greek New Comedy.

      Afranius: Born *c.* 150 BC; wrote *togatae*, i.e. comedies based on Italian customs and characters, as distinct from *palliatae*, i.e. comedies with a Greek setting, like those of Plautus and Terence.

58. *Epicharmus*: A Sicilian, writing in the first quarter of the fifth century BC. He seems to have been fond of mythological burlesque.

  Plautus: Born in Umbria, died some time after 184 BC. He was popular and productive, writing over twenty comedies. Horace, with his classical point of view, was rather unfair to Plautus; see vv. 171–6.

59. *Caecilius*: Came to Rome as a prisoner from northern Italy; died in 168 BC. His comedies, of which only fragments survive, were admired for their plots and emotional power.

  Terence: From North Africa, died not long after 160 BC. He was more refined, yet also more realistic than the exuberant Plautus.

62. *Livius*: Livius Andronicus from Tarentum wrote comedies, tragedies, and a translation of the *Odyssey* in the second half of the third century BC.

71. *Orbilius*: From Beneventum, taught in Rome from 63 BC. He was then fifty years of age. He lived to be a hundred and was honoured with a statue in his home town.

79. *Atta*: Died 77 BC. Composer of *togatae*, of which eleven titles survive.

80. *flowers and saffron*: The stage was sprinkled with essence of saffron; there is no other reference to flowers.

82. *Aesopus*: A tragic actor in the first half of the first century BC.

  Roscius: A popular and wealthy actor who was particularly effective in comedy; he died about 63 BC.

86. *Numa's Salian Hymn*: Pompilius Numa, second king of Rome, was renowned for his piety. He is supposed to have instituted the Salii, or priests of Mars. By the end of the first century BC their hymns were barely intelligible even to the priests themselves.

91. *what would now be old*: I.e. works which conventional Romans admired as old were once new to the Greeks.

93. *Greece abandoned war*: After her victories over the Persians in the first part of the fifth century.

107. *But what likes . . . change*: This line comes after v. 100 in the manuscripts. Lachmann, however, put it here, and many editors agree that this is an improvement.

112. *Parthian liar*: Since the disaster at Carrhae (53 BC) the Parthians had been a source of anxiety to Rome. But there is no evidence that they were more often guilty of treachery than the Romans themselves.

132–3. *Where would innocent . . . a poet*: A playful allusion to Horace's *Carmen Saeculare* (17 BC).

143. *Silvanus*: The Roman god of uncultivated land, who had to be placated when inroads were made into his domain.

144. *Genius*: The spirit which watched over a man's life and was coextensive with it; cf. *Epistles* II. 2. 187–9.

145. *Fescennines*: Ribald songs sung at country festivals of marriage and harvest.

152. *a law*: There was a law against defamation in the twelve tables.

158. *metre of Saturn*: The saturnian was an early type of Latin verse, used by Livius Andronicus and by Naevius.

163. *Aeschylus*: (525/4–456 BC) His first victory was in 484 BC. The *Oresteia* was produced in 458.

    Thespis: Took the first step in turning choral lyric into tragic drama. He won the prize at Athens *c*. 534 BC.

    Sophocles: (*c*. 496–406 BC) His best-known tragedies are *Antigone* and *Oedipus Tyrannus*.

193. *Corinth*: Captured and looted in 146 BC.

194. *Democritus*: See note on *Epistles* I. 12. 12. He was known as the laughing philosopher, no doubt because he wrote a treatise 'On Cheerfulness'.

200. *deaf ass*: This combines two traditional ideas of futility: talking to a deaf person, and talking to an ass.

202. *Gargan forest*: Garganus was a mountainous promontory on the coast of north-east Apulia.

    Tuscan Sea: Off the west coast of Italy.

217. *gift so worthy of Phoebus*: The library in the temple of Apollo on the Palatine, which was dedicated by Augustus in 28 BC.

233. *Choerilus*: An epic poet from Iasos in Caria, who attached himself to Alexander. Horace misrepresents the story, if we may judge from the pseudo-Acron, who says that Alexander gave Choerilus a gold piece for every good line. The poet received only seven pieces in all.

239. *Apelles*: A famous painter of the fourth century BC. His works included a portrait of Alexander holding a thunderbolt.

240. *Lysippus*: A celebrated sculptor from Sicyon; most of his works fell within the latter half of the fourth century BC.

244. *Boeotian climate*: The proverbial stupidity of the Boeotians was attributed to the heavy air of their valleys and lake basins.

250. *talks*: Horace's *Sermones*, which in the main avoided the grand style.

255. *Janus*: His temple was closed three times in the reign of Augustus. This was a ritual signifying peace.

256. *the Parthian*: See note on *Epistles* I. 12. 27.

262–3. *a thing that causes merriment . . . approval*: One doesn't wish to be celebrated by a poet whose lines are memorably ridiculous.

268. *closed box*: A box containing the book; also a coffin. As great poets ensure survival, bad poets ensure extinction.

269. *the street that deals in . . . incense*: The *vicus Tuscus* (Etruscan Street) with a pun on *tus* (incense).

Epistle II. 2

1. *Florus*: See *Epistles* I.3. 1–2.

26. *Lucullus*: See note on *Epistles* I. 6. 40.

30. *the king*: Mithradates of Pontus or Tigranes of Armenia; they made

an alliance against Rome and were engaged by Lucullus in the third
Mithradatic war.

42. *harm was done ... wrath of Achilles*: A reference to the opening of
the *Iliad*. Achilles harmed the Greeks by withdrawing from battle as a
protest against the removal of Briseis by Agamemnon.

43. *Athens the good*: I have translated *bonae Athenae* as 'Athens the good'
in view of its connection with moral philosophy; others take *bonae* as
'kind' or 'dear'.

45. *the Academy*: The school established by Plato *c.* 385 BC in a park
(named after the hero Academus) in the outskirts of Athens. To search
for truth *inter silvas Academi* has a hint of humorous self-depreciation.

47–8. *the raw recruit*: Horace served as a tribune in the army of Brutus.

49. *Philippi*: In east Macedonia; site of the battle (42 BC) between the
forces of Antony and Octavian and those of Brutus and Cassius.

53. *hemlock*: Used as a drug to reduce fever.

60. *Bion*: (*c.* 325–*c.* 255 BC) From Borysthenes north-west of the Black
Sea. He was an important figure in the development of the popular
sermon or 'diatribe'. In Horace's work the diatribe is represented by
the *Satires*, iambics by the *Epodes* and lyric by the *Odes*.

69. *Quirinal ... Aventine*: Two of the seven hills on which Rome was
built.

80. *narrow path*: This was recommended by Callimachus and his suc-
cessors as against the broad highway.

81–6. *The soul ... the lyre*: The sequence of thought seems to be: even in
Athens, with its favourable conditions, dedicated souls fail to get
anything done and make themselves ridiculous; so (*a fortiori*) why
should I try to compose in Rome?

89. *'Gracchus'*: Of the two Gracchi, Tiberius (d. 133 BC) and Gaius
(d. 122 BC), the latter was the more famous orator.
   'Mucius': there were three distinguished lawyers called Mucius
Scaevola: Publius (Consul 133 BC), Quintus (Consul 117 BC), and
Quintus (Consul 95 BC). Horace was probably thinking of the first,
who was a contemporary of the Gracchi.

94. *temple*: A reference to the library in the temple of Apollo; the Greek
spaces were already well stocked.

97. *Samnites*: Gladiators whose combats were protracted because of their
heavy armour.

99. *'Alcaeus'*: See note on *Epistles* I. 19. 29.

100. *'Callimachus'*: (*c.* 305–*c.* 240 BC) A scholar-poet from Cyrene who
made his career in Alexandria. His theory of poetry (and his practice),
which represented a reaction against the long epic, had a strong influ-
ence in Rome, not least upon writers of elegy. As Propertius spoke of
himself as the Roman Callimachus (IV.1.64) Horace may well be
glancing at him.

101. *'Mimnermus'*: See note on *Epistles* I. 6. 5. Propertius (I. 9. 11) said

that in matters of love a line of Mimnermus had more power than the whole of Homer.

110. *Censor*: This magistrate had the power to remove from the senate any members who had proved unworthy of their position.

114. *Vesta's temple*: As this represented the hearth of the state, Horace seems to be speaking of words which claim to have a legitimate status in the poetic language of Rome. To explain the metaphor more precisely we would need further evidence.

117. *Cato*: The Censor, who was Consul in 195 BC.
Cethegus: M. Cornelius Cethegus was Consul in 204 BC.

158. *bronze and balance*: The jurist Gaius (1. 119) describes the symbolic act of conveying property (*mancipatio*) whereby one of five witnesses held a balance and the purchaser touched it with a coin of bronze, which he then handed to the vendor.

159. *use*: Property could also be acquired by *usucapio*, i.e. possession for a certain period.

160. *Orbius*: Unknown. Horace is now drawing on another sense of 'use', viz. 'benefit', as if having the benefit of a piece of property was as good as owning it.

167. *Aricia*: Fifteen miles south-east of Rome.
Veii: Ten miles north-west of Rome.

172. *as if anything were 'ours'*: Having read 160ff. one might want to point out that after enjoying the benefit of a farm (and paying rent) for fifty years, the tenant would still not end up as the owner. Horace answers by saying, in effect, 'So what? Eventually the owner himself ends up dead.'

177–8. *Lucanian . . . Calabria*: Lucania and Calabria are large areas in the south of Italy.

179. *Orcus*: God of the underworld.

184. *Herod*: Herod the Great, who reigned in Judaea from 39–4 BC, had famous groves of date-palms near Jericho.

188. *mortal god*: The Genius is the divine projection of the man's self. It shares his fortune and characteristics, and does not survive his death.

209. *Thessalian*: Thessaly in northern Greece was remote and backward, hence mysterious.

The Ars Poetica

6. *Pisos*: According to Porphyrion, these were L. Calpurnius Piso (Consul 15 BC) and his sons. No sons have been certainly identified but see pp. 19–21 of my commentary.

50. *Cethegi*: An old patrician family.

55. *Caecilius and Plautus*: See notes on *Epistles* II. 1. 58–9.

60a. *and others . . . place*: The words in italics are supplied by conjecture.

64. *Neptune welcomed ashore*: I.e. the construction of a harbour.

79. *Archilochus*: See note on *Epistles* I. 19. 24.

80. *sock and the stately buskin*: Comedy and tragedy, as represented by their footwear. The 'sock' was a kind of slipper.

90. *Thyestes' banquet*: See note on Persius 5. 8.

94. *Chremes*: The angry father was a stock figure in New Comedy; the Chremes of Terence's *Heautontimorumenos* was not the only character of that name.

96. *Peleus*: Experienced many troubles (including exile on two occasions) before marrying Thetis and becoming the father of Achilles.

   Telephus: Son of Hercules, went to Achilles in a pitiful condition begging him to heal the wound which he had inflicted.

118. *Colchian*: A fierce barbarian from the region east of the Black Sea.

   Assyrian: A soft, effeminate type, representing oriental luxury.

120. *dishonoured*: The text *honoratum* ('honoured') gives the wrong sense. I have translated Nisbet's conjecture *inornatum* ('deprived of honour'); cf. *Odes* IV. 9. 31.

123. *Medea*: The princess from Colchis who protected Jason but was later abandoned by him and took a terrible revenge. The most famous treatment of the story is that of Euripides.

   Ino: Another tragic heroine, but of a more pathetic kind than the fierce Medea. She was driven mad by Hera for nursing the infant Dionysus.

124. *Ixion*: Murdered Eioneus having promised him a generous sum for the hand of his daughter. He was purified by Zeus, but repaid him by attempting to violate Hera.

   Io: Loved by Zeus and then turned into a heifer. After many wanderings she reached Egypt, where she was restored to human shape.

   Orestes: Murdered his mother Clytemnestra to avenge the death of his father Agamemnon.

136. *cyclic poet*: The epic cycle was a collection of post-Homeric epics artificially arranged in a series so as to run from the creation of the world to the end of the heroic age. The particular poet referred to by Horace has not been identified.

137–8. *Of Priam's fate . . . promise*: A paraphrase of the opening of the *Odyssey*.

145. *the cannibal king . . . Charybdis*: The figures mentioned come from *Odyssey* 10. 100f., 9. 187f., and 12. 81f.

146. *Diomedes' return*: I.e. some cyclic poet began his account of Diomedes' return from Troy with the death of the hero's great-uncle Meleager. Homer does not waste time on such tedious preliminaries.

172. *he puts things . . . the future*: A difficult and controversial line. Following Bentley, I have adopted *spe lentus* instead of *spe longus*, and *pavidus futuri* instead of *avidus futuri*. The reading *avidus futuri* would mean 'longs for the future'. Even if it is true that the typical old man is eager for the future (which I doubt), Horace would hardly have used the dynamic *avidus* along with *iners* (listless).

186. *Atreus*: Murdered the sons of his brother Thyestes and served them to their father at dinner.

187. *Procne*: Served her son Itys to her husband Tereus in revenge for Tereus' rape and mutilation of her sister Philomela. When pursued by Tereus, Procne changed into a nightingale (or a swallow).

    Cadmus: The founder of Thebes, eventually went to Illyria with his wife Harmonia, where they were both turned into large but harmless snakes.

220. *he-goat*: Horace is alluding to the derivation of tragedy from *tragos*, the Greek for he-goat.

221. *satyrs*: A reference to the origin of satyric drama.

237-8. *Davus . . . Pythias . . . Simo*: Comic characters; the first a slave, the second a slave-girl, and the third an old man.

239. *Silenus*: The teacher and guardian of Bacchus, seen here as a dignified figure.

253. *trimeters*: An iambic metron consisted of two feet; hence a trimeter had six.

254. *At a time in the past*: Glosses over an unsolved crux.

259. *noble*: Not in Horace's judgment, but in that of Accius' admirers. For Accius, see note on *Satires* I. 10. 53.

270. *Plautus*: See note on *Epistles* II. 1. 58.

275. *Thespis*: See note on *Epistles* II. 1. 163.

278. *Aeschylus*: See note on *Epistles* II. 1. 163.

281. *Old Comedy*: Its three main representatives are named in *Satires* I. 4. 1.

292. *Children of Numa*: The Calpurnius Piso family claimed to trace its descent from King Numa.

293. *stilus*: The blunt end of the stilus was used as an eraser.

295. *Democritus holds*: Probably in his book on poetry.

    talent: *Ingenium*.

296. *technique*: *Ars*.

300. *Licinus*: Unknown.

301. *three Anticyras*: Anticyra in Phocis on the Gulf of Corinth produced hellebore, which was used in the treatment of madness. Three Anticyras, therefore, meant something like 'three times the output of Anticyra'.

309. *Moral sense*: *Sapere*.

310. *Socrates' school*: A vague phrase denoting 'writers on moral philosophy'.

343. *wholesome and sweet*: *Utile* and *dulce*.

349. *[when you want . . . a treble]*: This line is probably spurious. The fault it describes is not a minor one, and there is a difficulty over the word *persaepe*. See Brink's note.

357. *Choerilus*: See note on *Epistles* II. 1. 233.

370. *Messalla*: See note on *Satires* I. 10. 28.

371. *Aulus Cascellius*: Born *c.* 104 BC. He may not have been still alive, but his reputation survived.

375. *Sardinian honey*: This was bitter.

387. *Tarpa*: See note on *Satires* I. 10. 38.

388. *the ninth year*: Probably an allusion to Cinna's *Zmyrna*, which according to Catullus 95 finally saw the light in the ninth year.

392. *Orpheus*: The moral progress brought about by Orpheus is ascribed to his poetry.

394. *Amphion*: See note on *Epistles* I. 18. 42.

401. *Tyrtaeus*: A Spartan elegiac poet of the seventh century BC.

404. *Pierian*: The district of Pieria in Thessaly was associated with the Muses.

405. *a king's favour*: Simonides, Pindar, and Bacchylides sought the patronage of rulers in fifth-century Sicily.

414–15. *Delphi*: There were musical competitions at the Pythian games.

437. *fox's hidden malice*: In Aesop's fable the crow, congratulated on his singing by the cunning fox, drops the piece of cheese.

438. *Quintilius*: Quintilius Varus of Cremona, the friend of Horace and Virgil, died in 24/23 BC. See *Odes* I. 24.

454. *lunar goddess*: Diana; cf. 'lunacy'.

464–6. *how Empedocles ... the first time*: Empedocles associated cold blood with dullness, which is apparently why Horace calls him *frigidus*, an adjective which could be used in a literary context. See also *Epistles* I. 12. 20n.

472. *a gruesome place*: A place struck by lightning was fenced off and consecrated. Cf. Persius 2. 26.

PERSIUS

Prologue

1. *cart-horse spring*: A deflationary translation of the Greek Hippocrene, the name given to the spring of the Muses on Mount Helicon. It was produced by a kick from Pegasus.

2. *dreamed*: Hesiod (*Theogony* 22ff.) tells how the Muses appeared to him on Mount Helicon and inspired him to write poetry. In the third century BC the Alexandrian poet Callimachus told in his *Aetia* (Origins) how he had been transported in a dream to Mount Helicon where he too had been instructed by the Muses. Ennius (239–169 BC), the father of Roman poetry, related in the introduction to his *Annals* how he had gone to the mountain of the Muses. Falling asleep there he dreamed that Homer's ghost expounded the doctrine of transmigration and told him that he now possessed Homer's soul. In the late twenties Propertius says (III. 30) that he dreamed he was on Mount Helicon contemplating a poem on Roman history when Apollo appeared to him and advised him to sing about love. It is not clear why Persius mentions Parnassus instead of Helicon. Perhaps he found it in another

Greek poet or perhaps he used it for metrical convenience. The alter-
ation does not appear to provide any additional satirical effect. For
discussion of these questions see J. H. Waszink, *Mnemosyne* 15 (1962),
113–32, O. Skutsch, *Studia Enniana* (London, 1968), 124–9, and
Ennius' *Annals* (Oxford 1986) 147–50.

4. *Pale Pirene*: A spring at Corinth, sacred to the Muses, where Bellero-
phon succeeded in catching Pegasus. Persius implies that the pallor
conventionally attributed to poets came from drinking the waters of
Pirene.

  Helicon's Maids: The Muses.

5–6. *whose portraits are entwined . . . ivy*: Established poets whose busts
were to be seen in the public libraries.

7. *a semi-clansman*: As a satirist Persius feels that he does not wholly
belong to the company of poets. Cf. Horace, *Satires* I. 4. 39ff.

  bardic rites: The Latin is *sacra*. Cf. Ovid, *Ex Ponto* III. 4. 67 and
IV. 8. 81. Writing poetry is seen as a celebration of the Muses.

14. *Pegasus' nectar-flow*: See n. 1 above.

Persius 1

4–5. *Are you worried . . . What the hell*: The sense is: 'the Roman reader
will prefer Labeo to me, but it would be foolish to worry about
such a thing.' Attius Labeo was a contemporary who had produced a
popular translation of Homer.

  'Polydamas and the Trojan ladies': An allusion to the *Iliad* 22. 100
and 105, where Hector fears the reproach of Polydamas and the Trojan
ladies. Here there is the further implication that the Roman aristocracy
is effeminate – an idea developed in vv. 19ff.

8. *Is there anyone in Rome who hasn't –*: The sense is completed in
v. 121, which says that every man Jack has an ass's ears.

19. *The mighty sons of Rome*: The Latin is *'ingentis . . . Titos'*. The Tities,
along with the Ramnes and Luceres, made up the three tribes of early
Rome. Their descendants get a perverted thrill from a recitation of
sentimental poetry.

22–3. *You old fraud . . . 'Whoa there!'*: These are difficult lines. I take the
'ears' in v. 23 as standing for the audience. This audience will puff up
the poet with praise until he is on the point of bursting. For a defence
of this view see *Classical Review* 20 (1970) 282–5. Others accept
Madvig's conjecture, *'articulis'* (joints) for the manuscripts' *'auriculis'*
(ears), translating 'are you, at your age, collecting titbits for other
people's ears – titbits to which you will have to say "no" wrecked as
you are in your joints and flesh' – i.e. disabled by gout and dropsy.

24. *frothy yeast . . . fig-tree*: The yeast and fig-tree represent the feelings
which burst out of the poet's heart. Actually Persius speaks of the liver
(*iecur*), which was often regarded as the seat of strong emotion.

34. *Phyllis*: A Thracian princess who hanged herself after being deserted

by Demophon the son of Theseus. See Ovid, *Heroides* 2 and the notes on p. 289 of Palmer's edition.

Hypsipyle: A princess of Lemnos who saved her father when all the other men on the island were killed. She bore Jason two sons, was captured by pirates, and sold into slavery. She figured in tragedy (Euripides) and romantic epic (Apollonius, Statius, and Valerius Flaccus). See also Ovid, *Heroides* 6.

42. *cedar oil*: This was used to preserve books.

43. *mackerel . . . incense*: Pages from unwanted books were used for cooking fish and wrapping incense. See Catullus 95. 8 and Horace, *Epistles* II. 2. 269.

50. *Attius' Iliad*: See note on vv. 4–5 above.

51. *hellebore*: According to Pliny hellebore was taken not only as a cure for madness but also to clear the heads of students.

53. *citrus*: An African tree with fragrant wood; used for high quality furniture.

56. *airy doodler*: The rich man produces trifles of no weight, in spite of his corpulence.

58–60. *Janus . . . Apulia*: The god Janus had two faces and could therefore see behind him. The stork's bill was imitated by bringing the fingers into sharp contact with the thumb. It was a rude gesture, like the ass's ears and the protruding tongue. The dog-star Sirius rises at the end of July. Apulia, a district in southern Italy, is mentioned here because of Horace, *Epodes* 3. 15–16: 'nor was so great a heat ever cast by the stars on thirsty Apulia.'

65. *the critical nail*: The fingernail was used to test the tightness and smoothness of a carpenter's joint.

66. *a cord*: To mark a straight line the workman would rub chalk on a cord, stretch it along the required line, pull it away from the surface and then let it snap back.

68. *the royal way of life . . . dinners*: The Latin is '*in mores, in luxum, in prandia regum/dicere*'. This could mean 'to attack the behaviour, the luxury, and the dinners of grandees', and it is often taken in that way. Yet it hardly seems in character for the poetaster to denounce vice, whereas feasts like those of Thyestes and Tereus were a common theme, suited to impassioned rhetoric. Cf. 5. 8.

72. *Pales' holiday*: The rustic festival of Pales, reputedly the anniversary of Rome's foundation, took place on 21 April. One feature of the purificatory ritual was jumping through the flames of a bonfire. See J. G. Frazer on Ovid, *Fasti* 4. 785.

73–5. *Quintius*: I.e. Quintius Cincinnatus. Livy 3. 26 tells how in 458 BC the Roman Senate appointed Cincinnatus Dictator to save the city from the Sabines. The official messengers found him at the plough. After his wife had fetched his toga from their cottage, the officials hailed him as Dictator and summoned him to take charge of the army.

The *lictor* was a magistrate's attendant with various police duties; hence I have translated the word by 'sergeant'.

76–8. *Nowadays one man . . . by woe*: Some scholars print vv. 76 and 78 as questions and give them to Persius' adversary. This would imply that Persius was lamenting the neglect of Accius and Pacuvius. But Roman tragedy is satirized by Lucilius and Horace, and by Persius elsewhere (see 5. 7ff.). And so it would be odd if he were defending it here. See Introduction, p. xxviii.

Accius: (170–c. 85 BC) A writer who adapted numerous Greek tragedies to the Roman stage. He is called 'the old Bacchanal' because tragedy arose in connection with the worship of Bacchus.

Pacuvius: Another early tragedian (220–c. 130 BC), nephew of Ennius. One of his plays concerned Antiopa, a Boeotian princess who was made pregnant by Jupiter. She escaped from her angry father but was caught and thrown into a dungeon by her uncle. Persius is apparently quoting from the play. See *Remains of Old Latin*, vol. 2, pp. 158–71.

85. *Pedius*: Pedius Blaesus was prosecuted for corruption in AD 59 (Tacitus, *Annals* 14. 18). Persius probably chose his name rather than that of another criminal because of Horace I. 10. 28, where Pedius Publicola is mentioned as speaking in court. Admittedly Publicola is a defence counsel, not a defendant. But Persius' reminiscences are often imprecise. The point about Pedius' style is also probably due to the Horatian passage, for there Horace is recommending the use of direct simple Latin unmixed with Greek. Therefore we are not entitled to infer that Pedius Blaesus defended himself in the manner satirized by Persius.

87. *is Romulus wagging his tail?*: I.e. is Rome guilty of perversion?

93–5. *'Berecyntian Attis . . . arms and the man'*: These passages illustrate certain objectionable features of contemporary poetry, but we cannot always be sure of what they are.

Berecyntian Attis: According to Ovid's version of the myth (*Fasti* 4. 221–44) Attis, a Phrygian boy, was loved by the goddess Cybele. She imposed a vow of chastity on him which he broke by making love to a nymph. Cybele killed the nymph, and Attis castrated himself in a frenzy of grief and remorse. The tale itself was morbid, romantic, and unRoman. The adjective *Berecyntius*, referring to Mount Berecyntus in Phrygia which was sacred to Cybele, was a pedantic flourish. It contained the Greek y, which sounded sweet and exotic to Roman ears. (It was pronounced like the French u.) Finally a five-syllable word of that metrical pattern in that position in the line was in Persius' view an affectation. The only other example in his work is the sarcastic *'hyacinthina'* (another Greek word) in 1. 32. He would not have approved of Ovid's *'Cybeleius Attis'* (*Metamorphoses* 10. 104) or his *'Berecyntius heros'* (*ibid.* 11. 106).

The dolphin: The word is *delphin*, a later form of the Greek nominative *delphis*.

Nereus: A sea-god, here used for the sea – a device found in elegy (Tibullus) and silver epic (Valerius Flaccus). The metonymy, itself rather 'poetic', becomes grotesque when Nereus is sliced by a dolphin.

Apennines: Persius objects to the practice, which was popular among the neoterics, of ending the hexameter with a word of four long syllables like '*Appennino*'. Quintilian, who cites this very example, calls the practice 'over-effeminate' (*praemolle*) – see his *Institutio Oratoria* IX. 4. 65. The affectation, however, is hardly confined to the last word. If the context was similar to that of Ovid, *Heroides* 16. 107–12, where a ship is built with timber taken from the mountains of the Troad, and if the long range of the Apennines is thought of as a *dorsum* or spine as in Suetonius, *Julius Caesar* 44 ('*per Appennini dorsum*'), then the conceit of stealing a rib would be sufficiently silly. I should make it clear that this is only a hypothesis and that Persius simply says 'the long Apennines'. But one has to have *some* working hypothesis about the line's context.

96. '*Arms and the man*': The opening words of the *Aeneid*.

98. *limp-held wrist*: A drooping posture was also an effeminate affectation. Cf. Quintilian I. 11. 9.

99–102. '*They filled their frightening horns . . . restorative Echo*': A description of the female devotees of Bacchus. The scene is outlandish and emotional; the sound self-consciously musical; the vocabulary markedly Greek in colouring (*Mimalloneis* – 'Bacchanalian', *bombis* – 'boomings', *Bassaris* – 'Bassarid', *lyncem* – 'lynx', *Maenas* – 'Maenad', *corymbis* – 'ivy', *euhion* – 'euhoe!', *echo* – 'echo').

106. *pummel the back-rest . . . bitten nails*: Pummelling the back of one's couch and biting one's nails are signs that writing poetry is hard and exasperating work.

109–10. *the rolling r . . . dog*: R was called the dog letter because it sounded like a growl. See Lucilius 3–4 (Warmington). Some scholars (most recently W. S. Anderson in *Classical Quarterly* 52, 1958) take the view that the growl is attributed to satire, not to the baronial porches.

112–14. *You erect a notice . . . else to piss*: Persius compares the objects of his satire to monuments which one is forbidden to deface. The snakes are the guardian spirits of the place. Several inscriptions similar to the notice described by Persius are cited by Villeneuve in his edition. One, from the Golden House of Nero, also contains two snakes.

115. *Lupus*: L. Cornelius Lentulus Lupus, Consul in 156 BC, Censor in 147, and Leader of the Senate from 130.

Mucius: Q. Mucius Scaevola, Consul 117 BC. Both these men were opponents of Scipio Aemilianus. See the index of A. E. Astin, *Scipio Aemilianus*, Oxford, 1967.

116–18. *While his friend . . . well-blown nose*: Horace rarely goes in for playful banter at the expense of his friends. Persius seems to mean that Horace's satirical strokes make his friends laugh, and then too late they realize that they themselves have the faults in question.

119–21. *Am I forbidden . . . AN ASS'S EARS*: King Midas, a legendary king of Phrygia, judged that Pan was superior to Apollo in a music contest; so Apollo gave him ass's ears. He managed to conceal these from everyone except his barber. The latter, bursting with the secret, whispered it into a hole in the ground, but the reeds heard it and repeated it when the wind blew. For this, and for the story of the golden touch, see Ovid, *Metamorphoses* 11. 90ff. See also Introduction, p. xxix.

123–4. *Cratinus . . . Eupolis, and the Grand Old Man*: (I.e. Aristophanes) The chief representatives of fifth-century Athenian comedy. Cf. Horace, *Satires* I. 4. 1.

127. *Greek-style sandals*: The idea that Greek sandals are something which calls for comment is found in Cicero, *Rab. Post.* 27, Livy 29. 19. 12, and Suetonius, *Tiberius* 13. Here the man who scoffs at Greek sandals represents a provincial mentality.

128. *'Hey one-eye!'*: The man who shouts this insult is geographically as well as intellectually provincial – he is an Aedile of Arretium. But even as he framed the description Persius was thinking of the man's Horatian counterpart, whose name was Aufidius Luscus – Mr One-eye, (*Satires* I. 5. 34–6). Therefore the choice of this particular insult appears to be due to an association of ideas.

132. *abacus*: Here an object like a tray covered with sand.

  Nones-girl: Plutarch (*Camillus* 33) tells how on the Nones of July (7 July) serving-girls, elaborately decked out, would go around chaffing and joking with the men they met. This was part of a festival known as the *Nonae Caprotinae*, i.e. 'the Nones of the wild fig-tree'. For a brief account of this fertility rite see H. J. Rose, *Religion in Greece and Rome*, Harper Torchbooks, 1959, pp. 217–18. An exhaustive treatment is given by S. Weinstock (under *Nonae Caprotinae*) in Pauly-Wissowa XVII. 1. 849–59. This explanation of *nonaria* was first given, I believe, by F. Morice in *Classical Review* 4 (1890) 230. It seems more convincing than the scholiast's view, which is that *nonaria* is a prostitute who plies her trade from the ninth hour.

134. *Calliroë*: The heroine of some popular work, possibly one like Chariton's novel but more likely something in Latin in view of the character's hostility to things Greek.

Persius 2

1. *Macrinus*: An older contemporary who studied in the house of Servilius Nonianus. See O. Jahn's commentary (1843) xxxvii–viii.

14. *'That's his third wife . . . burying'*: I.e. 'some people have all the luck.'

The husband would expect a legacy, and so wishes for the death of his wife.

17–23. *Well now ... 'Good God!'*: The sense is 'If a dubious character like Staius is indignant at the prayer, surely Jupiter himself must be scandalized by it.' Therefore v. 20 must be ironical, and Persius must be joking in v. 19 when he says 'Or perhaps you balk at that?'

26–8. *You don't lie buried ... abhorrence*: If a man was struck by lightning in a grove he was buried where he fell. The spot was then railed off and regarded as sacred. The crone is Tuscan because most of the ancient religious rituals were Etruscan in origin. Cf. v. 60.

32–4. *protects his forehead ... evil eye*: The middle finger was called '*infamis*' because it was used to simulate the penis in rude gestures. Such gestures were often employed to ward off the evil eye. Saliva was also used extensively in magic and medicine. For references see the long note of Jahn.

36. *Licinian domains*: Domains like those of Licinus, a freedman of Julius Caesar's. Under Augustus he was a financial official in Gaul, where he acquired enormous wealth.

Crassus: M. Licinius Crassus made a huge fortune by buying up the property of men who were killed in Sulla's proscriptions. By 60 BC he was one of the three most powerful men in the country, the others being Pompey and Caesar. He was killed in 53 BC when leading a campaign against the Parthians.

54. *Your heart ... expelling the drops*: The greedy man's heart forces out drops of sweat.

55–8. *Smearing the faces ... beards of gold*: Since he himself is so excited by gold he assumes that it is equally pleasing to the gods.

59. *Numa*: The second king of Rome, esteemed for his simple piety.

Saturn: A divine figure in whose reign Italy was supposed to have enjoyed an era of unexampled peace.

65. *Calabrian fleece*: Calabria is a district on the heel of Italy, which was well known for its wool.

70. *dolls*: These presents signified the end of girlhood.

71. *Messalla*: (64 BC–AD 8) An aristocrat who was a distinguished general, orator, and patron of letters. See Horace, *Satires* I. 10. 85. His son L. Aurelius Cotta Messalinus was notorious for his dissolute habits.

Persius 3

1. The opening words, '*nempe haec assidue*', may possibly be spoken by Persius, in which case they mean 'Always the same story!' The parallel with Horace II. 3, however, suggests that they belong to the companion who breaks in on the sleeping student. For a defence of the mise-en-scène adopted in the translation see *Classical Review* 20 (1970) 286–8.

4–5. *as the shadow ... dial*: The time is about 11 a.m.

10. *two-tone parchment*: The two sides of the parchment are different in colour. The hair has been removed with pumice.

29. *parade ... in full regalia*: The knights (*equites*) used to parade on horseback to be inspected by the Censor.

31. *Natta*: The name occurs in Horace, *Satires* I. 6. 124, but there the character is mean rather than extravagant.

39. *Sicily's brazen bull*: Phaleris was tyrant of Acragas in Sicily in the middle of the sixth century BC. His victims were roasted alive inside a bronze bull.

40. *the blade dangling*: Damocles was a courtier of Dionysius of Syracuse (*c.* 430–367 BC). When he praised the tyrant's happiness, Dionysius offered to show him what such a life was really like. Damocles was then clothed in purple, and a magnificent feast was set before him. But just above his head hung a sword, attached to the ceiling by a horse's hair.

45. *Cato*: M. Porcius Cato (95–46 BC), a man of austere principles and inflexible will. He upheld the old republican constitution against Pompey, Caesar, and Crassus. Eventually when a choice became necessary he supported Pompey against Caesar. After Pompey's death he continued to resist Caesar in Africa. Finally, after the battle of Thapsus, he committed suicide rather than surrender. See the account of his life given by Plutarch.

53. *the learned Porch*: The Porch or Colonnade in question was built at Athens about 460 BC and decorated with pictures by Polygnotus. One represented the battle of Marathon. From 300 BC on, the building was used by Zeno and his successors, and so their philosophy came to be associated with the Porch or Stoa.

56. *Pythagoras' Ч*: The old form of the Greek capital U; the stem stands for the unreflecting life of infancy and childhood, the branches for the straight and crooked paths of virtue and vice. The Latin is '*quae Samios diduxit littera ramos*' – 'the letter which separates the Samian branches'. The adjective Samian is transferred from the letter to the branches. The letter is Samian because Pythagoras came from the island of Samos off the coast of Asia Minor.

65. *Doctor Craterus*: Comes from Horace, *Satires* II. 3. 161.

73–6. *jars piled in a barrister's ... a survivor*: The successful lawyer has more presents than he can use.

79. *Arcesilas*: A Greek philosopher who was Head of the Academy in the middle of the third century BC.

     Solon: Reformed the economy and constitution of sixth-century Athens, and gave expression to his ideas in poetry. He was counted as one of the seven wise men of Greece.

83. *sick old fool*: This is taken in a wholly general sense by Jahn, Conington, and Villeneuve, and it is true that the doctrine mentioned in the next line was held by more than one philosophical school. Yet it is

hard to believe that a Roman reader would not have construed '*gigni/ de nihilo nihilum, in nihilum nil posse reverti*' as a parody of Lucretius, e.g. 1.150, 237, 248. In that case Persius had Epicurus chiefly in mind.

92. *Surrentine*: A light wine from Sorrento, often recommended for invalids.

106. *men whose caps proclaim them citizens*: These slaves had been emancipated by the deceased either just before he died or else through his will. Freedmen shaved their heads and wore a felt skull-cap.

Persius 4

11. *you can see the straight . . . crooked*: The straight represents the virtuous mean, the crooked the two faults of defect and excess.

12. *the rule misleads . . . standard*: This seems to refer to cases where the right action is not to be seen as a mean between two extremes.

16. *Anticyra*: In addition to the Anticyra in Phocis on the gulf of Corinth (see Horace, *Satires* II. 3. 83 and 166) there was also an Anticyra on the Malian gulf some thirty-five miles further north.

22. *Baucis*: The name of an old woman, taken from Ovid, *Metamorphoses* 8. 640 ff.

25. *Vettidius*: Unknown.

26. *Cures*: A Sabine town.

28. *On a public holiday . . . cross-road shrines*: The festival referred to is the Compitalia, which took place in early January. The yoke and the plough were hung up as a sign that work had come to an end.

48–9. *if you carefully whip . . . a weal*: The Latin is '*amarum/si puteal multa cautus vibice flagellas*', literally 'if careful you whip the harsh well with many a weal.' No one knows for certain what this means. The well was the place where money-lenders used to congregate; so 'well' may be used to denote 'interest'.

Persius 5

4. *Parthian*: The Parthians were Rome's traditional enemy in the east. As such they were an appropriate subject for a historical Roman epic. The actual expression is modelled on Horace, *Satires* II. 1. 15.

8. *Thyestes*: Engaged in a long and horrible struggle with his brother Atreus for the throne of Mycenae in the Peloponnese. At one stage Atreus lured him back from exile and served him dinner. When the meal was over Atreus, to show him what he had eaten, uncovered a dish containing the heads, hands, and feet of his two baby sons.

  Procne: On finding that her husband Tereus had violated and mutilated her sister Philomela, Procne murdered her son Itys and served his body up to Tereus. See Ovid, *Metamorphoses* 6. 424–674.

9. *Sweetman*: Glycon, a tragic actor, who in Persius' view was rather a ham.

22. *Cornutus*: L. Annaeus Cornutus, born *c.* AD 20 at Leptis in Libya. He came to Rome, probably as a slave in the household of Seneca or one of his relations. He was then emancipated and became a teacher of rhetoric and philosophy. With Caesius Bassus he produced a post-humous edition of Persius' Satires. Soon after the poet's death Cornutus was exiled by Nero. He was a man of wide erudition, writing on many subjects including Aristotle, Greek mythology, and Virgil.

30. *purple band*: At the age of sixteen a Roman boy would exchange his *toga praetexta*, with its border of purple, for a plain white toga.

31. *locket*: The *bulla*, containing a charm against the evil eye, was worn around the neck. When the boy reached maturity it was dedicated to the household gods.

33. *Subura*: A seedy old street specializing in victuals and vice.

48–9. *the even Scales . . . harmonious lives*: 'The *horoscopus*, the sign of the zodiac which is rising at the moment of birth, presides over the first year of a child's life, the next over the second, and so on until the child is twelve years old and the zodiac exhausted; then the first sign presides over his thirteenth year and the wheel goes round again.' A. E. Housman, *Classical Quarterly* 7 (1913) 19. The Scales and the Twins are, of course, Libra and Gemini.

50. *with Jove's help . . . power*: 'In the genitures of Persius and Cornutus the planets Jupiter and Saturn had the same relative positions, and such positions that the benignant Jupiter counteracted the maleficent Saturn,' A. E. Housman, ibid. 21.

64. *Cleanthes*: Born 331 BC, he was Head of the Stoic school from 263 until his death in 232. He gave to Stoicism a strongly religious colouring, maintaining that the universe was a living being with God as its soul.

73–4. *Jack . . . voters' list*: Jack becomes John Smith when he acquires citizen rights.

76. *whirl*: A slave was touched with the Praetor's rod, and his master turned him around saying 'I wish this man to be free.'

82. *cone-caps*: A freed slave wore a distinctive cap; cf. 3. 106.

90. *Sabinus*: Masurius Sabinus, a distinguished jurist of the first half of the first century AD, who wrote a standard work on civil law in three books.

103. *Melicerta*: A sea deity.

112. *Lord of Lucre*: Mercury. The saliva signifies greed.

115. *batch*: The Latin *'farina'* (flour) suggests a metaphor from baking.

123. *Bathyllus' satyr routine*: Bathyllus of Alexandria was a freedman of Maecenas. He won great fame as a comic mime.

126. *Crispinus' scrapers . . . baths*: Crispinus and the baths come from Horace, *Satires* I. 3. 138–9.

132. *Lady Greed*: Avaritia.

134. *Pontus*: An area on the south coast of the Black Sea.

139. *scraping the bottom of the barrel*: The Latin is '*regustatum digito terebrare salinum*' – 'to scrape a hole in your well-used salt-cellar'.

148. *Veientine*: From Veii in Etruria.

151. *What you live is ours*: I.e. a day which has been lived to the full is a valuable possession which cannot be taken away. Cf. Horace, *Odes* III. 29. 41–8. Luxury will share it; hence 'ours'.

161–74. '*Davus, look . . . genuine break*': This interchange is based on the opening scene of Menander's *Eunuch*.

166. *Goldie*: The girl is a Greek freedwoman called Chrysis. Her door is wet and her lover's torch is extinguished because she has thrown down a bucketful of water. Cf. Horace, *Satires* II. 7. 90–91. Other explanations, referring to rain, tears, and ointment, are much less convincing.

175. *stick*: The Praetor's rod.

176. *the charms of whitened Ambition*: Persius is referring to the glamour of the hustings. The Latin is '*cretata Ambitio*' – 'Ambition in her whitened toga'. Men seeking public office had their togas whitened with chalk; hence they were '*candidati*'. Political ambition is here personified as a dangerous vamp. I follow those who place a comma after '*sui*' in v. 176, and take '*palpo*' as an ablative. The theory that '*palpo*' is a nominative is not well based.

179. *Flora*: The Italian goddess of blooming plants. Her festival began on 28 April and was gradually extended to 3 May. It was conducted by the Aediles, who would win popularity by staging shows and distributing food. The licentiousness of the celebrations was much deplored by the serious minded.

180. *Herod*: Herod the Great, king of the Jews (*c.* 73–4 BC) Persius is referring to the Sabbath.

185. *exploding egg*: According to the scholiast, priests used to put eggs on the fire and watch where the moisture came out. If the egg burst it was regarded as a bad omen.

186. *Cybele's towering eunuchs*: Cybele was the name given to the great mother goddess of Phrygia. Her priests castrated themselves and dedicated the severed parts to her; they then continued in her service but dressed as women. The object of the rite seems to have been an attempt to give the goddess more of the *mana* which she needed for the task of reproduction. The priests were known as Galli, because (according to tradition) the water from the river Gallus made men mad. This derivation is suspect but no other has been accepted.

   Isis: The Egyptian goddess had many aspects. When angered she would sometimes punish the delinquent with blindness. The rattle was a mystical object used in her worship. Plutarch (*De Iside* 63) says that it signified that all things had to be kept in motion; he adds that it was used to repel the evil god Typhon (or Set).

187. *they fill you with gods*: Persius says this instead of saying 'they inspire

the fear of the gods. For the swelling caused by a god, cf. Martial IV. 43. 7.

191. *offers a clipped coin . . . Greeks*: The centurions see philosophy as something foreign and contemptible.

Persius 6

1. *Bassus*: Caesius Bassus, a lyric poet mentioned with qualified approval in Quintilian X. 1. 96. After Persius' death he edited the satires. He is said to have died in the eruption of Vesuvius in AD 79.

5. *you're an expert . . . love*: Bassus seems to have written on love rather in the Horatian vein.

7-8. *I'm wintering here . . . sea*: The sentence *hibernat meum mare* is controversial. Presumably the sea is Persius' sea (*meum*) because he has known and loved the place from his boyhood. Some scholars take *hibernat* as the equivalent of *hiemat* ('is rough'), pointing out that according to some ancient authorities the water became warmer as the sea became rough. But (1) it seems odd (even for Persius) to say 'the sea is rough' when one means only to convey that the water is warm. (2) *Hibernare* normally means 'to pass the winter'. (3) The description of the inlet running back behind the cliff does not suggest rough water. (4) There is a logical sequence of ideas in a stretch of water spending the winter where the cliffs offer protection and the coastline withdraws.

9. *'Good people . . . worth it!'*: A quotation from Ennius. Warmington (*Remains of Old Latin*, vol. 1) prints it as fragment 14 of the *Annals*. Skutsch, however, assigns it to the *Satires* (*Studia Enniana*, 25–9).

10-11. *Ennius the wise . . . Pythagoras' peacock*: The soul of Homer is said to have descended to Ennius via a peacock. 'In Pythagorean southern Italy, and apparently elsewhere, the peacock is a symbol of immortality.' Also 'he is the bird of Samos and thus connected with Pythagoras' (Skutsch, *Studia Enniana*, 153). For Ennius' dream see note on Prologue v. 2.

17. *poke my nose . . . flat*: A miser would keep examining the seal of his wine-jar to check whether it was still intact, even though the wine itself wasn't worth drinking.

28. *Bruttium*: An area covering the toe of Italy.

30. *the mighty gods from the stern*: A ship carried on its stern images of the gods to whom it was entrusted.

33. *carting around his picture*: I.e. as a beggar.

38. *Bruty*: The Latin name is Bestius. In making these complaints the heir is of course hypocritical, for he wanted a bigger legacy for himself. In Horace, *Epistles* I. 15. 37 we hear of a man who denounces luxury like Bestius. There appears to have been something rather suspect about Bestius' sermons. Perhaps he had once been a notorious spendthrift and then, after ruining himself, had become a fountain of austere wisdom. He may also have been a Lucilian figure.

39. *fancy ideas*: The Latin is *sapere . . . nostrum hoc maris expers*, which
can be interpreted in two ways, (1) by taking *maris expers* as 'unmixed
with sea-water', and (2) by taking it as 'destitute of virility'. In Horace
II. 8. 15 we hear of unsalted Chian wine being served at Nasidienus'
dinner-party. Like other items on the menu this was intended to be a
sign of the host's exquisite refinement. We know from Galen (10. 833)
that certain Greek wines, including one from Chios, were left unsalted
(cf. Pliny, *Natural History* 14. 73 and 75). Now if Persius was follow-
ing Horace, the fancy ideas are, like the pepper and dates, unnecessary,
exotic, and decadent. If he has changed Horace, then *maris* comes not
from *mare* (sea) but from *mas* (male), and the phrase means 'unmanly'.
The two interpretations are not far apart in general sense, and neither
is in any way absurd. If we ask 'What did Persius mean by *maris*?'
and 'How would his readers have understood it?' the best answer
is probably that the word had both meanings. The pun cannot be
reproduced in English, but one can choose a word which will include
both senses, hence the translation 'fancy'.

The actual content of the ideas is not specified (though they are
clearly of a hedonistic kind), and so it seems rather over-precise to
connect them solely with gastronomy, as Nisbet tentatively proposed.

43–7. *Caligula . . . the Empress has ordered . . . Rhine*: Caligula was the
Emperor Gaius (AD 12–41). Suetonius (*Caligula* 43ff.) gives an
account of his farcical campaign against the Germans and of the
subsequent triumph in which fake prisoners were compelled to march.
The yellow wigs mentioned by Persius were to be part of their disguise.
The Empress in question was Caesonia, Caligula's fourth wife.

52. *'That field . . . stones'*: The heir is afraid to voice his objections, because
if the crowd hears him he will be stoned to death. This is Hermann's
interpretation, accepted by Housman. Certainty is impossible.

55–6. *the beggars' hill at Bovillae*: Bovillae was eleven miles down the
Appian Way from Rome. The beggars' hill was the hill of Virbius some
four miles farther on. Hippolytus, who was brought back to life by
Aesculapius at the request of Diana, was worshipped with her at Aricia
under the name of Virbius. As travellers toiled up the hill on their way
south, the beggars would accost them.

61. *why shout for the baton*: Life is here represented as a relay race.

62. *offering a purse*: Mercury, who brought gain, was often portrayed as
carrying a purse.

68. *boy*: Here Persius addresses his servant. The sermon is resumed in
v. 69.

77. *fat Cappadocians*: Slaves from Cappadocia, which was on the west of
the Euphrates between Pontus in the north and Cilicia in the south.

80. *Chrysippus' heap*: The puzzle of the heap may be illustrated by placing
a coffee bean on a table and asking a friend if it makes a heap. He will
say no. Add another bean and repeat the question. Eventually, when

you have added bean x, he will say 'yes, that *is* a heap.' Then you take off bean x and say 'Do you mean that a single bean makes it a heap?' The process also operates in reverse.

Chrysippus (*c.* 280–207 BC) was converted to Stoicism by Cleanthes and succeeded him as Head of the school. He was a vigorous apologist and a formidable logician.

Select Bibliography

GENERAL

Anderson, W. S., *Essays on Roman Satire*, Princeton, 1982
Braund, S. H., *Roman Verse Satire*, Greece and Rome Survey, Oxford, 1992
Coffey, M., *Roman Satire*, second edition, Bristol, 1989
Rudd, N., *Themes in Roman Satire*, London, 1986
Van Rooy, C. A., *Studies in Classical Satire*, Leiden, 1965

LUCILIUS

Texts and Commentaries

Krenkel, W., *Lucilius, Satiren*, Berlin, 1970
Marx, F., c. *Lucilii Carminum Reliquiae*, Lipsiae, 1904–5, reprinted 1963

Translation

Warmington, E. H., *Remains of Old Latin*, volume 3, Loeb Classical Library, 1957

Background

Astin, A. E., *Scipio Aemilianus*, Oxford, 1967
Gruen, E. S., *Culture and National Identity in Republican Rome*, Ithaca, 1992

Interpretation

Cambridge History of Classical Literature, volume 2, Cambridge, 1982, chapter 7

HORACE

Texts and Commentaries

Brink, C. O., *Horace on Poetry: The 'Ars Poetica'*, Cambridge, 1971
Horace on Poetry: Epistles, Book II, Cambridge, 1982

Brown, P. M., *Horace, Satires I*, Warminster, 1993 (with translation)
Kiessling, A. and Heinze, R., *Q. Horatius Flaccus, Satiren*, sixth edition, Leipzig, 1921
Lejay, P., *Oeuvres d'Horace. Satires*, Paris, 1911
Mayer, R., *Horace, Epistles I*, Cambridge, 1994
Muecke, F., *Horace, Satires II*, Warminster, 1993 (with translation)
Rudd, N., *Horace, Epistles II and Ars Poetica*, Cambridge, 1989
Shackleton Bailey, D. R., *Horatius, Opera*, Stutgardiae, 2001

Translations

Fairclough, H. R., *Horace, Satires, Epistles, and Ars Poetica*, Loeb Classical Library, 1929
MacLeod, C., *Horace, Epistles*, Roma, 1986

Background

Millar, F. and Segal, E. (ed.), *Caesar Augustus: Seven Aspects*, Oxford, 1984
Cambridge Ancient History, second edition, volume 10, chapters 1–4

Interpretations

Brink, C. O., *Horace on Poetry*, Cambridge 1963, 156–77
Costa, C. D. N. (ed.), *Horace*, London, 1973, chapters 3, 4 and 5
Fraenkel, E., *Horace*, Oxford, 1957
Freudenburg, K., *The Walking Muse*, Princeton, 1993
Gowers, E., *The Loaded Table*, Oxford, 1993, chapter 3
Kilpatrick, R. S., *The Poetry of Friendship: Horace, Epistles I*, Edmonton, 1986
   The Poetry of Criticism: Horace, Epistles II, Edmonton, 1989
Lyne, R. O. A. M., *Horace: Behind the Public Poetry*, New Haven and London, 1995
MacLeod, C., 'The Poetry of Ethics: Horace, *Epistles I*,' *Collected Essays*, Oxford, 1981
Rudd, N., *The Satires of Horace*, Cambridge, 1966
   (ed.) *Horace 2000*, London, 1993, chapters 1, 2 and 4
Shackleton Bailey, D. R., *Profile of Horace*, London, 1982
Stack, F., *Pope and Horace*, Cambridge, 1985
Williams, G. W., *Tradition and Originality in Roman Poetry*, Oxford, 1968
Woodman, T and West, D. (ed.) *Quality and Pleasure*, Cambridge, 1974, chapter 5
   Poetry and Politics in the Age of Augustus, Cambridge, 1984, chapter 2

PERSIUS

Texts and Commentaries

Clausen, W. V., *A. Persi Flacci et D. Iuvenalis Saturae*, second edition, Oxonii, 1992

Harvey, R. A., *A Commentary on Persius*, Leiden, 1981

Jenkinson, J. R., *Persius. The Satires*, Warminster, 1980 (with translation)

Lee, G. and Barr, W., *The Satires of Persius*, Liverpool, 1987 (with translation)

Translation

Ramsay, G. G., *Juvenal and Persius*, Loeb Classical Library, 1918; now replaced by S. M. Braund, 2004

Background

Griffin, M. T., *Nero, The End of a Dynasty*, New Haven and London, 1984

Rudich, V., *Political Dissidence under Nero*, London and New York, 1993

Interpretations

Bramble, J. C., *Persius and the Programmatic Satire*, Cambridge, 1974

Morford, M., *Persius*, Boston, 1984

Rudd, N., *Lines of Enquiry*, Cambridge, 1976, chapter 3

Sullivan, J. P. (ed.), *Critical Essays on Roman Literature. Satire*, London, 1963, chapter 2

  Literature and Politics in the Reign of Nero, Ithaca and London, 1985, chapter 2

N.B. For further bibliography (including periodical literature) see Braund's Survey (under General, above).

Index of the More Important Names and Topics

Numbers in brackets indicate that the persons are referred to, but not named, in the text.

Notes are indicated only when they contain a reference which is independent of the text. When they comment directly on the text they can be found by means of the appropriate line number.

READ MORE IN PENGUIN

In every corner of the world, on every subject under the sun, Penguin represents quality and variety – the very best in publishing today.

For complete information about books available from Penguin – including Puffins, Penguin Classics and Arkana – and how to order them, write to us at the appropriate address below. Please note that for copyright reasons the selection of books varies from country to country.

In the United Kingdom: Please write to *Dept. EP, Penguin Books Ltd, Bath Road, Harmondsworth, West Drayton, Middlesex UB7 0DA*

In the United States: Please write to *Consumer Services, Penguin Putnam Inc., 405 Murray Hill Parkway, East Rutherford, New Jersey 07073-2136.* VISA and MasterCard holders call 1-800-631-8571 to order Penguin titles

In Canada: Please write to *Penguin Books Canada Ltd, 10 Alcorn Avenue, Suite 300, Toronto, Ontario M4V 3B2*

In Australia: Please write to *Penguin Books Australia Ltd, 487 Maroondah Highway, Ringwood, Victoria 3134*

In New Zealand: Please write to *Penguin Books (NZ) Ltd, Private Bag 102902, North Shore Mail Centre, Auckland 10*

In India: Please write to *Penguin Books India Pvt Ltd, 11 Community Centre, Panchsheel Park, New Delhi 110017*

In the Netherlands: Please write to *Penguin Books Netherlands bv, Postbus 3507, NL-1001 AH Amsterdam*

In Germany: Please write to *Penguin Books Deutschland GmbH, Metzlerstrasse 26, 60594 Frankfurt am Main*

In Spain: Please write to *Penguin Books S. A., Bravo Murillo 19, 1°B, 28015 Madrid*

In Italy: Please write to *Penguin Italia s.r.l., Via Vittorio Emanuele 45/a, 20094 Corsico, Milano*

In France: Please write to *Penguin France, 12, Rue Prosper Ferradou, 31700 Blagnac*

In Japan: Please write to *Penguin Books Japan Ltd, Iidabashi KM-Bldg, 2-23-9 Koraku, Bunkyo-Ku, Tokyo 112-0004*

In South Africa: Please write to *Penguin Books South Africa (Pty) Ltd, P.O. Box 751093, Gardenview, 2047 Johannesburg*

PENGUIN CLASSICS

THE FROGS AND OTHER PLAYS   ARISTOPHANES

THE WASPS / THE POET AND THE WOMEN / THE FROGS

'This is just a little fable, with a moral: not too highbrow for you, we hope,
but a bit more intelligent than the usual knockabout stuff'

The master of ancient Greek comic drama, Aristophanes combined
slapstick, humour and cheerful vulgarity with acute political observations.
In *The Frogs*, written during the Peloponnesian War, Dionysus descends
to the Underworld to bring back a poet who can help Athens in its darkest
hour, and stages a great debate to help him decide between the traditional
wisdom of Aeschylus and the brilliant modernity of Euripides. The clash
of generations and values is also the object of Aristophanes' satire in *The
Wasps*, in which an old-fashioned father and his loose-living son come to
blows and end up in court. And in *The Poet and the Women*, Euripides,
accused of misogyny, persuades a relative to infiltrate an all-women
festival to find out whether revenge is being plotted against him.

David Barrett's introduction discusses the Athenian dramatic contests in
which these plays first appeared, and conventions of Greek comedy – from
its poetic language and the role of the Chorus to casting and costumes.

Translated with an introduction by David Barrett

PENGUIN CLASSICS

LYSISTRATA AND OTHER PLAYS   ARISTOPHANES

LYSISTRATA / THE ACHARNIANS / THE CLOUDS

'But he who would provoke me should remember
That those who rifle wasps' nests will be stung!'

Writing at a time of political and social crisis in Athens, Aristophanes
(*c*. 447–*c*. 385 BC) was an eloquent, yet bawdy, challenger to the
demagogue and the sophist. In *Lysistrata* and *The Acharnians*, two pleas
for an end to the long war between Athens and Sparta, a band of women
and a lone peasant respectively defeat the political establishment. The
darker comedy of *The Clouds* satirizes Athenian philosophers, Socrates
in particular, and reflects the uncertainties of a generation in which all
traditional religious and ethical beliefs were being challenged.

For this edition Alan H. Sommerstein has completely revised his
translation of these three plays, bringing out the full nuances of
Aristophanes's ribald humour and intricate word play, with a new
introduction explaining the historical and cultural background to
the plays.

Translated with an introduction by Alan H. Sommerstein

PENGUIN CLASSICS

PROMETHEUS BOUND AND OTHER PLAYS
AESCHYLUS

PROMETHEUS BOUND / THE SUPPLIANTS / SEVEN AGAINST THEBES / THE PERSIANS

'Your kindness to the human race has earned you this.
A god who would not bow to the gods' anger – you
Transgressing right, gave privileges to mortal men'

Aeschylus (525–456 BC) brought a new grandeur and epic sweep to the drama of classical Athens, raising it to the status of high art. In *Prometheus Bound* the defiant Titan Prometheus is brutally punished by Zeus for daring to improve the state of wretchedness and servitude in which mankind is kept. *The Suppliants* tells the story of the fifty daughters of Danaus who must flee to escape enforced marriages, while *Seven Against Thebes* shows the inexorable downfall of the last members of the cursed family of Oedipus. And *The Persians*, the only Greek tragedy to deal with events from recent Athenian history, depicts the aftermath of the defeat of Persia in the battle of Salamis, with a sympathetic portrayal of its disgraced King Xerxes.

Philip Vellacott's evocative translation is accompanied by an introduction, with individual discussions of the plays, and their sources in history and mythology.

Translated with an introduction by Philip Vellacott